THE

HILGENDORF-HAAG

CONNECTION

March 2018

THE

HILGENDORF-HAAG

CONNECTION

James P. Barber

THE OTHER ROAD PUBLISHING

THE HILGENDORF-HAAG CONNECTION
The Other Road Publishing
630 Nancy Street, Warsaw, Indiana 46580
www.jamespbarber.com

©⃝(i) James P. Barber, 2018

Printed in the United States of America.

First Edition, 2018

ISBN: 978-0692075814

All photos were provided by members of the Hilgendorf/Haag family.

The family descendant charts at the end of the book were created with the Legacy Family Tree genealogy software, version 9.0.

CONTENTS

INTRODUCTION

This Hilgendorf-Haag Family Tree is based upon the best information available at the time of publication. There are several on-line sources utilized in the research for the family tree. These include Ancestry, Family Search, and Find-A-Grave among others. Additional information was obtained at the La Porte County Public Library.

Access to international resources that are available through sources such as Ancestry were not directly used. The Ancestry account used for research did not include international access. Accordingly, secondary sources at Ancestry were utilized. This meant reliance upon the research that others had done in completing Hilgendorf and Haag family trees for the international – specifically German – family information.

These secondary family trees are normally consulted as a last resource, especially in the case of international information, and in particular for the German records for the Hilgendorf and Haag families. With not always a way to verify the information placed in these family trees by their authors, a close examination of the logic used in placing the German families on these trees was employed.

Generally, there were two or three different trees to select from when looking at the German ancestors. Close examination of the earliest family member that was uncovered through my own primary research was used when looking back at the earlier German ancestors. The German birthplace of the earliest known ancestor was given heavy weight when examining the German ancestors. Geographical family patterns did exist with these very early families. And, in addition, simple common sense rules out some very obvious errors.

Unfortunately, many researchers simply copy what others have done without question. So, again, while not having access to the original German documents, the best research methods were applied in selecting the most likely German ancestry of the Hilgendorf and Haag families.

For ancestors living in America, sources such as U.S. Federal Census records, birth certificates, death certificates, marriage certificates, wills, cemetery records, school yearbooks, city directories, newspaper articles and photographs were used to confirm and verify all relationships. Family trees created by others were little-used, as, again, there is a concern over others simply copying unsubstantiated information. These other family trees were only consulted as a last resort to look into possible clues when there were questions and roadblocks.

This book is organized by family and by family generation, where the first generation is the earliest known ancestor. While each family is shown with as much detail as possible, from one generation to the next, the family tree follows the main family line that brings the Hilgendorf and Haag families together with the marriage of Clarence John Hilgendorf and Leatha Cecelia Haag in 1940.

Each generation begins with a simplified chart of the family relationships for the generation that is being presented. This simple chart shows individuals and there spouse(s) and children with their birth and death information. With each generation, there is an overview of the specific individual leading to the Hilgendorf-Haag union as well as the siblings of that person. This is done to present an overview of that generation.

In many cases background information about times and places is provided. For example, there is general background provided about the places where the families originated in Germany. Additionally, many relevant documents and, where available, photographs are included with these narratives.

A complete family tree in the form of a descendant chart follows at the end of the book after all of the general family information for each generation. Details on birth, death and marriage are included where available.

Separate descendant charts have been created for each family line. Within each family, each generation begins on a new page, and each individual is given a number in the chart. In this manner, children of each generation are numbered on their parents' chart; then, that number is carried over to that child's generation on the child's page. There is an F or an M after the generation number designating female or male.

Other notes on the descendant charts: First, place names are designated with city/township, county, state and country in that order where available. Secondly, as you get deeper into a family narrative, you will notice names in italics behind a specific individual's name. This is done to show the line from which that individual is descended in reverse order (parent, grandparent, great-grandparent and so on). The number with each name is that individual's number for reference purposes. This will become clear as you look at these family charts.

Since these charts are created using a genealogy software package, each chart contains its own page numbers. Each chart has an index of names and places that reference the page numbers within that individual chart. Besides the Hilgendorf and Haag descendant charts, there are some other smaller charts that show some additional family lines.

The German Connection
of the
Hilgendorf and Haag Families

Prussia and Germany

Both the Hilgendorf and the Haag families arrived in the United States from Germany. They were, however, from very different areas. The Hilgendorfs immigrated from northeast Germany, while the Haags came from southwestern Germany.

Until 1871, however, Germany as a nation did not exist. In 1871, German states united to create the German Empire under Prussian leadership. Prior to that time, the area that contains today's Germany was known as the Kingdom of Prussia. In fact, Prussia covered a much larger area than today's Germany, extending east into Poland and Russia. This area was controlled by monarchies, a land of feudal empires and working peasants.

This area was turbulent over many centuries as far back as the Roman Empire. Centuries of struggle eventually led to the abolishment of the monarchies in November 1918. The nobility lost its political power during the German Revolution of 1918-1919. The Kingdom of Prussia was thus abolished in favor of a republic – the Free State of Prussia, a state of Germany from 1918 until 1933.

In 1933, Prussia lost its independence as a result of the Prussian coup, when the Nazi regime was successfully establishing laws in pursuit of a unitary state. With the end of the Nazi regime, the division of Germany into allied-occupation zones and the separation of its territories to the east, which were incorporated into Poland and the Soviet Union, the State of Prussia ceased to exist in 1945.

The Hilgendorf and Haag families immigrated relatively close to one another in time. Most of the earlier census records note that they were from Prussia which, of course, is correct. Later census records, however, note their origin as Germany.

The Hilgendorfs appear to have come to America about 1856, while the Haags arrived a bit earlier, about 1841. Exact points of entry into the United States are not known; however, most Germans immigrating at the time the Hilgendorfs did would have come to the Midwest with many going to Ohio, Wisconsin, Indiana and Missouri. By 1880, Wisconsin had more German Americans than any other state. And, in fact, the research finds many Hilgendorfs in these areas in the 1850-1880 time-frame.

THE HILGENDORFS AND MECKLENBURG, GERMANY

It seems the Hilgendorf family comes from an area of Germany known today as Mecklenburg, or Mecklenburg-Vorpommern. Nearly every Hilgendorf located during the research was from this area of Germany. Mecklenburg is located in northeast Germany on the Baltic Sea.

Traditionally, Mecklenburg has always been one of the poorer German areas. The reasons for this may vary, but one factor that stands out is that agriculturally the land is poor and cannot produce at the same level as other parts of Germany.

Mecklenburg had the highest percentage of emigrants of any of the German states. While conditions in other areas improved, Mecklenburg peasants had little reason to hope for a better future. After living in grinding poverty with limited freedom and few opportunities, many saw immigration as a new chance at life. In addition, industrialization, which arrived late in Mecklenburg, forced many already marginal peasants out of their jobs.

In 1857 alone, 1.2 percent of the population of Mecklenburg left. The great majority went to the U.S. Nearly ninety percent came from agricultural lands, with landless people, particularly those closely supervised by a noble, being the most likely to leave.

Like many German territories, Mecklenburg was sometimes partitioned and re-partitioned among different members of the ruling dynasty. After three centuries of partition, Mecklenburg was united in 1934 by the Nazi government. After World War II, the Soviet government occupying eastern Germany merged Mecklenburg with the smaller neighboring region of Western Pomerania to form the state of Mecklenburg-Vorpommern. Mecklenburg contributed about two-thirds of the geographical size of the new state and the majority of its population. Also, the new state became home for many refugees expelled from former German territories seized by the Soviet Union and Poland after the war. The Soviets changed the name from Mecklenburg-Western Pomerania to Mecklenburg in 1947.

In 1952, the East German government ended the independent existence of Mecklenburg, creating 3 districts out of its territory: Rostock, Schwerin and Neubrandenburg. Finally, during German reunification in 1990, the state of Mecklenburg-Vorpommern was revived, and is now one of the 16 states of the Federal Republic of Germany.

THE HAAGS AND WUERTTEMBERG, GERMANY

Much like Mecklenburg, Wuerttemberg, or Baden-Wuerttemberg, has a turbulent history, and, as with most of Germany, it begins with the Roman Empire. More recently, after World War II, the Allies established three federal states in the territory of modern-day Baden-Wuerttemberg: Wurttemberg-Hohenzollern, Baden, and Wurttemberg-Baden. Baden and Wurttemberg-Hohenzollern were occupied by France, while Wurttemberg-Baden was occupied by the United States. In 1949, each state became a founding member of the Federal Republic of Germany. On 16 December 1951, Wurttemberg-Baden, Wurttemberg-Hohenzollern and Baden voted in favor of a joint merger. Baden-Wuerttemberg officially became a state in Germany on 25 April 1952.

The western part of this territory bounced back and forth between Germany and France, eventually ending up in Germany. The French area immediately across the border is known as Alsace-Lorraine. The Haags at some point moved just west a bit from Wuerttemberg to the state of Saarland. This area is still contiguous to Alsace-Lorraine, France. As we will later see, there were likely very close ties with the Haag family to that area of France.

Wuerttemberg's economy was very agricultural, its most important product being wine. The peasantry harvested such grains as rye, barley, hay, and oats. Other products, wool, wood, cloth, linen, and glass and metal wares, followed in importance. Frequent trading partners were the area's southwestern cities and the Swiss Confederation. Though it had no central business hub, the area was a breadbasket for its neighbors.

THE HAAGS AND SAARLAND, GERMANY

Saarland is Germany's smallest state and has a very turbulent past. In the Middle Ages, Saarland, then known simply as Saar, consisted of several small territories, the largest of which was centered on the city of Saarbrücken, today's state capital. From 1381 to 1793 Saarbrücken was ruled by the local nobility. The territory around Saarbrücken, though inhabited by German-speaking people, was much influenced by France.

Saar became a French province in 1684, but in 1697 France was forced to surrender all of Saar except for one small town. From 1792 to 1815 France again occupied Saar, together with the entire west bank of the Rhine.

With the final defeat of Napoleon in 1815, France was forced to cede most of Saar to Prussia, which made the area part of its Prussian Rhine province. When Alsace-Lorraine was added to the German Empire in 1871, Saar ceased to be a boundary state and experienced rapid industrial development based on its own coal deposits and the iron-ore deposits of Lorraine.

After World War I, Saar's coal mines were awarded to France, and Saarland was placed under the administration of the League of Nations for fifteen years, at the end of which time the inhabitants of Saar voted for its return to Germany.

In 1945, following World War II, French military forces occupied Saarland, and two years later the first Saar state parliament adopted a constitution that called for an autonomous Saar in an economic union with France. By 1954, however, West Germany's renewed prosperity was attracting the sympathies of most Saarlanders, and France and the Federal Republic of Germany agreed to a statute that provided for Saar's autonomy under a European commissioner.

This new status was to be approved by a referendum; however, 68 percent of Saar's voters rejected the statute and the separation of Saar from Germany. In 1956, the French agreed to the return of Saar to West Germany, and on January 1, 1957, Saarland finally achieved its present status as a federal state of Germany.

GERMAN IMMIGRATION TO THE UNITED STATES

Immigration to the United States from Europe overwhelmingly increased in the mid-1800s. From 1840 to 1880, the Germans were the largest group of immigrants. Following the Revolutions of 1848 in the German states, a wave of political refugees fled to America. The majority of the immigrants at that time came from two countries: 1.6 million from Ireland, and 1.3 million from Germany (principally from the southwestern states of Wuerttemberg, Baden, and Bavaria). The mass migration from Germany had begun in the 1830s, but the peak decades were the 1850s and the 1880s.

Immigration from Mecklenburg began in earnest in the early 1800's, accelerated through mid-century and began slowing after the German unification in 1871. It is estimated that during the peak years from 1850-1860 as many as 50,000 Mecklenburgers, about 9% of the population, emigrated primarily through the port of Hamburg, Germany. This resulted in the Mecklenburgers comprising 25% of the traffic through Hamburg during this period.

It was a dangerous and difficult trip across the Atlantic. Germans began the journey by making their way to a port city. During the high peaks of emigration there was a steady flow of traffic on the roads to the ports made up of families pushing carts loaded with their belongings. In Germany, most emigrants left from Bremerhaven or Hamburg. Some made their way to Britain in the early eighteenth century, hoping to find passage to North America from there. Others went to Rotterdam, Holland, or Le Havre, France, and sought a ship there. They were often robbed or swindled when they arrived in ports.

Emigrants were required to bring certain items on board, such as eating utensils, bedding in the form of straw sacks and some food items. Often the promises made by agents and ship captains were not held, and traveling became an arduous adventure. A letter written by an emigrant in America advised travelers to bring a jug of whiskey which would help during seasickness.

The conditions on the sailing ships that took the German immigrants across the Atlantic were terrible. Many people could not afford to purchase a first- or second-class ticket, and so they traveled in steerage, the lower decks of the ship that were designed to carry cargo. Aside from being miserably overcrowded, the accommodations often lacked clean drinking water and adequate toilet and washing facilities. Rats, head lice, and bedbugs were common, and infectious diseases spread quickly. In later years, steamships would shorten the voyage, and regulations on ships would correct some of the worst abuses of travelers. Even so, throughout the eighteenth and nineteenth centuries, many immigrants faced misery and even death to get to the United States. Despite the hard trip, for over a century Germans immigrated by the hundreds of thousands to the United States.

DNA

In 2014, Marti (Hilgendorf) Barber, daughter of Clarence Hilgendorf and Leatha Haag submitted a DNA test through Family Tree DNA (https://www.familytreedna.com/). Now, there are a number of typical DNA tests that can be taken. The three common tests are:

1. mtDNA: The mtDNA test follows the maternal line. That is, it follows the mother and her mother and her mother's mother and so on back in time. It only follows the females. The test can be performed on a male or a female, however.

2. Y-DNA: The Y-DNA test follows the paternal line. It looks at the father, his father, his father's father and so on. It only follows the male line, and only males can take this test. None of the Y-DNA is passed to the female.

3. Autosomal: The chromosomes in Autosomal DNA are inherited from both parents (unlike maternal mtDNA and paternal Y-DNA). If you are going to have a DNA test done, this is the one I would recommend first. It is also less expensive than the others.

It was the Autosomal DNA test that Marti took in 2014. Autosomal DNA is inherited from both parents, and includes some contributions from further generations (grandparents, great-grandparents, and so on). Your autosomes essentially contain a complete genetic record, with all branches of your ancestry contributing a piece of your autosomal DNA.

For each of your twenty-two pairs of autosomal chromosomes, you received one from your mother and one from your father. Before they passed these chromosomes down to you, the contents were randomly jumbled in a process called "recombination" (this is why you and your siblings are all a little different from each other).

Your parents, in turn, received their chromosomes from their parents (your grandparents). Your autosomal DNA, therefore, contains random bits of DNA from your great-grandparents, great-great grandparents, and so on.

Both men and women can take this type of test. Compared to Y-DNA and mtDNA tests, it is broader but shallower. It can find matches in any branch of your family tree. It is not limited to just the narrow paternal or maternal lines. This autosomal DNA test only works when people share relatively recent ancestors. Relationships out to the second cousin level are virtually certain to show up. The chance of finding a match with a particular relative begins to decline slightly with third cousins. It can still detect many of your relatives at the fourth and fifth cousin levels and occasionally beyond that.

The fun part of this Autosomal DAN test is that it includes an estimate of your overall ethnic ancestry. Autosomal DNA tests use DNA population studies to determine your biogeographical ancestry. Essentially, they tell you what proportion of your total ancestry originated in different populations around the world. This gets to the deep ancestral roots of origin, often indicating one's roots to 10,000, 20,000 or even 50,000 years ago.

So, here is what was learned about Marti's ancestry.

She is 96% European, and that European ancestry is broken down as follows:
- 38% Scandinavian
- 24% British Isles
- 19% Southern Europe
- 10% Eastern Europe
- 4% Finland and Northern Siberia
- 1% Western and Central Europe

The remaining non-European 4% is Central Asian.

While 96% European is not unusual, it is fun to look at the mix. There is a bit of interesting analysis of the Scandinavian and Finland/Siberia connection. Thousands of years ago there was a land bridge between Denmark and Norway. This led to a mixing of the peoples from the Scandinavian area, including Finland, and today's Germany. So, the large percentage of Scandinavian in the mix may not be all that surprising. The 4% Central Asian; well, how that came to be will take someone else to do a lot of digging.

Baltic Sea

Schleswig-Holstein

Hamburg

Mecklenburg-Vorpommern

Bremen

Brandenburg

Niedersachsen

Berlin

Sachsen-Anhalt

Nordrhein-Westfalen

Sachsen

Hessen

Thüringen

France

Rheinland-Pfalz

Saarland

Bayern

Baden-Württemberg

Germany

This map of Germany highlights the states of Mecklenburg-Vorpommern, Baden-Wuerttemberg, and Saarland. The Hilgendorfs are from Mecklenburg-Vorpommern, and the Haags are from Baden-Wuerttemberg and Saarland.

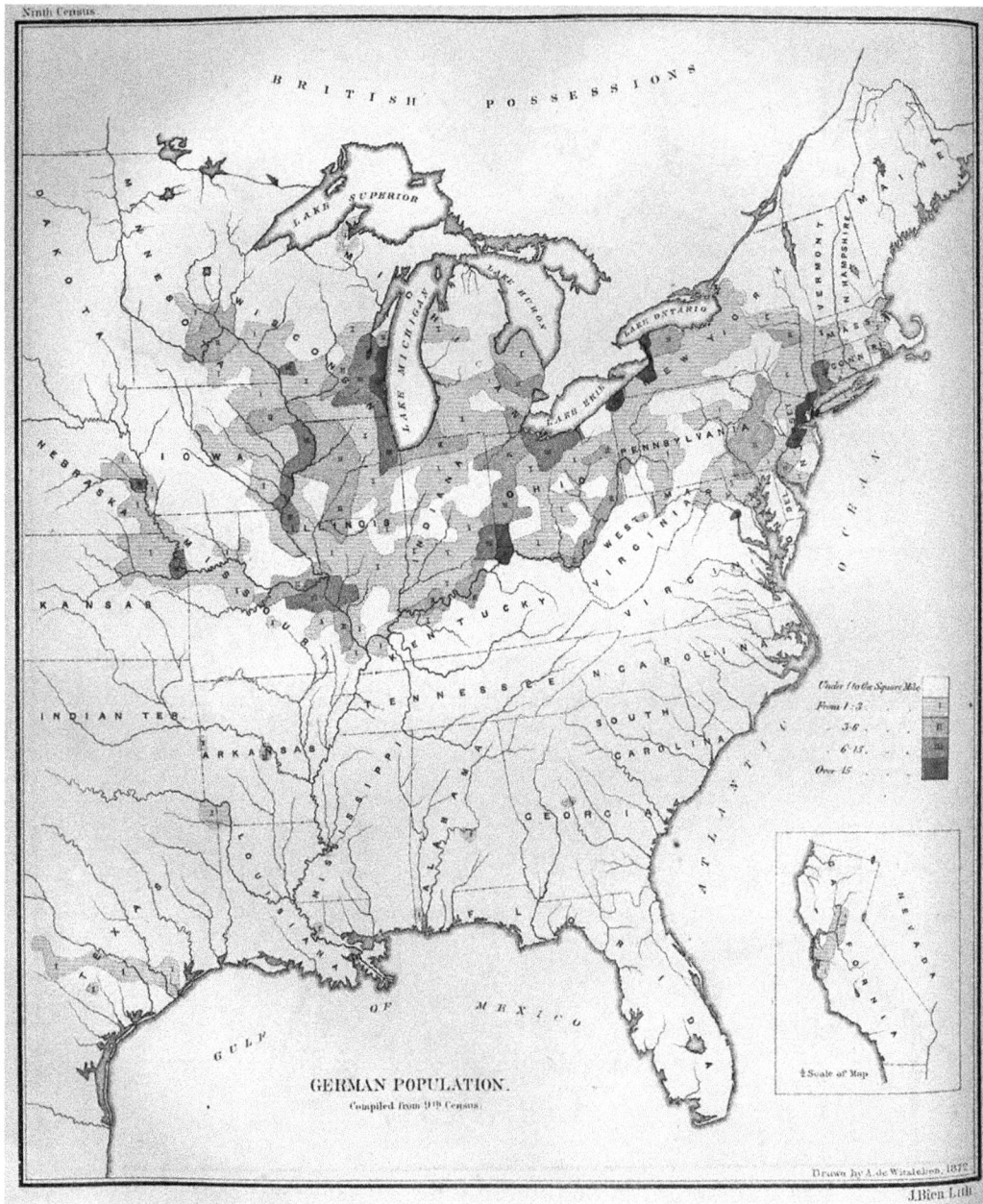

U.S. German Population – 1870

This map shows the distribution of the population of German immigrants based upon the 1870 United States Federal Census. The map was produced in 1872.

Southwestern Indiana

This map of southwestern Indiana counties shows a number of the locations referenced in the book.

Illinois

This map of most of the counties of Illinois shows a number of the areas referenced in the book.

HILGENDORF
THE FIRST GENERATION:
JOHANN C. HILGENDORF (1824-1897)

FAMILY CHART

<u>Johann (John) C. Hilgendorf</u> – b. 26 April 1824, d. 4 March 1897
    Spouse: Maria (Mary) – b. 1 March 1823, d. 1 September 1902
    Children:
        Friederike Hilgendorf – b. 21 June 1848, d. 30 January 1920
        Wilhelmina (Minnie) Hilgendorf – b. 30 March 1852, d. 31 August 1907
        Ludwig (Louis) Hilgendorf – b. 20 December 1859, d. 12 March 1928
        <u>John Edward Hilgendorf</u> – b. 20 October 1862, d. 30 September 1942

Note: The names in **<u>underlined bold</u>** above, and at each generation similarly, represent the descendant line that will be followed ultimately leading to the Hilgendorf-Haag union. Each chapter represents one family generation. Only the family that is **<u>underlined bold</u>** is followed at each generation, or chapter. Thus, detail is provided for the underlined individual and that person's siblings in each chapter. So, this first chapter is about Johann (John) C. Hilgendorf, and the next chapter will be about John Edward Hilgendorf. Siblings will be studied in the order of birth in each chapter.

INTRODUCTION

The Hilgendorf name is more common than perhaps expected. The research into the Hilgendorf family proved to be difficult with not only the number of Hilgendorf families, but also because of multiple occurrences of the names Johann and Maria. These are the names of the earliest ancestors that can be confirmed with the information available.

In the process of research, all available information is obtained before turning to family trees that have been created by others. This is because there are many trees that merely copy other trees that may contain incorrect information. Some researchers take the easy route and pick up the most convenient information without question.

So, I found a number of Johann (John) Hilgendorfs in Indiana and Wisconsin, as well as in Illinois. Indiana and Wisconsin were two of the most common states in which German immigrants from the state of Mecklenburg, Germany, settled in the period 1820-1871. This was at the time of a second wave of German immigration; those in this wave of immigrants often settled in Ohio, Wisconsin, Indiana, Missouri, and Texas.

LOCATING JOHANN C. HILGENDORF

The roots of the Hilgendorf family are a bit muddled at the time of Johann Hilgendorf. There were numerous Johann Hilgendorfs, and multiple Hilgendorfs of the name Johann with a spouse by the name of Maria. And, many with births within several years of one another. Finding the correct set of Johann and Maria Hilgendorf was further hampered by lack of access to the international records. As I researched, one family of particular interest of many Johann Hilgendorf family trees was found to have remained centered in Illinois. This Johann, or John, also had a wife by the name of Mary, and they are buried in Illinois.

A number of sources contain a Johann Michel Hilgendorf as the early ancestor of the Hilgendorfs. Michael was married to Maria Rossow, so this appears to look good at first glance. As with many others, one of the sources of information is a La Porte census record and a La Porte death record for Johann in 1897. I do agree that these La Porte sources are for our Johann Hilgendorf. The problem arose when I discovered that Johann's La Porte burial record indicates that his middle initial was C. Further research brought into question the children of Johann Michel versus Johann C.

After many hours of research, comparison and a process of elimination, I was able to conclude that Johann C. and Johann Michel are two different individuals.

Another common mistaken Johann is Johann Juergen Andreas Hilgendorf. His birth and death dates are not a very good fit, and his wife was not Maria (although some family trees do have Maria Rossow as his wife).

To further complicate matters, all of these Johanns were born somewhere in Mecklenburg, Germany. Without access to the international records, I was only able to observe some very basic information for the German records. Three records contain a Johann Hilgendorf with a middle name containing the letter C. There is Johann Christoph Hilgendorf born in Pomerania, Germany. Pomerania extended from what is today Poland into the northeastern part of the present state of Mecklenburg. Next is Johann Christian Martin Hilgendorf. He was born in Rostock, Germany. Rostock is midway in Mecklenburg located on the Baltic Sea. The third record related to a marriage in Pomerania and contained Johann Carl Christian Hilgendorf and his wife Maria Christiana Catharina Rohrdanz. Perhaps this is our Johann and Maria, but we cannot be certain.

JOHANN C. HILGENDORF (1824-1897)

We do not know exactly when and where the family arrived in America, but their location in Indiana would not be out of line with immigration in the 1850s. We do know with certainty that Johann, or John, and Maria, or Mary, are living in La Porte in 1870 based upon that year's census. There is no indication of where they lived prior to that date, nor have any other earlier census records been located for them.

Most immigrants had their names "Americanized." Johann was commonly changed to John. Mary was the easy choice for Maria; although, it appears Maria did use her actual given name in some cases. It seems evident that Johann and Maria were married in Germany likely before 1848. This is based upon census records, and one child, Friederike Hilgendorf, born in Germany in 1848.

The 1870 census for La Porte shows them with one child at home, Mena (Wilhelmina, or Minnie), who was born about 1851 in Prussia. The next census for La Porte in 1880 includes two children at home, Ludwig and John, born in 1859 and 1862 respectively, in Indiana. This indicates that Johann and Maria came to America after 1851 and prior to 1859. This would be consistent with the large wave of German immigrants in that time, and especially the large number from Mecklenburg.

Johann Hilgendorf may have come to the United States in 1857, consistent with the range of 1851 to 1859. A passenger ship record lists a J. Hilgendorf born about 1824 who immigrated into New York on 13 Nov 1857. He was aboard the ship *Elise Ruebcke* that departed from Hamburg, Germany. Records show that he was a German-born laborer bound for Chicago. It also notes that his compartment was in steerage.

The steerage area of the ship was used to accommodate passengers traveling on the cheapest class of ticket, and offered only the most basic amenities, typically with limited toilet use, no privacy, and poor food. Many immigrants to the United States in the late 18th and early 19th century traveled in this area of the ships. Please note that it has not been determined with any certainty that J. Hilgendorf traveling on the *Elise Ruebcke* is our Johann Hilgendorf.

The Index to U.S. Naturalization records indicates that John became a naturalized citizen of the United States on 18 Feb 1881. These records do not indicate the date of arrival in America, however.

In the 1880 census, Johann's occupation is listed as "Laborer." An index to La Porte city directories for 1893 and 1894 list John Hilgendorf at 1506 Scott Street where his occupation is simply noted, again, as "laborer." In 1902 John's widow Mary is listed at this Scott Street address. It does appear that son John E. Hilgendorf lived at this address. It is likely that his parents lived with him on Scott Street.

The 1900 census does confirm that Mary is living with her son John and his family. The census record notes that Mary had eight children, four of whom are living. Only those four children have been located. This census also indicates that Mary immigrated into the United States in 1856. She would have been about 33 at that time. Note that this fits closely with the possible immigration time of John as noted previously.

The census records place John's birth in 1824 and Mary's birth in 1823. Cross-referencing this against cemetery records in La Porte, there is a record of John and Mary in the Saint John's Cemetery in La Porte. According to this information, Johann was born 26 April 1824, and Maria was born 1 March 1823. Their dates of death are 4 March 1897 and 1 September 1902, respectively. Mary's death certificate does use the name Maria. Because Maria is on her death certificate, that is likely the name she typically used.

John and Mary are buried at Saint John's Cemetery in La Porte. They are in Section A-60, Row 9, Lots 3 and 4.

Page No. _91_

Inquiries numbered 7, 16, and 17 are not to be asked in respect to infants. Inquiries numbered 11, 12, 15, 16, 17, 19, and 20 are to be answered (if at all) merely by an affirmative mark, as /.

SCHEDULE 1.—Inhabitants in _LaPorte City_ , in the County of _LaPorte_ , State of _Indiana_ , enumerated by me on the ____ day of _____, 1870.

Post Office: _LaPorte Ind_   _C. Loomis_ , Ass't Marshal.

		The name of every person whose place of abode on the first day of June, 1870, was in this family.	Age	Sex	Color	Profession, Occupation, or Trade of each person, male or female.	Value of Real Estate	Value of Personal Estate	Place of Birth, naming State or Territory of U.S.; or the Country, if of foreign birth.	Father of foreign birth	Mother of foreign birth	If born within the year	If married within the year	Attended school	Cannot read	Cannot write	Whether deaf and dumb, blind, insane, or idiotic.	Male Citizen	Denied
1	2	3	4	5	6	7	8	9	10	11	12	13	14	15	16	17	18	19	20
1		Harloff, Mena	10	F	W	At Home			Indiana	/	/			/					
2		— Charles	8	M	W	At Home			Indiana	/	/								
3		— Bertha	6	F	W	At Home			Indiana	/	/								
4																		1	
5		Heidendorf, John	47	M	W	Day Laborer	400	150	Prussia										
6		— Mary	38	F	W	Keeping House			Prussia									1	
7		— Mena	18	F	W	At Home			Prussia										
19	285	822	Heidendorf, John	47	M	W	Day Laborer	400	150	Prussia x	/	/							1
20			— Mary	38	F	W	Keeping House			Prussia x	/	/							
21			— Mena	18	F	W	At Home			Prussia x	/	/							
22	709	823	Mersault, Christ	43	M	W	Day Laborer		250	Prussia x	/	/							1
23			— Caro		F														
34		826	McHale, Christ	36	M	W	Day Laborer			Mecklenburg x	/	/							1
35			— Sophia	36	F	W	Keeping House			Mecklenburg	/	/							
36			— Lewis	9	M	W	At Home			Indiana	/	/							
37			— Ida	6	F	W	At Home			Indiana	/	/							
38			— Freak	4	M	W	At Home			Indiana	/	/							
39	62	827	Hetke, Henry	36	M	W	Day Laborer		350	Mecklenburg	/	/							1
40			— Sophia	28	F	W	Keeping House			Mecklenburg x	/	/							

No. of dwellings, _7_   No. of white females, _20_   No. of males, foreign born _7_   No. of insane, ___
" families, _8_   " colored males, ___   " females, " _8_
" white males, _20_   " " females, ___   " blind,

Johann C. Hilgendorf – 1870 Federal Census for La Porte, La Porte Co., Indiana

The above image shows a portion of a page from the 1870 census. The highlighted area shows the John (Johann C.) Hilgendorf (misspelled Hildendorf) family. In addition to 47-year-old John are his wife Mary (Maria), age 38, and daughter Mena (Wihelmina, Minnie), age 18.

D. [7–296.]

Page No. 64
Supervisor's Dist. No. 5
Enumeration Dist. No. 87

Note A.—The Census Year begins June 1, 1879, and ends May 31, 1880.
Note B.—All persons will be included in the Enumeration who were living on the 1st day of June, 1880. No others will. Children BORN SINCE June 1, 1880, will be OMITTED. Members of Families who have DIED SINCE June 1, 1880, will be INCLUDED.
Note C.—Questions Nos. 13, 14, 22 and 23 are not to be asked in respect to persons under 10 years of age.

SCHEDULE 1.—Inhabitants in La Porte, in the County of La Porte, State of Indiana enumerated by me on the Seventeenth day of June, 1880.

Gustav Drebing, Enumerator.

Line	Dwelling	Family	Name	Color	Sex	Age	Relationship	Single	Married	Occupation	Place of Birth	Father's Birthplace	Mother's Birthplace
1	509	514	Eggert August	W	M	48			/	Laborer	Mecklenburg	Mecklen"	Mecklen
2			— Carlina	W	F	46	Wife		/				
3			— Christian	W	M	10	Son	/		At School	Indiana		
4			— Minna	W	F	9	Daughter	/					
5			— Emma	W	F	7	—	/					
6			— Herman	W	M	6	Son	/					
7			— Friedrich	W	M	3	—	/					
10	510	515	Hacker Hermuth	W	M	49			/	Laborer	Mecklenburg	—	
38			Hilgendorf John	W	M	56			/	Laborer	Germany		
40			— Maria	W	F	57	Wife		/				
41			— Ludwig	W	M	18	Son	/		Blacksmith App"	Indiana		
43			— John	W	M	16	—	/		Tailor App"			
46	517	522	Hilgendorf John	W	M	56			/	Laborer	Germany	Germany	Germany
47			— Maria	W	F	57	Wife		/				
48			— Ludwig	W	M	18	Son	/		Blacksmith App"	Indiana		
49			— John	W	M	16	—	/		Tailor App"			

Note D.—In making entries in columns 9, 10, 11, 12, 15 to 23, an affirmative mark only will be used—thus /, except in the case of divorced persons, column 11, when the letter "D" is to be used.
Question No. 12 will only be asked in cases where an affirmative answer has been given either to question 10 or to question 11.
Question No. 14 will only be asked in cases when a gainful occupation has been reported in column 13.
In column 7 an abbreviation in the name of the month may be used, as Jan., Apr., Dec.

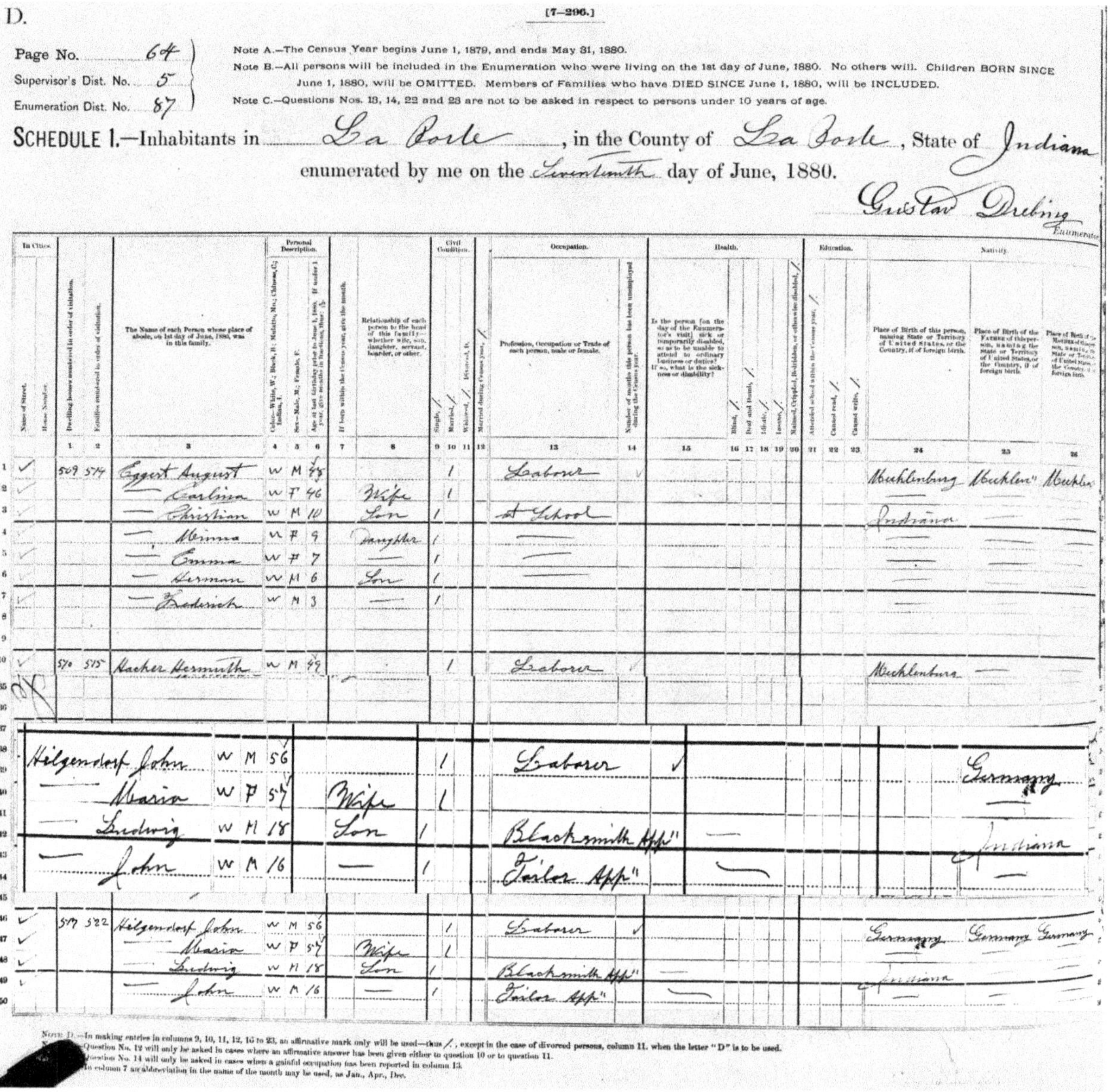

Johann C. Hilgendorf - 1880 Federal Census for La Porte, La Porte Co., Indiana

The above image shows a portion of a page from the 1880 census. The highlighted area shows the John (Johann C.) Hilgendorf family. Included are John, Maria, and sons Ludwig and John.

```
H   425
```

Family name	Given name or names
Hilgendorf	**John**
Address	
X	
Certificate no. (or vol. and page)	Title and location of court
Vol.-1854-1888-Pg.-348	Cir. Ct.-LaPorte Co.,Ind.
Country of birth or allegiance	When born (or age)
Germany	X
Date and port of arrival in U. S.	Date of naturalization
X	Feb. 18, 1881
Names and addresses of witnesses	
X	
X -	

U. S. Department of Labor, Immigration and Naturalization Service.   Form No. 1 IP.

Johann C. Hilgendorf – Naturalization Index Record

This is an index to the naturalization record of John (Johann C.) Hilgendorf. John became a naturalized U.S. citizen on 18 February 1881.

Maria Hilgendorf – Death Certificate

This is a copy of Maria Hilgendorf's death certificate. She died on 1 September 1902, about five years after John. The cause of death is listed as Cancer of Omentum. The omentum is a fat pad that lays on top of the intestines.

Johann C. and Maria Hilgendorf Grave

This is the grave marker for Johann C. and Maria Hilgendorf in St. John's Lutheran Cemetery, La Porte, Indiana. The family name Hilgendorf can be seen at the base of the marker. Johann and Maria are in Section A-60, Row 9, Lots 3 and 4. There are two small markers next to this larger marker with the German words Vater (Father) and Mutter (Mother) on them.

Johann C. and Maria Hilgendorf Grave

These are two of the faces on the marker shown on the preceding page. The face shown on the left above reads, "Johann C. Hilgendorf, GEB., 26 April 1824, GEST., 4 Marz 1897." GEB is the abbreviation for the German word Geboren, which means born. GEST. Is the abbreviation for the German word Gestorben, which means died. Marz, of course, is March. The face shown on the right above reads, "Maria Ehefrau Von, J. C. Hilgendorf, GEB., 1 Marz 1823, GEST., 1 Sept. 1902. The German Ehefrau Von translates to wife of.

Johann C. and Maria Hilgendorf Grave

A third face on the Johann C. and Maria Hilgendorf grave marker reads, "Hier Ruhen In, Frieden, Johann C. und Maria, Hilgendorf." The translation from German is, "Here Rest in, Peace, Johann C. and Maria, Hilgendorf."

HILGENDORF

THE SECOND GENERATION:

JOHN EDWARD HILGENDORF
(1862-1942)

FAMILY CHART

Friederike Hilgendorf – b. 21 June 1848, d. 30 January 1920
    Spouse: William L. Blankschein – b. 21 April 1845, d. 16 November 1893
    Children:
        Emma Blankschein – b. unknown, d. 1883
        Fred L. Blankschein – b. 1869, d. 1 February 1926
        George Blankschein – b. 7 August 1878, d. 22 June 1955
        Charles (Carl) Julius Blankschein – b. 24 October 1880, d. 1 January 1960
        Walter Blankschein – b. 13 November 1882, d. 7 March 1959

Wilhelmina (Minnie) Hilgendorf – b. 30 March 1852, d. 31 August 1907
    Spouse: Theodore Martin – b. unknown, d. unknown
    Children:
        Louisa Martin – b. January 1880, d. unknown
        John Martin – b. March 1882, d. unknown
        Paul Martin – b. August 1887, d. unknown
        Louis Martin – b. June 1893, d. unknown

Ludwig (Louis) Hilgendorf – b. 20 December 1859, d. 12 March 1928
    Spouse: Wihelmina Raddatz – b. 14 December 1863, d. 29 August 1942
    Children:

Paul Herman Hilgendorf – b. 3 June 1884, d. 16 January 1952
Leo Hilgendorf – b., August 1887, d. unknown
Elsie Caroline Hilgendorf – b. 21 February 1889, d. March 1986
Lawrence Hilgendorf – b. 5 November 1891, d. 1 September 1892
Clara Hilgendorf – b. 7 December 1892, d. 14 December 1918
Alfred Hilgendorf – b. 7 August 1895, d. 14 May 1896
Ruth Hilgendorf – b. 26 March 1897, d. 1 May1989
Herbert Clarence Carl Hilgendorf – b. 21 March 1899, d. 7 August 1980
Herman Hilgendorf – b. 12 November 1901, d. 28 May 1964
Edna Hilgendorf – b. 6 May 1904, d. 111 January 1937

John Edward Hilgendorf – b. 20 October 1862, d. 30 September 1942
    Spouse: Fredericka (Rickie) Kuch – b. 3 April 1866, d. 2 March 1935
    Children:

        Arthur John Hilgendorf – b. 1 July 1885, d. 18 January 1958
        Walter Frederick Hilgendorf – b. 19 March 1887, d. 21 February 1951
        Edwin William John Hilgendorf – b. 4 October 1893, d. 1956
        Mabel Louise Hilgendorf – b. 13 May 1897, d. 17 April 1985
        Nora W. Hilgendorf – b. 28 June 1899, d. 23 January 1992
        William A. Hilgendorf – b. 30 December 1901, d. 21 January 1979
        George F. Hilgendorf – b. 21 December 1904, d. 13 December 1966
        John Martin Leiter Hilgendorf – b. 30 September 1909, d. 15 March 1976

INTRODUCTION

In this chapter we will look at the children of Johann and Maria Hilgendorf. As previously indicated, we will follow the bold underlined names above as we move towards the blending of the Hilgendorf and Haag families, in this instance John E. Hilgendorf. Each of the siblings of John is studied to add more context to the life of the family. The siblings are reviewed in their order of birth.

FRIEDERIKE HILGENDORF (1848-1920)

Friederike was born 7 October 1848 in Germany. No records were found of her birth, but it is most likely that she was born in Mecklenburg. In various records, the names Fredericka, Rickie, Ricka and Rica are used. The shortened versions of Fredericka seem to have been common. There were several alternate birth dates for Rica. Some records note 1840, 1845, 1848 and 1850. 1848 seems to be the most likely date of her birth. Her gravestone uses the date of 1845, and maybe that is the correct date. However, her death certificate is either 1840 or 1848, and some census records would seem to indicate 1849-1850.

Rica was married to William (Wilhelm) L. Blankschein on 21 September 1867 in La Porte, Indiana. William was also of German descent born in1845. On 11 February 1890, he became a naturalized citizen.

In 1870, they are in La Porte where William is working in a woolen mill, likely Fox Woolen Mills which had been established in 1858. At this time 21-year-old Rica is keeping house and tending to 8-month-old Frederick.

William died in 1893, and in 1900 we find Rica living at 312 Fox Street next door to son Fred who lives at 310 Fox Street. At home with Rica are three sons: George, 21, who works as a clerk; Carl (or Charles), 19, who works as a day laborer; and Walter, 18, who also works as a day laborer. A day laborer was an unskilled worker who was paid by the day.

In 1910, Rica is living with her son Walter and his wife Elizabeth at 312 Fox Street. Walter and Elizabeth have no children at this time. Walter is now working in a skilled position as a finisher in a carriage factory. While there were several carriage businesses in La Porte at this time, the largest was the La Porte Carriage Company located at 506 Indiana Avenue (the corner of Indiana Avenue and State Street). This industry was a generally thriving trade at this time. In 1903 there were 36,184 such businesses in the country, and 1,497 of these were located in Indiana, making it the tenth largest state for this trade.

The next census in January 1920 finds Rica still living with Walter and Elizabeth at the same 312 Fox Street address. Elizabeth's father is also living with them at this time. Interestingly, the census does not list any employment for Walter.

Rica died later that year on 21 June 1920. She is buried next to her husband Wilhelm and daughter Emma in Saint John's Lutheran Cemetery in La Porte. They are in Section A-62, Row 9, Lots 3-5.

Page No. 95

☞ Inquiries numbered 7, 16, and 17 are not to be asked in respect to infants. Inquiries numbered 11, 12, 15, 16, 17, 19, and 20 are to be answered (if at all) merely by an affirmative mark, as /.

SCHEDULE 1.—Inhabitants in _La Porte City_, in the County of _La Porte_, State of _Indiana_, enumerated by me on the ___ day of ___, 1870.

157

Post Office: _La Porte Ind_ _C Loomis_, Ass't Marshal.

1	2	3	4	5	6	7	8	9	10	11	12	13	14	15	16	17	18	19	20	
		The name of every person whose place of abode on the first day of June, 1870, was in this family.	Age	Sex	Color	Profession, Occupation, or Trade of each person, male or female.	Value of Real Estate	Value of Personal Estate	Place of Birth, naming State or Territory of U. S.; or the Country, if of foreign birth.	Father of foreign birth	Mother of foreign birth	If born within the year	If married within the year	Attended school within the year	Cannot read	Cannot write	Whether deaf and dumb, blind, insane, or idiotic			
1		Miller, Charles	5	m	W	At Home			Indiana		/									1
2		Carr, Maria	23	F	W	At Home			Indiana	/	/									2
3	85 797	Kober, Charles	36	m	W	Tailor	1200	175	Saxony	X	/	/						/		3
4		— Margaret	40	F	m	Keeping House			Denmark	X	/	/								4
5		— Rosa	13	F	m	At Home			Indiana	/	/		/							5
6		— Doris	3	m	W	At Home			Indiana	/	/		/							6
14		— Frederick	2	m	W	At Home			Indiana	/	/									14
15	85 799	Blankschein, Wm	24	m	W	Works in Woolen Mill	800		Prussia	X	/	/						/		15
16		— Rica	21	F	W	Keeping House			Prussia	X	/	/								16
17		— Frederick	8/12	m	W	At Home			Indiana	/	/	Oct								17
18																				18
19																				19
20	85 799	Blankschein, Wm	24	m	W	Works in Woolen Mill	800		Prussia	X										20
31		— Rica	21	F	W	Keeping House			Prussia	X										31
32		— Frederick	8/12	m	W	At Home			Indiana											32
33																				33
34	740 803	Anderson, Earl	38	m	W	Day Laborer			Sweden	X	/	/						/		34
35		— Sophia	38	F	W	Keeping House			Sweden	X	/	/								35
36		— Augusta	19	F	W	At Home			Sweden	X	/	/								36
37		— Emily	11	F	W	At Home			Sweden	X	/	/								37
38		— August	9	m	W	At Home			Sweden	X	/	/								38
39		— Albion	1/12	m	W	At Home			Indiana	/	/	May								39
40	741 804	Loover, James	48	m	W	Ret Hardware Merchant	20	3000	Pennsylvania									/		40

Friederike Hilgendorf – 1870 Federal Census for La Porte, La Porte Co., Indiana

The above image shows a portion of a page from the 1870 census. The highlighted area shows William Blankschein, his wife Rica (Friederike Hilgendorf) and their 8-month-old son Frederick.

Friederike Hilgendorf – 1900 Federal Census for La Porte, La Porte Co., Indiana

The above image shows a portion of a page from the 1900 census. The highlighted area shows Ricky (Rica/Friederike Hilgendorf) Blankschein, now widowed, living with her three sons George, Carl and Walter.

Friederike Hilgendorf – 1910 Federal Census for La Porte, La Porte Co., Indiana

The above image shows a portion of a page from the 1910 census. The highlighted area shows Rika (Hilgendorf) Blankschein at age 60 living with her son Walter and his wife.

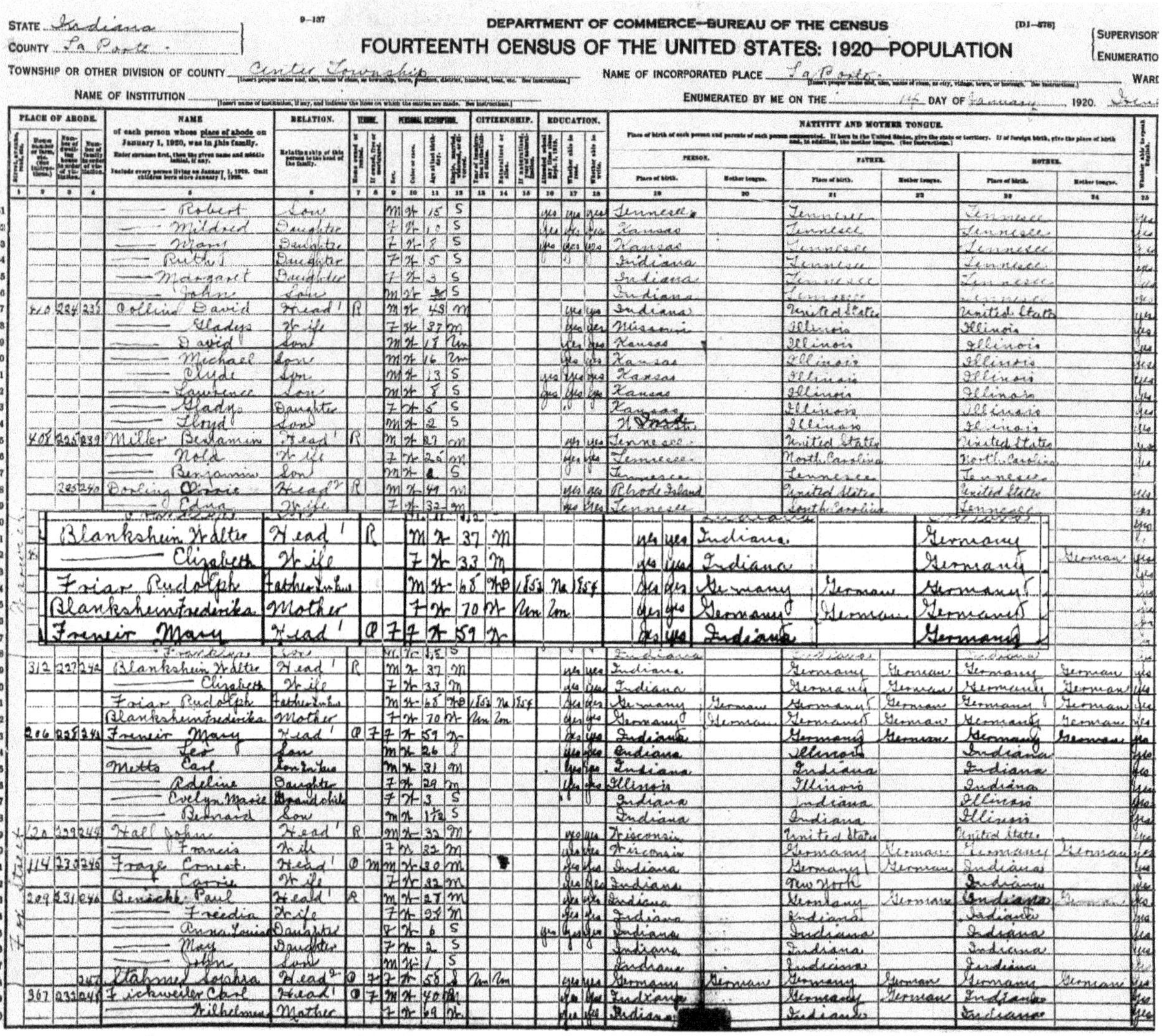

Friederike Hilgendorf – 1920 Federal Census for La Porte, La Porte Co., Indiana

The above image shows a portion of a page from the 1920 census. The highlighted area shows Frederika (Hilgendorf) Blankschein still living with her son Walter and his wife. His wife's father is also living with them.

Friederike (Hilgendorf) Blankschein – Death Certificate

This is a copy of Frederika (Hilgendorf) Blankschein's death certificate. She died on 30 January 1920. The cause of death is listed as Lobar Pneumonia with a contributory cause of Influenza.

WILHELMINA (MINNIE) HILGENDORF (1852-1907)

Wilhelmina, shortened to Minnie, was born in March of 1851 or 1852 in Germany. Census records indicate her birth in 1852, while her death certificate indicates 1851. She makes her first appearance in the 1870 census as the 18-year-old daughter of John and Maria. She subsequently married Theodore Martin (or Marten/s) on 15 March 1880 in La Porte.

In June of 1880, Minnie and Theodore are living in Colehour, Cook County, Illinois. That town no longer exists, but it appears to have been a neighborhood between the Calumet River and Calumet Park, about 15 miles from Gary, Indiana, just over the Indiana state line. In 1880 Minnie and Theodore have a 5-month-old daughter, Louisa, born in January.

A divorce for Minnie and Theodore was filed on 2 April 1898 in Charlevoix County, Michigan. The record notes that the couple had four children. The complainant is the husband, and he is filing for divorce for the reason of desertion. The divorce was contested, but it was granted on 2 April 1898.

The 1900 La Porte census finds Minnie as a divorced mother with three children at home: John, 18, working in a carriage shop; Paul, 12; and Louis, 6. All the children were born in Illinois. So, while no further information has been located on her husband, it is likely he was from Illinois as they had moved there after being married. At the time of the 1900 census, Minnie and her children are living at 1512 Scott Street, next door to her brother at their parents' former home at 1506 Scott Street.

The 1900 census also notes that Minnie immigrated to America in 1856. That corresponds with other information placing Johann and Maria's family immigration about 1856.

Minnie's death certificate lists her date of death as 30 March 1907. Minnie is buried in Section A-60, Row 9, Lot 1, near her parents, in Saint John's Lutheran Cemetery in La Porte.

Wilhelmina Hilgendorf – 1880 Federal Census for Colehour, Cook Co., Illinois

Wihelmina (Minnie) Hilgendorf Martin appears in the highlighted portion of the 1880 census with her husband Theodore Martin and their 5-month old daughter Louisa.

Wilhelmina Hilgendorf – 1900 Federal Census for La Porte, La Porte Co., Indiana

Wihelmina (Minnie) Hilgendorf Martin appears in the highlighted portion of the 1900 census with her sons John, Paul and Louis. Minnie is divorced and now living in La Porte.

Wilhelmina (Hilgendorf) Martin – Death Certificate

This is a copy of Wilhelmina (Hilgendorf) Martin's death certificate. She died on 31 August 1907. The cause of death is listed as Heart Disease.

Wilhelmina (Hilgendorf) Martin Grave

This is a photo of Wilhelmina (Hilgendorf) Martin's grave marker in St. John's Lutheran Cemetery, La Porte, Indiana. Note that the birth year is listed as 1853; whereas, research seems to place her birth in 1851 or 1852. She is buried Section A-60, Row 9, Lot 1, near her parents.

LUDWIG (LOUIS) HILGENDORF (1859-1928)

Ludwig appears alternately as Louis and Ludwig in the census records for 1880 and 1900. In the 1880 census, Ludwig is an 18-year-old apprentice blacksmith living at home with his parents in La Porte. La Porte city directories for 1893 and 1894 shows Louis at a blacksmith shop at 601-605 Clay Street. In the 1900 census, Louis is married to Wilamine (note, the spelling for this name varies greatly in the records), and he is a blacksmith. At this time, they have been married for 18 years.

In the 1900 census there are six children living at home with Louis and Wilhelmina: Paul,15; Leo, 12; Elsie, 11; Clara, 7; Ruth, 3; and Herbert, 1. In the census, it notes that they had ten children, six of whom are living. According to the 1910 census, they had eight children, and eight are living.

Wilhelmina was born in Germany according to the census records and immigrated to America in 1864. Her maiden name appears to be Raddatz, although it has also been noted as Rothets. In the 1930 census, it appears as though the census taker began to write Mecklenburg for the country of birth but wrote the word German over that. So, we can surmise that Wilhelmina was born in Mecklenburg, Germany. As previously noted, located in northeast Germany, Mecklenburg has traditionally been one of the poorer German areas.

While there is no address in the 1880 census, in 1900 the family is living at 307 Fox Street in La Porte. They remain at this address the rest of their lives.

In 1910, the couple now has a new child, Edna, age 8. The oldest daughter, Elsie, is working as a seamstress. Louis is still a working blacksmith, but the census record notes that he owns his own shop. The address for his business is 712-714 Madison Street.

The 1920 census reveals that son Herbert, age 20, is now also employed as a blacksmith, in all likelihood working with his father. Son Herman, age 18, is a clerk in the woolen mill. There are now four children at home: Ruth, Herbert, Herman and Edna. Also living with them is Wilhelmina's mother, Wilhelmina Raddatz.

Louis died in 1928, an in the 1930 census daughter Edna is living with Wilhelmina. In the last available census, which is for the year 1940, Wilhelmina is a 76-year-old widow with no others listed living with her.

There are La Porte City directories that show the family for 1893, 1894, 1896, 1902, 1907, 1910, 1923 and 1926. It appears Louis was a blacksmith all of his life. He is shown associated with two businesses: Wild & Hilgendorf in 1893-1894 and Eggenbrecht & Hilgendorf in 1910. The first business was listed at 601 and 605 Clay Street, while the second business may have been at 712-714 Madison Street.

The 1904 city directory lists three children living with Louis and Wilhelmina: Leo, a fireman; Elsie, a milliner; and Paul, a weaver. The 1910 directory lists Clara and Elsie both working at Buckingham. Buckingham refers to Buckingham Brothers Skirt Company in La Porte.

The 1923 directory notes that Louis is a blacksmith at 712-714 Madison Street. Paul, now married to Louise, is noted as a blacksmith working for Louis. Edna is still at home working as a seamstress. Herbert is also at home and employed as a mechanic. In the 1926 directory, the last prior to Louis' death, he is listed in the business section under the heading Blacksmith. Son Paul is still living with Louis and Wilhelmina.

Louis and Wilhelmina are buried in Saint John's Lutheran Cemetery in La Porte. They are in Section E-27, Row 4, Lots 1 and 2. Buried in this same section in Lots 3 and 4 are children Clara Hilgendorf and Figg Hilgendorf. Figg's birth year is listed as 1904. Based upon this information, this would be Edna who was born in May of 1904. Further research found that Edna's married name was Figg.

Louis and Wilhelmina's Son Paul is also buried in Saint John's in Section I-20, Lot 1, and his wife Louise is next to him in Lot 2. Son Herbert and his wife Laura are buried in Pine Lake Cemetery, as are son Herman and his wife Veronica.

1900 Census
La Porte, La Porte County, Indiana
Louis Hilgendorf

TWELFTH CENSUS OF THE UNITED STATES.

SCHEDULE No. 1.—POPULATION.

B

State _Indiana_
County _La Porte_
Township or other division of county _Center Township_
Name of incorporated city, town, or village, within the above-named division. _City of La Porte_
Name of Institution _____
Supervisor's District No. _67_
Enumeration District No. _46_
Sheet No. _17_
Ward of city _3_
Enumerated by me on the ____ day of June, 1900. _Charles H. Provisdau_ Enumerator.

Louis (Ludwig) Hilgendorf – 1900 Federal Census for La Porte, La Porte Co., Indiana

Louis (Ludwig) Hilgendorf appears in the highlighted portion of the 1900 census with his wife Wilhelmina and their children Paul, Leo, Elsie, Clara, Ruth and Herbert.

Louis (Ludwig) Hilgendorf – 1910 Federal Census for La Porte, La Porte Co., Indiana

Louis (Ludwig) Hilgendorf appears in the highlighted portion of the 1910 census with his wife Minnie and their children Elsie, Clara, Ruth, Herbert and Edna.

Louis (Ludwig) Hilgendorf – 1920 Federal Census for La Porte, La Porte Co., Indiana

Louis (Ludwig) Hilgendorf appears in the highlighted portion of the 1920 census with his wife Wilhelmina and their children Ruth, Herbert, Herman and Edna. Also living with them is Wilhelmina's mother, Wilhelmina Raddatz.

Louis (Ludwig) Hilgendorf – Death Certificate

This is a copy of Louis Hilgendorf's death certificate. He died on 12 March 1928. The cause of death is listed as Thrombo Phlebitis of Cerebral Venous (blood clot in the brain). A contributory cause noted is Meningitis (an acute inflammation of the protective membranes covering the brain and spinal cord).

Wilhelmina (Raddatz) Hilgendorf – Death Certificate

This is a copy of Wihelmina (Raddatz) Hilgendorf's death certificate. She died on 29 August 1942. The cause of death is listed as Gangrene of the Right Leg due to a blood clot. There is also note of another condition of Coronary Thrombosis (a blood clot in the heart).

Louis (Ludwig) and Wilhelmina (Raddatz) Hilgendorf Grave Markers

The above photos are of the grave markers for Louis and Wilhelmina Hilgendorf. They are buried in Saint John's Lutheran Cemetery, La Porte, Indiana. They are in Section E-27, Row 4, Lots 1 and 2. Buried in this same section in Lots 3 and 4 are children Clara Hilgendorf and Edna Hilgendorf.

JOHN EDWARD HILGENDORF (1862-1942)

John Edward Hilgendorf is the family line that we will follow as we move towards the Hilgendorf-Haag union. Looking through the census records and city directories for La Porte, we find that John is a tailor. In fact, in the 1880 census it is noted that at age 16 he is a tailor's apprentice. His wife, Fredericka Kuch/Cook/Pusch was born in September 1866 in Germany. She immigrated to the U.S. in 1868. Fredericka is often referred to as Ricka or Rickie in various records. Her last name Kuch is also noted as Cook, an obvious American pronunciation of her German name. I also found one source where the name appeared to be Pusch. It is not out of question that Pusch was misspelled as Kuch at some point, and Kuch could have then been Americanized to Cook.

In the 1900 census there are five children: Arthur, 15; Walter, 13; Edwin, 5; Mabel, 3; and Nora, 11 months. Also living with the family is John's mother Mary, a 78-year-old widow born in March 1823. They reside at 1506 Scott Street in La Porte. They are still at this address in 1902, but by 1904 they are living at 1208 Ridge Street. Subsequent directories list the address as 1206 Ridge Street. The 1902 directory, and all subsequent directories continue to list John's occupation as a tailor.

By 1910, there are seven children at home (and oldest son, Arthur, is no longer there): Walter, 23; Edwin, 17; Mabel, 12; Nora, 10; Willie, 8; Georgie, 5; and John, 6 months. Also living with the family is Walter's new wife, Minnie. In the 1910 census we see John's occupation listed as a tailor, as it would be for all ensuing years. Walter's occupation is also noted as a tailor. Edwin, age 17, is a painter at a carriage factory. It also notes in this census that Edwin was born in Wisconsin. All the other children were born in Indiana. Walter's wife Minnie is a weaver at a blanket factory.

In 1920, we find son Edwin is a laborer at a cycle works. Nora is a stenographer at a doctor's office and William is a trimmer at a baby carriage company. As in the 1910 census, the family is living at 1206 Ridge Street, which is where every subsequent record shows John through the 1940 census and a 1940 city directory.

By 1930 three children are still at home: Mabel, George and John. Mabel is 32, George is a 25-year-old painter in the buildings trade, and John is a 20-year-old polisher at a metal products company.

In the last available 1940 census, John is 77 years old and still listed as a tailor. At home are Mabel, 32 and single, and George, 35 and also single, working as a mechanic at an auto factory.

John's business address was listed in earlier directories as 708 Main Street (Lincolnway today). He is later listed as working at Low's clothing store. In the 1907 city directory John's occupation is listed as "merchant tailoring, cleaning and pressing." All other directories simply note tailor or merchant tailor.

John died 30 September 1942, while Fredericka had already passed in 1935. John's death certificate notes the cause of death as chronic hepatitis. They are buried in Pine Lake Cemetery in La Porte, possibly in the North Lawn section of the cemetery.

John Edward Hilgendorf – 1900 Federal Census for La Porte, La Porte Co., Indiana

John Hilgendorf appears in the highlighted portion of the 1900 census with his wife Ricky (Fredericka) and their children Arthur, Walter, Edwin, Mable and Nora. Also living with them is John's mother Mary (Maria).

John Edward Hilgendorf – 1910 Federal Census for La Porte, La Porte Co., Indiana

John Hilgendorf appears in the highlighted portion of the 1910 census with his wife Rica (Fredericka) and their children Walter, Edwin, Mabel, Nora, Willie, Georgie and John. Also living with them is Minnie, Walter's wife.

John Edward Hilgendorf – 1920 Federal Census for La Porte, La Porte Co., Indiana

John Hilgendorf appears in the highlighted portion of the 1920 census with his wife Fredericke and their children Edwin, Mabel, Nora, William, George and John.

John Edward Hilgendorf – 1930 Federal Census for La Porte, La Porte Co., Indiana

John (J. E. in the census) Hilgendorf appears in the highlighted portion of the 1930 census with his wife Fredericke and their children Mabel, George and John.

Deaths

JOHN E. HILGENDORF

John E. Hilgendrof, 79, of 1206 Ridge street, a tailor here for many years, died at his home at 10 o'clock this morning following an illness of 10 days. He was born in LaPorte Oct. 20, 1862, the son of Mr. and Mrs. John Hilgendorf, and had lived here all his life with the exception of five years in his early years.

He attended St. John's Lutheran school and was confirmed in that church. On March 29, 1886 he was married in LaPorte to Fredericka Cook, who died March 2, 1935.

Surviving are six sons, Arthur, Walter, Edwin, and William Hilgendorf, all of LaPorte; George, Camp Blanding, Fla., and John M., Detroit; two daughters, Miss Mabel Hilgendorf, at home; Mrs. John Lingard, LaPorte, 13 grandchildren and five great grandchildren.

The funeral services will be held at the O. M. Haverstock chapel Friday at 2:30, the Rev. Manfred E. Reinke officiating. Burial will be in Pine Lake cemetery. The body may be viewed at the Haverstock chapel from tomorrow noon until time for the rites Friday.

John E. Hilgendorf – Obituary

This is a copy of John Edward Hilgendorf's obituary from the *La Porte Daily Herald-Argus* of 30 September 1942.

John E. Hilgendorf – Death Certificate

This is a copy of John Edward Hilgendorf's death certificate. He died on 30 September 1942. The cause of death is noted as Chronic Hepatitis.

MRS JOHN E. HILGENDORF

Mrs. Fredericka Hilgendorf, age 68, wife of John E. Hilgendorf of 1206 Ridge street, passed away at 2 o'clock Saturday afternoon in the Holy Family hospital. She had been ill for the past three years.

The daughter of Christ and Hanna Cook, Mrs. Hilgendorf was born in Germany on Sept. 3, 1866. She had lived here practically all her life, however, for she came to this country from Germany when she was two years old.

On March 29, 1885, in LaPorte she was married to John E. Hilgendorf. The ceremony was performed by the Rev. Mr. Niedthammer. She was a member of St. John's Lutheran church.

Surviving are her husband; six sons, Arthur, Walter, Edwin, William, George and John M. Hilgendorf, all of LaPorte; two daughters, Miss Mable Hilgendorf and Mrs. John Lingard, both of LaPorte; one sister, Mrs. Charles Helt of LaPorte.

Funeral services will be held at 2 o'clock tomorrow afternoon at the residence. The Rev. Manfred E. Reinke will officiate and burial will be in Pine Lake cemetery with O. M. Haverstock in charge.

The body may be viewed at the home this afternoon and evening and until the time of the funeral.

Fredericka (Kuch/Cook) Hilgendorf – Obituary

This is a copy of Fredericka (Kuch/Cook) Hilgendorf's obituary from the *La Porte Daily Herald-Argus* of 4 March 1935.

Fredericka (Kuch/Cook) Hilgendorf – Death Certificate

This is a copy of Fredericka Hilgendorf's death certificate. She died on 2 March 1935. The cause of death is noted as Pulmonary Embolism (sudden blockage of a major blood vessel in the lung, usually by a blood clot).

HILGENDORF

THE THIRD GENERATION:

ARTHUR JOHN HILGENDORF
(1885-1958)

FAMILY CHART

Arthur John Hilgendorf – b. 1 July 1885, d. 18 January 1958
      Spouse: Mary Kramer – b. 21 January 1844, d. 6 December 1960
      Children:
            Arthur Hilgendorf Jr. - b. 27 May 1908, d. 1908?
            Lawrence Arthur Hilgendorf – b. 25 July 1909, d. 21 April 1999
            Clarence John Hilgendorf – b. 30 October 1910, d. 24 July 1990
            Roy A. Hilgendorf – b. 7 October 1912, d. 9 April 1970
            Wilbur C. Hilgendorf – b. 21 October 1914, d. 1 May 1943
            Raymond J. Hilgendorf – b. 5 July 1916, d. 7 June 1981
            Arthur Hilgendorf Jr. - b. 15 March 1919, d. 10 December 1922
            Marie J. Hilgendorf – b. 1 April 1922, d. 1 April 2009
            Doris Hilgendorf – b. 23 July 1924, d. 30 June 2012

Walter Frederick Hilgendorf – b. 19 March 1887, d. 21 February 1951
      Spouse: Minnie Pusch – b. 30 October 1888, d. 19 February 1912
      Spouse: Emma E. Mellenthin – b. 24 July 1894, d. 5 January 1991
      Children:
            Norman W. Hilgendorf – b. 18 March 1914, d. 15 February 1994
            Mildred Emma Hilgendorf – b. 30 September 1915, d. 12 July 2012
            Donald John Hilgendorf – b. 19 July 1917, d. 30 October 1999

Edwin William John Hilgendorf – b. 4 October 1893, d. 1956
    Spouse: Ella H. - b. 13 May 1894, d. 1 January 1973

Mabel Louise Hilgendorf – b. 13 May 1897, d. 17 April 1985

Nora W. Hilgendorf – b. 28 June 1899, d. 23 January 1992
    Spouse: John Thomas Lingard – b. 28 February 1891, d. 22 March 1974

William A. Hilgendorf – b. 30 December 1901, d. 21 January 1979
    Spouse: Louise Pflugshaupt – b. 24 February 1901, d. 30 June 1986
    Children:
        Elaine Ruth Hilgendorf – b. 28 January 1925
        Viola June Hilgendorf – b. 24 November 1928, d. 25 August 2016
        Ronald William Hilgendorf – b. 25 September 1939

George F. Hilgendorf – b. 21 December 1904, d. 13 December 1966
    Spouse: Katherine Lucille Lindborg – b. 17 October 1905, d. 20 January 1993

John Martin Leiter Hilgendorf – b. 30 September 1909, d. 15 March 1976
    Spouse: Ruth Ervin – b. 19 June 1908, d. 18 December 2000

ARTHUR JOHN HILGENDORF (1885-1958)

Arthur John Hilgendorf is the first-born son of John Edward Hilgendorf and Fredericka (Cook) Hilgendorf. Born in 1885, Arthur is living at home with his parents at 1506 Scott Street in La Porte in 1900. In 1902 he is working as a farm laborer, and his occupation is listed simply as laborer in a 1904 city directory. At that time he is still at home with his parents, now at 1208 Ridge Street.

Having married Mary (Marie) Kramer in 1907, in 1913 Arthur and Mary are at 1116 Ridge Street, and he is employed as a moulder at Niles & Scott Co. in La Porte. He would remain at the Ridge Street address for the remainder of his life. In 1917, Arthur is still at Niles & Scott, but by 1923 he is working as a coremaker at La Porte F&F Co.

In the 1920 census, Arthur and Marie have five children: Lawrence, 10; Clarence, 9; Roy, 7; Wilbur, 5; and Raymond, 3. Several years later, there was a change in Arthur's direction as we find that in 1929 he is now working as a confectioner with a business at 111 Clement Street. This store was just behind his house on Ridge Street. From this time through 1952 he serves in this capacity and as a grocer at 111 Clement Street. In the 1954 city directory, there is no occupation listed. Perhaps he has retired from his business at this point.

The 1930 census notes the following children at home: Lawrence, 20; Clarence, 19; Roy, 17; Wilbur, 15; and Raymond, 13; Marie, 8; and Doris, 5. This census notes that Arthur is the proprietor of a grocery store. Lawrence is working as a pressman at a printing company.

In the 1940 census, four children are living at home with Arthur and Mary. This year finds Clarence, 29; Wilbur, 25; Marie, 18; and Doris, 15, still at home with their parents. Arthur's occupation is noted as a salesman at a retail confectionery. Clarence is working as a stocking clerk at an automobile brake factory (most likely Bendix Corporation in South Bend), Wilbur is a laborer at an automobile radiator business.

Records of two other children who do not show up in any of the census records have been located. The first is Arthur Hilgendorf Jr. who was born on 27 May 1908, making him the first child of Arthur and Mary. The birth certificate notes that this is the first child of Mary and there are no other children. We might assume that he died soon after birth, but no death record has been located. There is no indication of any complications at birth. Added to this, however, is the fact that he was born about six months after Arthur and Mary were married. So, perhaps he was premature and did not live long. But, again, there are no indications of this on the birth record. There is also a place on the birth record to check whether the child was born alive or not, but nothing is checked in this location.

The other child located was also Arthur Hilgendorf Jr. This son was born 15 March 1919, placing him between between Ray and Marie. His death record has been found, but no birth record. This death record clearly notes both the birth and death dates – 15 March 1919 and 10 December 1922. The dates on the documents for these two children are very clear, and all other information is very clear as to parents, addresses, etc.; there is no mistake that these two Arthur

Juniors are the children of Arthur and Mary Hilgendorf.

I have been unable to locate a 1910 census record for the family to see if the first Arthur Jr. was still with the family at the time. Strangely, the 1920 census does not show the second Arthur Jr., even though he did not die until 1922. Perhaps he was ill from birth and living under some type of care. Unfortunately, with the lack of information available, we may never know the answer. His death certificate notes the cause of death as "lobar pneumonia – both lungs" and a secondary factor of "Measles." He is buried in Pine Lake Cemetery.

Most records indicate that Arthur John Hilgendorf was born in Indiana. The 1930 census, however, lists his place of birth as Wisconsin. This is the only record found to date that indicates Wisconsin as his birthplace. His wife Mary was born in Indiana.

Arthur passed away on 18 January 1958. Mary followed on 6 December 1960. Arthur and Mary are buried in Pine Lake Cemetery in La Porte in the North Dewberry section.

Arthur John Hilgendorf – 1920 Federal Census for La Porte, La Porte Co., Indiana

Arthur Hilgendorf appears in the highlighted portion of the 1920 census with his wife Marie (Mary) and their children Lawrence, Clarence, Roy, Wilbur and Raymond.

Arthur John Hilgendorf – 1930 Federal Census for La Porte, La Porte Co., Indiana

Arthur Hilgendorf appears in the highlighted portion of the 1930 census with his wife Mary and their children Lawrence, Clarence, Roy, Wilbur, Raymond, Marie and Doris.

Arthur John Hilgendorf – 1940 Federal Census for La Porte, La Porte Co., Indiana

Arthur Hilgendorf appears in the highlighted portion of the 1940 census with his wife Mary and their children Clarence, Wilbur, Marie and Doris.

Arthur John Hilgendorf – World War I Draft Registration Card

REGISTRATION CARD—(Men born on or after April 28, 1877 and on or before February 16, 1897)

SERIAL NUMBER	1. NAME (Print)			ORDER NUMBER
U 457	Arthur	John	Hilgendorf	
	(First)	(Middle)	(Last)	

2 PLACE OF RESIDENCE (Print)   1115 Ridge St., LaPorte, Ind.

(Number and street)   (Town, township, village, or city)   (County)   (State)

[THE PLACE OF RESIDENCE GIVEN ON THE LINE ABOVE WILL DETERMINE LOCAL BOARD
JURISDICTION; LINE 2 OF REGISTRATION CERTIFICATE WILL BE IDENTICAL]

3. MAILING ADDRESS   same

[Mailing address if other than place indicated on line 2. If same insert word same]

4. TELEPHONE	5. AGE IN YEARS	6. PLACE OF BIRTH
1404 L (old)	56	LaPorte
	DATE OF BIRTH	(Town or county)
	July 1st, 1885	LaPorte, Ind.
(Exchange) (Number)	(Mo.) (Day) (Yr.)	(State or country)

7. NAME AND ADDRESS OF PERSON WHO WILL ALWAYS KNOW YOUR ADDRESS

Mrs. Mary Hilgendorf, 1115 Ridge St., LaPorte, Ind.

8. EMPLOYER'S NAME AND ADDRESS   self employed

9. PLACE OF EMPLOYMENT OR BUSINESS   107 Clement, LaPorte, Ind.

(Number and street or R.F.D. number)   (Town)   (County)   (State)

I AFFIRM THAT I HAVE VERIFIED ABOVE ANSWERS AND THAT THEY ARE TRUE.

D. S. S. Form 1
(Revised 4-1-42)   (over)   16—21630   *Arthur Hilgendorf*

(Registrant's signature)

Arthur John Hilgendorf – World War II Draft Registration Card

Arthur Hilgendorf and Mary Kramer

These undated photos of Arthur and Mary seem likely to have been shortly before their marriage.

Arthur John Hilgendorf and Mary Kramer on their Wedding Day, 17 December 1907

Couple To Mark 50th Year

MR. AND MRS. ARTHUR HILGENDORF

Mr. and Mrs. Arthur Hilgendorf will observe their golden wedding anniversary with an open house from 2 to 5 o'clock at their home, 1116 Ridge street, on Sunday afternoon. Relatives, friends and neighbors are invited. The six children of the couple will be hosts. Mr. and Mrs. Hilgendorf were married Dec. 18, 1907 at St. Joseph's parsonage. For 27 years Mr. Hilgendorf was proprietor of a grocery and confectionery store on Clement street. He is now retired. The couplee are in fair health.

Arthur and Mary Hilgendorf on their 50th Anniversary in 1957.

Arthur Hilgendorf Storefront

A recent photo of the site of Arthur Hilgendorf's store at 111 Clement Street, La Porte, Indiana. The store was located behind the family's home at 1116 Ridge Street.

Arthur Hilgendorf Store

This is an undated photo of the interior of Arthur Hilgendorf's store located at 111 Clement Street, La Porte, Indiana.

The Arthur Hilgendorf Family

This is an undated photo of the Arthur Hilgendorf family. It was likely taken in the late 1930s. Arthur and Mary are seated in front. From left to right the others are: Lawrence, Doris, Wilbur, Roy, Ray, Marie, and Clarence (Dutch).

Mathias and Katherine (Berg) Kramer – Mary's Parents

This is an undated photo of Mathias and Katherine (Berg) Kramer and three of their children. Mathias and Katherine were Mary's parents.

Arthur John Hilgendorf – Death Certificate

This is a copy of Arthur John Hilgendorf's death certificate. He died on 18 January 1958. The cause of death is entered as Chronic Myocarditis (inflammation of the heart muscle, chronic indicating that symptoms reappeared later after a previous episode).

INDIANA STATE BOARD OF HEALTH
DIVISION OF VITAL RECORDS
MEDICAL CERTIFICATE OF DEATH

Local No. 60 235

State No. '60 042534

1. PLACE OF DEATH		2. USUAL RESIDENCE (Where deceased lived. If institution: Residence before admission)
a. COUNTY LaPorte		a. STATE Indiana — b. COUNTY LaPorte
b. CITY, TOWN, OR LOCATION LaPorte	c. Length of Stay in 1b	c. CITY, TOWN, OR LOCATION LaPorte Indiana
d. NAME OF HOSPITAL OR INSTITUTION (If not in hospital, give street address) Holy Family Hospital		d. STREET ADDRESS 1116 Ridge St.
e. IS PLACE OF DEATH INSIDE CITY LIMITS? YES ☒ NO ☐		e. IS RESIDENCE INSIDE CITY LIMITS? YES ☒ NO ☐ — f. IS RESIDENCE ON A FARM? YES ☐ NO ☒

3. NAME OF DECEASED (Type or print)	First Mary	Middle	Last Hilgendorf	4. DATE OF DEATH Month Day Year 12/6/60

5. SEX female	6. COLOR OR RACE white	7. MARRIED ☐ NEVER MARRIED ☐ WIDOWED ☒ DIVORCED ☐	8. DATE OF BIRTH Jan.21,1884	9. AGE (In years last birthday) 76	IF UNDER 1 YEAR Months Days	IF UNDER 24 HRS. Hours Min.

10a. USUAL OCCUPATION housewife	10b. KIND OF BUSINESS OR INDUSTRY home	11. BIRTHPLACE LaPorte Indiana	12. CITIZEN OF WHAT COUNTRY? USA

13. FATHER'S NAME Mathia Kramer	14. MOTHER'S MAIDEN NAME Katie Bergland

15. WAS DECEASED EVER IN U. S. ARMED FORCES? no	17a. INFORMANT'S NAME Lawrence Hilgendorf

17b. INFORMANT'S ADDRESS R # 4 LaPorte Indiana	17c. RELATIONSHIP TO DECEASED son

18. CAUSE OF DEATH (Enter only one cause per line for (a), (b), and (c).)
PART I. DEATH WAS CAUSED BY:
IMMEDIATE CAUSE (a) Cerebral Embolism — INTERVAL BETWEEN ONSET AND DEATH 48 hours

Conditions, if any, which gave rise to above cause (a) stating the underlying cause last.
DUE TO (b)_____
DUE TO (c)_____

PART II. OTHER SIGNIFICANT CONDITIONS CONTRIBUTING TO DEATH BUT NOT RELATED TO THE TERMINAL DISEASE CONDITION GIVEN IN PART I (a)

19. WAS AUTOPSY PERFORMED? YES ☐ NO ☐

20a. ACCIDENT ☐ SUICIDE ☐ HOMICIDE ☐	20b. DESCRIBE HOW INJURY OCCURRED.

20c. TIME OF INJURY Hour Month Day Year a.m. p.m.

20d. INJURY OCCURRED WHILE AT WORK ☐ NOT WHILE AT WORK ☐
20e. PLACE OF INJURY
20f. CITY, TOWN, OR LOCATION — COUNTY — STATE

21. ATTENDING PHYSICIAN: I certify that I attended the deceased from July 1955 to 12/6/60 and last saw her alive on 12/6/60. Death occurred at 11:35 A.M. (C.S.T.) on the date stated above; and to the best of my knowledge, from the causes stated.

22. HEALTH OFFICER: I certify that I investigated cause of death of deceased and find that death occurred at ____ M (C.S.T.) from causes stated and on above date.

23a. Signature of Attending Physician or Health Officer Francis B Filck 2d	23b. ADDRESS 1201 Maple	23c. DATE SIGNED 12/8/60

24a. BURIAL, CREMATION, REMOVAL (Specify) burial	24b. DATE 12/9/60	24c. NAME OF CEMETERY OR CREMATORY Pine Lake Cemetery	24d. LOCATION LaPorte Ind.

DATE REC'D BY LOCAL HEALTH OFFICER 12-7-60
SIGNATURE OF HEALTH OFFICER Russ Ulsey Jr. M.D.
25. FUNERAL DIRECTOR Haverstock, LaPorte Ind. — ADDRESS

S.B.H.—6-24-3—Revised 1955 U. S. Department Health, Education and Welfare. Form Approved Budget Bureau No. 68-R375

EMBALMER'S NAME L.F.Judey 4136
LICENSE No.
FUNERAL DIRECTOR'S LICENSE No. 109

Mary (Kramer) Hilgendorf – Death Certificate

This is a copy of Mary (Kramer) Hilgendorf's death certificate. She died on 6 December 1960. The cause of death is listed as Cerebral Embolism (a blockage of a brain vessel by a clot or plaque). This is one form of a stroke.

WALTER FREDERICK HILGENDORF (1887-1951)

In the 1910 census Walter is living at home at 1206 Ridge Street and working as a tailor, apparently following in his father's footsteps. He is recently married to Minnie Pusch. Minnie is a weaver at a blanket mill. Unfortunately, Minnie died on 19 February 1912. It is unknown what happened to Minnie. It appears that Walter and Minnie did not have any children together.

On 28 August 1913, Walter married Emma Mellenthin. By 1920, Walter and Emma are living at 607 Division Street and have three children: Norman, 5; Mildred, 4; and Donald, 2. We know they were at this location as early as 1917 as this is the address on his World War I draft registration card. His occupation in the 1920 census is a draftsman at a building construction company.

In 1913 Walter was employed as a draftsman at the building company Griewank Brothers in La Porte. Apparently his work as a tailor was not suitable for some reason. We do not know yet the exact year, but Walter next went into a business partnership with Walter Shrader to form Hilgendorf & Shrader, a retail lumber and coal company located at 507 Brighton Street. This business is listed in a 1923 city directory.

Walter and Emma continued to live at 607 Division Street. This address appears through 1947 city directories. In 1949, their address is listed as 706 Lakeside Street. Walter died in 1951, and Emma died in 1991. Walter and Minnie are buried in Pine Lake Cemetery in La Porte in the Cherry section. Emma appears to be in the Dew section at Pine Lake Cemetery.

Walter Frederick Hilgendorf – 1920 Fed. Census for La Porte, La Porte Co., Indiana

Walter Frederick Hilgendorf appears in the highlighted portion of the 1920 census with his wife Emma and their children Norman, Mildred and Donald.

Walter Frederick Hilgendorf – 1930 Fed. Census for La Porte, La Porte Co., Indiana

Walter Frederick Hilgendorf appears in the highlighted portion of the 1930 census with his wife Emma and children Norman, Mildred and Donald.

INDIANA STATE BOARD OF HEALTH
Division of Vital Records
CERTIFICATE OF DEATH

Local No. 48
Death No. 4920

1. PLACE OF DEATH	2. USUAL RESIDENCE (Where deceased lived. If institution: residence before admission)
a. COUNTY LaPorte 346	a. STATE Indiana b. COUNTY LaPorte
b. CITY OR TOWN LaPorte c. LENGTH OF STAY (in this place)	c. CITY OR TOWN LaPorte Indiana 346
d. FULL NAME OF HOSPITAL OR INSTITUTION 607 Division	d. STREET ADDRESS 607 Division St

3. NAME OF DECEASED (Type or Print)	a. (First) Walter	b. (Middle) F.	c. (Last) Hilgendorf	4. DATE OF DEATH 2-21-51 19

| 5. SEX male | 6. COLOR OR RACE white | 7. MARRIED NEVER MARRIED WIDOWED DIVORCED (Specify) married | 8. DATE OF BIRTH March 19, 1887 | 9. AGE (In years) 63 |

| 10a. USUAL OCCUPATION Owner | 10b. KIND OF BUSINESS OR INDUSTRY Coal Dealer | 11. BIRTHPLACE LaPorte Indiana | 12. CITIZEN OF WHAT COUNTRY? USA |

| 13. FATHER'S NAME John Z. Hilgendorf | 14. MOTHER'S MAIDEN NAME Fredricka (unknown) |

| 15. WAS DECEASED EVER IN U.S. ARMED FORCES? No | 16. SOCIAL SECURITY No. | 17. INFORMANT (NAME AND ADDRESS) Mrs. Emma Hilgendorf, LaPorte Ind. |

MEDICAL CERTIFICATION

18. CAUSE OF DEATH		INTERVAL BETWEEN ONSET AND DEATH
I DISEASE OR CONDITION DIRECTLY LEADING TO DEATH (a)	Coronary thrombosis	12 hours
ANTECEDENT CAUSES DUE TO (b)	Arteriosclerosis	5 years
DUE TO (c)		
II OTHER SIGNIFICANT CONDITIONS		

| 19a. DATE OF OPERATION None | 19b. MAJOR FINDINGS OF OPERATION No operation 42.01-012 | 20. AUTOPSY? Yes ☐ No ☒ |

| 21a. ACCIDENT SUICIDE HOMICIDE None | 21b. PLACE OF INJURY Omit | 21c. (CITY, TOWN, OR TOWNSHIP) Omit (COUNTY) (STATE) |
| 21d. TIME OF INJURY Omit | 21e. INJURY OCCURRED While at Work ☐ Not While at Work ☐ | 21f. HOW DID INJURY OCCUR? Omit |

| 22a. ATTENDING PHYSICIAN I certify that I attended the deceased from 2/20/51 19 to 2/21/51 8:30A 19 and that death occurred at M from causes stated and on above date | 22b. HEALTH OFFICER I certify that I investigated cause of death of deceased and find that death occurred at M from causes stated and on above date |
| 23a. Signature of Attending Physician or Health Officer W.B. Martin M.D. | 23b. ADDRESS 821 Michigan Avenue, La Porte | 23c. DATE SIGNED 2/23/51 |

| 24a. BURIAL, CREMATION, REMOVAL (Specify) Burial | 24b. DATE 2-25-51 | 24c. NAME OF CEMETERY OR CREMATORY Pine Lake Cemetery | 24d. LOCATION LaPorte Ind. |

| DATE REC'D BY LOCAL HEALTH OFFICER 2-26-51 | SIGNATURE OF HEALTH OFFICER Jm Nelson Kelly | 25. FUNERAL DIRECTOR Haverstock Funeral Home, LaPorte Ind. ADDRESS |

SRH 426 2

Walter F. Hilgendorf – Death Certificate

This is a copy of Walter Hilgendorf's death certificate. He died on 21 February 1951. The cause of death is listed as Coronary Thrombosis (a blood clot in the heart) with a prior condition of Arteriosclerosis (thickening and hardening of the walls of the arteries).

EDWIN WILLIAM JOHN HILGENDORF (1893-1956)

Edwin first appears in an index to Wisconsin births and christenings where he is shown as born 4 October 1893 in Milwaukee, Wisconsin. He next appears in the 1900 census in La Porte, Indiana, at age five along with siblings Arthur, Walter, Mabel and Nora. Also living with them at 1506 Scott Street is Mary Hilgendorf (wife of Johann/John), John's mother and Edwin's grandmother, who is 78 years old. It has not been determined why Edwin was born in Wisconsin.

In 1910, we find 17-year-old Edwin living with his parents at 1206 Ridge Street and working as a painter at a carriage factory. (The La Porte Carriage Company would have been one of the prominent carriage factories at this time). Siblings Walter, Mabel, Nora, Willie, George and John, as well Walter's wife Minnie, are also at the home.

Edwin registers for the World War I draft in 1917. He notes his age of 23 and place of residence at Ridge Street. In the 1920 census he is still at home and working as a laborer at a cycle factory. He is now 27 years old.

The 1930 census finds Edwin, 36, married to Ella Krebs, 35, and living at 401 Niles Street. It appears that they have been married about a year. Edwin is working as a fireman for the city of La Porte. Subsequent city directories find Edwin and Ella living at the same address, and Edwin continues to work for the fire department achieving a position of Assistant Fire Chief between 1947 and 1949.

It appears that Edwin died in 1956, and Ella passed in 1973. In the 1960 city directory, Ella was still living at 401 Niles Street. Both Edwin and Ella are buried at Woodlawn Cemetery in Forest Park, Illinois. The Find-a-Grave index locates them at that cemetery and notes Edwin's death as 1956. An index of burials in Pine Lake Cemetery, however, lists a death date as 1967. Apparently, Edwin was originally buried in Pine Lake Cemetery in La Porte, but he was reinterred at Woodlawn.

The Social Security Death Index notes Ella's last place of residence as Cook County, Illinois. It is likely they are buried in Illinois because Ella was born there. We could presume that she wanted to be buried there with her family. The Woodlawn Cemetery contains at least 14 members of the Krebs family. There is no record of any children for Edwin and Ella.

REGISTRATION CARD—(Men born on or after April 28, 1877 and on or before February 16, 1897)

SERIAL NUMBER	1. NAME (Print)			ORDER NUMBER
U 2329	Edwin William John Hilgendorf			
	(First)	(Middle)	(Last)	

2 PLACE OF RESIDENCE (Print)

401 Niles St.   LaPorte   LaPorte   Indiana
(Number and street)   (Town, township, village, or city)   (County)   (State)

[THE PLACE OF RESIDENCE GIVEN ON THE LINE ABOVE WILL DETERMINE LOCAL BOARD JURISDICTION; LINE 2 OF REGISTRATION CERTIFICATE WILL BE IDENTICAL]

3. MAILING ADDRESS

Same

[Mailing address if other than place indicated on line 2.   If same insert word same]

4. TELEPHONE	5. AGE IN YEARS	6. PLACE OF BIRTH
43539	48	Milwaukee
		(Town or county)
LaPorte (Number)	DATE OF BIRTH October 4 1893	Wis.
(Exchange)	(Mo.) (Day) (Yr.)	(State or country)

7. NAME AND ADDRESS OF PERSON WHO WILL ALWAYS KNOW YOUR ADDRESS

Mrs Ella Hilgendorf 401 Niles Street LaPorte.Ind

8. EMPLOYER'S NAME AND ADDRESS

City of LaPorte

9. PLACE OF EMPLOYMENT OR BUSINESS

8o1 Indiana Ave   LaPorte   LaPorte   Indiana
(Number and street or R.F.D. number)   (Town)   (County)   (State)

I AFFIRM THAT I HAVE VERIFIED ABOVE ANSWERS AND THAT THEY ARE TRUE.

Edwin W. Hilgendorf
(Registrant's signature)

D. S. S. Form 1
(Revised 4–1–42)   (over)   16—21630–2

Edwin William John Hilgendorf – World War II Draft Registration Card

MABEL LOUISE HILGENDORF (1897-1985)

Mabel first appears in the 1900 La Porte census as a five-year-old with her parents. In 1920 she is 12 in the census, and in 1920 she is 22, single, living at home with her parents and not working. Her middle initial is listed as H. in the census.

In 1930, she is still at home on Ridge Street, still single, and still not working. Her parents are ages 67 and 63. Her father is still working as a tailor, and brothers George and John are also at home. 1940 finds her at home with her 77-year-old father, and brother George. She is still single and does not work.

Mabel appears in La Porte city directories living at 1206 Ridge Street from 1924 through 1943. In 1947 she is employed in the factory at Ove Gnatt and residing at 207 McCollum Street. Her listing in 1949 says she works as an assembler. In the 1954 directory, she is listed as Mabel L. Hilgendorf. This is the only other appearance of a middle initial, and it does not match that of the 1920 census. I am assuming that this is the same individual, however. She is now a helper at the White Tower Nursing Home and living at 1202 1/2 Scott Street. Directories show the same information through 1960 where she is noted as a nurse's aide at White Tower.

The Social Security Death Index lists her death as April 1985. A listing of burial permits for Pine Lake Cemetery shows Mabel Louise Hilgendorf who died 17 April 1985. Her death certificate notes that Mabel was never married.

ID CERTIFICATE

85 017867

INDIANA STATE BOARD OF HEALTH
MEDICAL CERTIFICATE OF DEATH

Local No. **164**

State No. ....

FUNERAL HOME No. 406

FUNERAL DIRECTOR'S LICENSE No. 109

FUNERAL DIRECTOR'S SIGNATURE .... *Herman B Juday*

TYPE OR PRINT IN PERMANENT INK FOR INSTRUCTIONS SEE HANDBOOK

DECEASED—NAME	FIRST	MIDDLE	LAST	SEX	DATE OF DEATH (MONTH DAY YEAR)
1 Mabel	Louise	Hilgendorf	2 Female	3 04/17/85

RACE	AGE—Last Birthday	UNDER 1 YEAR		UNDER 1 DAY		DATE OF BIRTH	COUNTY OF DEATH
	(Yrs.)	MOS	DAYS	HOURS	MINS		
4 White	5a 87	5b		5c		6 05/13/97	7a LaPorte

DECEASED

CITY, TOWN OR LOCATION OF DEATH	HOSPITAL OR OTHER INSTITUTION—Name if not in either give street and number.	IF HOSP OR INST Indicate DOA OR Emer Rm Inpatient (Specify)
7b LaPorte	7c Fountainview Tr	7d Inpat.

STATE OF BIRTH If not in USA name country	CITIZEN OF WHAT COUNTRY	MARRIED, NEVER MARRIED, WIDOWED, DIVORCED (Specify)	SURVIVING SPOUSE If wife give maiden name	WAS DECEDENT EVER IN US ARMED FORCES? (Specify Yes or No)
8 INDIANA	9 USA	10 Never Married		12 No

SOCIAL SECURITY NUMBER	USUAL OCCUPATION (Give kind of work done during most of working life, even if retired)	KIND OF BUSINESS OR INDUSTRY
13	14a Homemaker	14b Home

USUAL RESIDENCE WHERE DECEASED LIVED IF DEATH OCCURRED IN INSTITUTION, GIVE RESIDENCE BEFORE ADMISSION

RESIDENCE—STATE	COUNTY	CITY, TOWN OR LOCATION
15a IN	15b LaPorte	15c LaPorte

STREET AND NUMBER	IS RESIDENCE ON A FARM?	INSIDE CITY LIMITS (Specify Yes or No)
15d 1900 Andrew Ave	15e YES ☐ NO ☒	15f No

IS DECEASED OF SPANISH DESCENT? IF YES SPECIFY MEXICAN, CUBAN, PUERTO RICAN, ETC
15g YES ☐ NO ☒

PARENTS

FATHER—NAME FIRST MIDDLE LAST	MOTHER—MAIDEN NAME FIRST MIDDLE LAST
16 John E. Hilgendorf	17 Fredericka Cook

INFORMANT—NAME (Type or print)	RELATIONSHIP	MAILING ADDRESS STREET OR RFD NO	CITY OR TOWN	STATE	ZIP
18a Marie Wineholt	Niec.	18b 3754 S. US 35	LaPorte	IN	46350

DISPOSITION

BURIAL, CREMATION, REMOVAL, OTHER (Specify)	CEMETERY OR CREMATORY—FUNERAL HOME	LOCATION CITY OR TOWN STATE
19a Burial	19b Pine Lake Cem.	19c LaPorte IN

DATE (MONTH DAY YEAR)	FUNERAL HOME—NAME AND ADDRESS (STREET OR RFD NO, CITY OR TOWN, STATE ZIP)
20a 04/20/85	20b HAVERSTOCK FUNERAL HOME, 602 MAPLE, LAPORTE IN. 46350

M.D. OR D.O.

To the best of my knowledge, death occurred at the time, date and place and due to the cause(s) stated.

21a (Signature) ▶ *John M. Gilroy Jr MD*	DATE SIGNED (Mo Day Yr) 21b 4-19-85	HOUR OF DEATH 21c 12:25 PM M

NAME OF ATTENDING PHYSICIAN (Type or Print)
21d Robert M. Kelsey M.D.

MAILING ADDRESS —PHYSICIAN
21e 1300 State St. LaPorte, IN. 46350

HEALTH OFFICER—SIGNATURE	DATE RECEIVED BY LOCAL HEALTH OFFICER
22a *James Agrecka M.D.*	22b 4-22-85

CONDITIONS IF ANY WHICH GAVE RISE TO IMMEDIATE CAUSE STATING THE UNDERLYING CAUSE LAST

CAUSE

23 PART I

IMMEDIATE CAUSE [ENTER ONLY ONE CAUSE PER LINE for (a), (b) AND (c)]	Interval between onset and death
(a) *Myocardial infarction*	
DUE TO, OR AS A CONSEQUENCE OF (b) *Arteriosclerotic Heart Disease*	
DUE TO, OR AS A CONSEQUENCE OF (c) *Atherosclerosis*	

PART II

OTHER SIGNIFICANT CONDITIONS—Conditions contributing to death but not related to cause given in PART I (a)	AUTOPSY (Specify Yes or No) 24 No

SBH 06-003   State Form 35430
REV.10/77

Mabel Louise Hilgendorf – Death Certificate

This is a copy of Mabel Louise Hilgendorf's death certificate. She died on 17 April 1985. The cause of death is listed as Myocardial Infarction (heart attack) with an underlying cause of Arteriosclerosis (thickening and hardening of the walls of the arteries).

NORA W. HILGENDORF (1899-1992)

Nora first appears with her family in the 1900 La Porte federal census. She is 11 months old at the time. We see her in the 1910 census at age 10 with the family. She is still with the family on Ridge Street in the 1920 census, and she is working as a stenographer at a doctor's office. After this she shows up in the 1923 and 1924 city directories. In 1923 she is a bookkeeper for doctors Bowel, Martin, Simon and Kimball. The next year she is listed as sec-treas for doctors Martin, Simon and Kimball.

In the 1938 La Porte City Directory, Nora is married to John Lingard and working as a book-keeper at 806 Maple Avenue. They live at 906 Ridge Street. They had married on 26 November 1927.

In the 1940 census, John and Nora are living at 906 Ridge Street. John works as an accountant at a farm implement factory (he retired from Allis-Chalmers). They continue to reside at this address through a 1960 La Porte City Directory.

John died in 1974, and Nora died in La Porte in 1992. No evidence has been found of any children from this marriage. John and Nora are buried in Pine Lake Cemetery in La Porte.

INDIANA STATE BOARD OF HEALTH
CERTIFICATE OF DEATH

Local No. 845   State No. 92-00197.2

TYPE/PRINT IN PERMANENT BLACK INK	1 DECEASED—NAME (First, Middle, Last) Nora W. Lingard	2 SEX Female	3a TIME OF DEATH 6:15 A.M	3b DATE OF DEATH January 23, 1992

5a AGE—Last Birthday (Years) 92	5b UNDER 1 YEAR	5c UNDER 1 DAY	6 DATE OF BIRTH JUN 28, 1899	7 BIRTHPLACE LaPorte, Indiana

DECEDENT

8a WAS DECEDENT A U.S VETERAN? No 8b YEAR LAST SERVED IN U.S. ARMED FORCES N/A 9a PLACE OF DEATH: HOSPITAL X Inpatient; ER/Outpatient; DOA; OTHER Nursing Home; Other; Residence

9b FACILITY NAME LaPorte Hospital 9c CITY, TOWN, OR LOCATION OF DEATH LaPorte 9d COUNTY OF DEATH LaPorte

10 MARITAL STATUS Widowed 11 SURVIVING SPOUSE NONE 12a DECEDENT'S USUAL OCCUPATION Housewife 12b KIND OF BUSINESS/INDUSTRY Homemaker

13a RESIDENCE—STATE Indiana 13b COUNTY LaPorte 13c CITY, TOWN, OR LOCATION LaPorte 13d STREET AND NUMBER 906 Ridge St.

13e ZIP CODE 46350 13f INSIDE CITY LIMITS No / X Yes 13g ON A FARM? X No / Yes 14 CITIZEN OF WHAT COUNTRY? USA 15 WAS DECEDENT OF HISPANIC ORIGIN? X No / Yes 16 RACE White 17 DECEDENT'S EDUCATION Elementary/Secondary Unknown / College

PARENTS
18 FATHER'S NAME John Hilgendorf 19 MOTHER'S NAME Frederica Cook

INFORMANT
20a INFORMANT'S NAME Marie Wineholt 20b MAILING ADDRESS 3754 S. SR 35, LaPorte, Indiana 46350 20c Relationship Niece

DISPOSITION
21a METHOD OF DISPOSITION: X Burial; Cremation; Donation; Entombment; Removal from State; Other 21b DATE AND PLACE OF DISPOSITION JAN 25, 1992 Pine Lake Cemetery 21c LOCATION LaPorte, Indiana

22a EMBALMER'S NAME Norman B. Juday 22b EMBALMER'S LICENSE NO FD01010436 23 WAS DEATH REPORTED TO CORONER? X No / Yes

24a SIGNATURE OF FUNERAL DIRECTOR Norman B. Juday 24b LICENSE NUMBER FD01010436 25 NAME, ADDRESS, AND LICENSE NUMBER OF FUNERAL HOME FH83004065 Haverstock Funeral Home Inc. 602 Maple Ave, La Porte, IN 46350

CAUSE OF DEATH
26 PART I
IMMEDIATE CAUSE a. Pulmonary embolus — Interval: 9mm
DUE TO b. Arterio sclerosis, Pulmonary Embolus — 2.5 years
DUE TO c. ___ — 1.5 years
d.

PART II Other significant conditions

27 WAS DECEDENT PREGNANT No 28a WAS AN AUTOPSY PERFORMED? No 28b WERE AUTOPSY FINDINGS AVAILABLE No

CERTIFIER
29a X CERTIFYING PHYSICIAN 29c MEDICAL LICENSE NO 01018955 29d DATE SIGNED JAN 31 1992
30 NAME AND ADDRESS Robert M. Kelsey M.D., 1300 State Street, LaPorte, IN 46350

HEALTH OFFICER
31 HEALTH OFFICER'S SIGNATURE K Aggarwal MD 32 DATE FILED JAN 31 1992

CORONER USE ONLY
33 MANNER OF DEATH X Natural; Accident; Suicide; Homicide; Pending Investigation; Could not be Determined
34g DATE PRONOUNCED DEAD

SBH06-004 State Form 10110 (R2/3-89) DEA CERT/PD 1

Nora W. Hilgendorf Lingard – Death Certificate

This is a copy of Nora W. Hilgendorf Lingard's death certificate. She died on 23 January 1992. The cause of death is entered as Pulmonary Embolus (a sudden blockage in a lung artery, usually caused by a blood clot).

WILLIAM A. HILGENDORF (1901-1979)

In the 1910 census, eight-year-old Willie is living with his parents in La Porte at 1206 Ridge Street. Still there in 1920, 18-year-old William is a trimmer at a baby carriage company. The 1923 La Porte city director finds him working as a woodworker at K-K Co. (Kumfy-Kab Co., a shoe-maker according to one source, at 305-306 Detroit Street). In 1924 he is married to Louise E. Pflugshaupt, living at 712 Ridge Street and is now an assistant foreman at K-K Co. It should be noted that in the 1920 census his middle initial is listed as F, and it is the same in the 1923 directory, but the 1924 directory lists his middle initial as E.

The 1930 census finds William and Louise with two children, Elaine, 5; and Viola 1. The 1931 city directory now shows his middle initial as A. All subsequent records on William list his middle initial as A. In 1938 he is working as a machinist at Deluxe Products. They still reside at 712 Ridge Street.

The 1940 census shows that William and Louise have another child, Ronald. All subsequent city directories through 1956 continue to show William's employment at Deluxe Products Company. A 1960 directory shows his employment as a laborer at Thanhardt-Burger Company.

William died in 1979, and Louise followed in 1986. They are buried in Patton Cemetery, Section Dev, Lot 170, Graves 1 and 2.

William A. Hilgendorf – 1930 Federal Census for La Porte, La Porte Co., Indiana

William A. Hilgendorf appears in the highlighted portion of the 1930 census with his wife Louise and children Elaine and Viola.

William A. Hilgendorf and Louise E. Pflugshaupt – Marriage License

William A. Hilgendorf and Louise E. Pflugshaupt were married in Starke County on 23 February 1924.

79-301545

INDIANA STATE BOARD OF HEALTH
MEDICAL CERTIFICATE OF DEATH

Local No. **018**

State No.

FUNERAL HOME No. 403		

1 DECEASED - NAME: William A. Hilgendorf   **2** SEX: Male   **3** DATE OF DEATH: January 21, 1979

4 RACE: White   **5a** AGE Last Birthday: 77   **5b** UNDER 1 YEAR   **5c** UNDER 1 DAY   **6** DATE OF BIRTH: 12-30-1901   **7a** COUNTY OF DEATH: La Porte

7b CITY, TOWN OR LOCATION OF DEATH: La Porte   **7c** HOSPITAL OR OTHER INSTITUTION: La Porte Hospital   **7d** IF HOSP. OR INST. Indicate DOA OR Emer. Rm. Inpatient: Inpatient

8 STATE OF BIRTH: Indiana   **9** CITIZEN OF WHAT COUNTRY: U.S.A.   **10** MARRIED NEVER MARRIED WIDOWED DIVORCED: Married   **11** SURVIVING SPOUSE: Louise E. Pflugshaupt   **12** WAS DECEDENT EVER IN U.S. ARMED FORCES?: No

13 SOCIAL SECURITY NUMBER: **14a** USUAL OCCUPATION: Machinist   **14b** KIND OF BUSINESS OR INDUSTRY: Auto Parts Mfg.

15a RESIDENCE - STATE: Indiana   **15b** COUNTY: La Porte   **15c** CITY, TOWN OR LOCATION: La Porte

15d STREET AND NUMBER: 712 Ridge Street   **15e** IS RESIDENCE ON A FARM?: YES ☐ NO ☒   **15f** INSIDE CITY LIMITS: Yes

15g IS DECEASED OF SPANISH DESCENT?: YES ☐ NO ☒

16 FATHER - NAME: John Hilgendorf   **17** MOTHER - MAIDEN NAME: Fredericka Cook

18a INFORMANT - NAME: Mrs. Louise Hilgendorf   **18b** MAILING ADDRESS: 712 Ridge Street, La Porte, Indiana 46350

19a BURIAL, CREMATION, REMOVAL, OTHER: Burial   **19b** CEMETERY OR CREMATORY: Patton Cemetery   **19c** LOCATION: La Porte, Indiana

20a DATE: January 23, 1979   **20b** FUNERAL HOME - NAME AND ADDRESS: Cutler Funeral Home Inc., 1104 Ind. Ave., La Porte, IN 46350

21a (Signature) Robert M. Kelsey Jr. M.D.   **21b** DATE SIGNED: January 22, 1979   **21c** HOUR OF DEATH: 12:05 P. M.

21d NAME OF ATTENDING PHYSICIAN: Robert M. Kelsey Jr., M.D.

21e MAILING ADDRESS - PHYSICIAN: 1206 Michigan Avenue, La Porte, Indiana 46350

22a HEALTH OFFICER - SIGNATURE: James Sprecker, M.D.   **22b** DATE RECEIVED BY LOCAL HEALTH OFFICER: 1-22-79

23 CAUSE
PART I — IMMEDIATE CAUSE
(a) Congestive Heart Failure
DUE TO OR AS A CONSEQUENCE OF
(b) Coronary Artery Disease
DUE TO OR AS A CONSEQUENCE OF
(c) Dehydration
PART II — OTHER SIGNIFICANT CONDITIONS: Rheumatoid Arthritis

24 AUTOPSY: No

SBH 06-003
REV 10/77

LICENSE No. 160   LICENSE No. 1689   EMBALMER'S NAME Robert F. Cutler Jr.   FUNERAL DIRECTOR'S SIGNATURE Robert F. Cutler Jr.

William A. Hilgendorf – Death Certificate

This is a copy of William A. Hilgendorf's death certificate. He died on 21 January 1979. The cause of death is noted as Congestive Heart Failure.

Louise (Pflugshaupt) Hilgendorf – Death Certificate

This is a copy of Louise (Pflugshaupt) Hilgendorf's death certificate. She died on 30 June 1986. The cause of death is listed as Congestive Heart Failure.

George F. Hilgendorf (1904-1966)

George first appears at age five in the 1910 census living with his parents at 1206 Ridge Street in La Porte. In the 1920 census he is 15 and at home. In a city directory in 1923 George is working as a woodworker at Kumfy-Kab Company and living at home. In 1924 and 1931 directories he is a painter at Claude DeMyer. The 1930 census shows him as a single 25-year-old at home.

In 1938 he is working at Bendix Corporation. The 1940 census finds him still at home with his 77-year-old widowed father and his 42-year-old sister Mabel. The census record notes that he is a mechanic at an automobile factory (Bendix). On 5 June 1942, George enlisted in the U.S. Army. A 1943 city directory shows the same.

In the 1947 city directory, we see that George has married Katherine Lindborg, and they are living at 308 Walker Street in La Porte. City directories from 1947 through 1951 show him working as a machinist at Bendix in South Bend. From 1951 on, he is living in South Bend with wife Katherine. They reside at 1333 N. Fremont Street. South Bend city directories from 1958 to 1960 show Katherine employed as a clerk at Tulsley's & Cruickshank in South Bend.

No record of any children has been located for George and Katherine. George died in South Bend on 13 December 1966. Katherine died on 20 January 1993 in La Porte. They are both buried in the North Lawn Section at Pine Lake Cemetery in La Porte.

George F. Hilgendorf – Death Certificate

This is a copy of George F. Hilgendorf's death certificate. He died on 13 December 1966. The cause of death is listed as Myocardial Infarction (heart attack).

INDIANA STATE BOARD OF HEALTH

CERTIFICATE OF DEATH

Local No. ....032....

State No. 93-001726

DECEASED—NAME (First, Middle, Last)			2 SEX	3a. TIME OF DEATH	3b. DATE OF DEATH (Mo, Day, Yr)
Katherine	Lucille	Hilgendorf	Female	8:04P M	January 20, 1993

4. SOCIAL SECURITY NUMBER	5a. AGE—Last Birthday (Years)	5b. UNDER 1 YEAR Months Days	5c. UNDER 1 DAY Hours Minutes	6 DATE OF BIRTH (Mo, Day, Yr)	7 BIRTHPLACE (City and State or Foreign Country)
	87			OCT 17, 1905	LaPorte, Indiana

8a. WAS DECEDENT A U.S. VETERAN?	8b. YEAR LAST SERVED IN U.S. ARMED FORCES?	9a. PLACE OF DEATH (Check only one. See instructions)
No	N/A	HOSPITAL: ☐ Inpatient ☐ ER/Outpatient ☐ DOA OTHER: ☐ Nursing Home ☐ Other (Specify) ☒ Residence

9b. FACILITY NAME (If not institution, give street and number)	9c. CITY, TOWN, OR LOCATION OF DEATH	9d COUNTY OF DEATH
98 Regency Place	LaPorte	LaPorte

10. MARITAL STATUS	11. SURVIVING SPOUSE (If wife, give maiden name)	12a. DECEDENT'S USUAL OCCUPATION (Give kind of work done during most of working life. Do not use retired)	12b. KIND OF BUSINESS/INDUSTRY
Widowed	NONE	Housewife	Homemaker

13a. RESIDENCE—STATE	13b. COUNTY	13c. CITY, TOWN, OR LOCATION	13d. STREET AND NUMBER
Indiana	LaPorte	LaPorte	98 Regency Place

13e. ZIP CODE	13f. INSIDE CITY LIMITS	14. CITIZEN OF WHAT COUNTRY?	15. WAS DECEDENT OF HISPANIC ORIGIN? (if yes, specify Cuban, Mexican, Puerto Rican, etc.)	16. RACE—American Indian, Black, White, etc. (Specify)	17. DECEDENT'S EDUCATION (Specify only highest grade completed) Elementary/Secondary (0-12) College (1-4 or 5 +)
46350	☒ No ☐ Yes 13g. ON A FARM? ☒ No ☐ Yes	USA	☒ No ☐ Yes	White	12

18. FATHER'S NAME (First, Middle, Last)			19. MOTHER'S NAME (First, Middle, Maiden Surname)	
Samuel	Lindborg		Mary	Olin

20a. INFORMANT'S NAME (Type/Print)	20b. MAILING ADDRESS (Street and Number or Rural Route Number, City or Town, State, Zip Code)	20c. Relationship
Anna Fridh	98 Regency Place, LaPorte, IN 46350	Sister

21a. METHOD OF DISPOSITION	21b. DATE AND PLACE OF DISPOSITION (Name of cemetery, crematory, or other place)	21c. LOCATION—City or Town, State
☒ Burial ☐ Entombment ☐ Removal from State ☐ Donation ☐ Other (Specify)	JAN 25, 1993 Pine Lake Cemetery	LaPorte, Indiana

22a. EMBALMERS NAME	22b. EMBALMERS LICENSE NO.	23. WAS DEATH REPORTED TO CORONER?
Norman B. Juday	FD01010436	☒ No

24a. SIGNATURE OF FUNERAL DIRECTOR	24b. LICENSE NUMBER (of Licensee)	25. NAME, ADDRESS AND LICENSE NUMBER OF FUNERAL HOME
Norman B. Juday	FD01010436	FH83004065 Haverstock Funeral Home Inc. 602 Maple Ave., LaPorte, IN. 46350

26. PART I   Enter the diseases, injuries, or complications that caused the death. Do not enter nonspecific terms, such as cardiac or respiratory arrest, shock, or heart failure. List only one cause on each line.

		Approximate Interval Between Onset and Death
IMMEDIATE CAUSE (Final disease or condition resulting in death)	a. RECURRENT ADENOCARCINOMA OF THE URETHRA	1 year 10 month
	DUE TO (OR AS A CONSEQUENCE OF):	
Conditions, if any, which gave rise to the immediate cause, stating the underlying cause last	b. ADENOCARCINOMA OF URETHRA	5 years 11 mont
	DUE TO (OR AS A CONSEQUENCE OF):	
	c.	
	DUE TO (OR AS A CONSEQUENCE OF):	
	d.	

PART II Other significant conditions - Conditions contributing to death but not previously stated in Part I	27. WAS DECEDENT PREGNANT OR 90 DAYS POSTPARTUM? (Yes or no)	28a. WAS AN AUTOPSY PERFORMED? (Yes or no)	28b. WERE AUTOPSY FINDINGS AVAILABLE PRIOR TO COMPLETION OF CAUSE OF DEATH? (Yes or no)
	No	No	No

29a. CERTIFIER (Check only one)	☒ CERTIFYING PHYSICIAN To the best of my knowledge, death occurred at the time, date, and place, and due to the cause(s) as stated. ☐ HEALTH OFFICER On the basis of examination and/or investigation, in my opinion, death occurred at the time, date, and place, and due to the cause(s) as stated. ☐ CORONER On the basis of examination and/or investigation, in my opinion, death occurred at the time, date, and place, and due to the cause(s) and manner as stated.

29b. SIGNATURE AND TITLE OF CERTIFIER	29c. MEDICAL LICENSE NO.	29d. DATE SIGNED (Month, Day, Year)
Beatrice M. Hernandez MD	33415	JANUARY 25, 1993

30 NAME AND ADDRESS OF PERSON WHO COMPLETED CAUSE OF DEATH (ITEM 26) (Type/Print)
Beatrice M. Hernandez M.D., 1007 Lincolnway, P.O. Box 250, LaPorte, IN. 46350

31. HEALTH OFFICER'S SIGNATURE	
K. Aggarwal MD	JAN 27 1993

33. MANNER OF DEATH	34a. DATE OF INJURY (Month, Day, Year)	34b. TIME OF INJURY	34c. INJURY AT WORK? (Yes or no)	34d. DESCRIBE HOW INJURY OCCURRED
☒ Natural ☐ Pending Investigation ☐ Accident ☐ Suicide ☐ Could not be Determined ☐ Homicide				

	34e. PLACE OF INJURY—At home, farm, street, factory, office building, etc. (Specify)	34f. LOCATION (Street and Number or Rural Route Number, City or Town, State)
5 cc BP 1-27-93		

34g. DATE PRONOUNCED DEAD (Month, Day, Year)	34h. MOTOR VEHICLE ACCIDENT? (Yes or no) If yes, specify driver, passenger, pedestrian, etc.

SBH06-004   State Form 10110 (R2/3-89)   DEA CERT/PD 1

Katherine Lucille (Lindborg) Hilgendorf – Death Certificate

This is a copy of Katherine Lucille (Lindborg) Hilgendorf's death certificate. She died on 20 January 1993. The cause of death is shown as Adenocarcinoma of the Urethra (cancer of the duct that transmits urine from the bladder to the exterior of the body).

JOHN MARTIN LEITER HILGENDORF (1909-1976)

John is six months old in the 1910 census of La Porte. The family is at 1206 Ridge Street. He next appears as a ten-year-old in the 1920 census with a middle initial of M. In the 1930 census John is a single 20-year-old living at home and working as a polisher at a metal products company. A 1931 city directory lists him as a metalworker. John's birth certificate does contain the two middle names Martin and Leiter.

John and Ruth Ervin were married on 23 June 1934. Ruth was born in Illinois. The 1940 census finds John and Ruth living at 211 1/2 Allen Street in La Porte. The census notes that he was at the same address in 1935.

A 1940 city directory lists John as a draftsman at Bastian-Morley Co. The next directory in which he is found is for 1949. He is now working as a tool engineer at Allis-Chalmers. He and Ruth are now living at 608 1/2 Maple Avenue.

In 1956 John is still with Allis-Chalmers, but they now live at 1536 1st Street. The last city directory for 1960 shows John still at Allis-Chalmers as a chief tool designer, and still living on 1st Street. At the time of his death, John and Ruth were living at 2306 Monroe Street in La Porte.

John died in 1976 and is buried in Pine Lake Cemetery in La Porte. Ruth died in 2000 and is also buried in Pine Lake Cemetery. No record of children has been found.

John Martin Leiter Hilgendorf – Birth Certificate

This is a copy of John Martin Leiter Hilgendorf's birth certificate. He was born in La Porte, Indiana, on 30 September 1909 to John and Ricka Hilgendorf.

John Martin Hilgendorf – Death Certificate

This is a copy of John Martin Hilgendorf's death certificate. He died on 15 March 1976. The cause of death is noted as Acute Myocardial Infarction (heart attack).

ATTENTION ESTATE: Disclosure of the SS# we need to pursue our responsibilities is voluntary and there will be no penalty for refusal.

Local No. .....454........

INDIANA STATE DEPARTMENT OF HEALTH

CERTIFICATE OF DEATH

043971

State No. ....

THE RECORDS IN THIS SERIES ARE CONFIDENTIAL PER IC 16-1-19-3

TYPE/PRINT IN PERMANENT BLACK INK

1 DECEASED—NAME (First, Middle, Last)		2 SEX	3a TIME OF DEATH	3b DATE OF DEATH (Month, Day, Yr)
Ruth	Hilgendorf	Female	5:30 A.M.	December 18, 2000

5a AGE—Last Birthday (Years)	5b UNDER 1 YEAR Months Days	5c UNDER 1 DAY Hours Minutes	6 DATE OF BIRTH (Mo. Day, Yr)	7 BIRTHPLACE (City and State or Foreign Country)
92			June 19, 1908	Carthage, Illinois

DECEDENT

8a WAS DECEDENT A U.S. VETERAN?	8b YEAR LAST SERVED IN U.S. ARMED FORCES?	9a PLACE OF DEATH (Check only one. See instructions)
No	N/A	HOSPITAL ☐ Inpatient ☐ ER/Outpatient ☐ DOA OTHER ☐ Nursing Home ☐ Other (Specify) ☒ Residence

9b FACILITY NAME (If not institution, give street and number)	9c CITY, TOWN, OR LOCATION OF DEATH	9d COUNTY OF DEATH
2306 Monroe Street	La Porte	La Porte

10 MARITAL STATUS (Specify)	11 SURVIVING SPOUSE (If wife, give maiden name)	12a DECEDENT'S USUAL OCCUPATION (Give kind of work done during most of working life. Do not use retired)	12b KIND OF BUSINESS/INDUSTRY
Widowed	N/A	Homemaker	Own Home

13a RESIDENCE—STATE	13b COUNTY	13c CITY, TOWN, OR LOCATION	13d STREET AND NUMBER
Indiana	La Porte	La Porte	2306 Monroe Street

13e ZIP CODE	13f INSIDE CITY LIMITS ☐ No ☒ Yes	14 CITIZEN OF WHAT COUNTRY?	15 WAS DECEDENT OF HISPANIC ORIGIN? ☒ No ☐ Yes (If yes, specify Cuban, Mexican, Puerto Rican, etc.)	16 RACE—American Indian, Black, White, etc. (Specify)	17 DECEDENT'S EDUCATION (Specify only highest grade completed) Elementary/Secondary (0-12) College (1-4 or 5 +)
46350		U.S.A.		White	12

13g ON A FARM? ☒ No ☐ Yes

PARENTS

18 FATHER'S NAME (First, Middle, Last)	19 MOTHER'S NAME (First, Middle, Maiden Surname)
Clarence Ervin	Lessie Tyler

INFORMANT

20a INFORMANT'S NAME (Type/Print)	20b MAILING ADDRESS (Street and Number or Rural Route Number, City or Town, State, Zip Code)	20c Relationship
Don Ervin	13045 Sherman, Warren, MI 48089	Brother

DISPOSITION

21a METHOD OF DISPOSITION ☒ Burial ☐ Cremation ☐ Removal from State ☐ Donation ☐ Other (Specify) ☐ Entombment	21b DATE AND PLACE OF DISPOSITION (Name of cemetery, crematory, or other place) December 20, 2000 Pine Lake Cemetery	21c LOCATION—City or Town, State LaPorte, Indiana

22a EMBALMER'S NAME	22b EMBALMER'S LICENSE NO	23 WAS DEATH REPORTED TO CORONER?
Dale A. Knouse	FD#08601420	☒ No ☐ Yes

24a SIGNATURE OF FUNERAL DIRECTOR	24b LICENSE NUMBER (of Licensee)	25 NAME, ADDRESS, AND LICENSE NUMBER OF FUNERAL HOME
Kent C	FDO1001609	Cutler Funeral Home, Inc. FH19500004 2900 Monroe St., La Porte,IN. 46350

CAUSE OF DEATH

26. PART I Enter the diseases, injuries, or complications that caused the death Do not enter nonspecific terms, such as cardiac or respiratory arrest, shock, or heart failure. List only one cause on each line.

Approximate Interval Between Onset and Death

IMMEDIATE CAUSE (Final disease or condition resulting in death)
a. Acute Myocardial Infarction — hours
DUE TO (OR AS A CONSEQUENCE OF)

Conditions, if any, which gave rise to the immediate cause, stating the underlying cause last
b. Arteriosclerotic Heart Disease — years
DUE TO (OR AS A CONSEQUENCE OF)

c.
DUE TO (OR AS A CONSEQUENCE OF)

d.

PART II Other significant conditions - Conditions contributing to death but not previously stated in Part I	27 WAS DECEDENT PREGNANT OR 90 DAYS POSTPARTUM? (Yes or no)	28a WAS AN AUTOPSY PERFORMED? (Yes or no)	28b WERE AUTOPSY FINDINGS AVAILABLE PRIOR TO COMPLETION OF CAUSE OF DEATH? (Yes or no)
	No	No	N/A

CERTIFIER

29a CERTIFIER (Check only one)
☒ CERTIFYING PHYSICIAN To the best of my knowledge, death occurred at the time, date, and place, and due to the cause(s) as stated
☐ HEALTH OFFICER On the basis of examination and/or investigation, in my opinion, death occurred at the time, date, and place, and due to the cause(s) as stated
☐ CORONER On the basis of examination and/or investigation, in my opinion, death occurred at the time, date, and place, and due to the cause(s) and manner as stated

29b SIGNATURE AND TITLE OF CERTIFIER	29c MEDICAL LICENSE NO	29d DATE SIGNED (Month, Day, Year)
Kenneth D. Shively MD	24055	12-18-00

30 NAME AND ADDRESS OF PERSON WHO COMPLETED CAUSE OF DEATH (ITEM 26) (Type/Print)
Kenneth D. Shively, MD, 900 I Street, LaPorte, IN 46350

HEALTH OFFICER

31 HEALTH OFFICER SIGNATURE	DATE FILED (Month, Day, Year)
Edwin C. Mueller MD	DEC 19 2000

33 MANNER OF DEATH ☐ Natural ☐ Accident ☐ Suicide ☐ Homicide ☐ Pending Investigation ☐ Could not be Determined	34a DATE OF INJURY (Month, Day, Year)	34b TIME OF INJURY	34c INJURY AT WORK? (Yes or no)	34d DESCRIBE HOW INJURY OCCURRED
	34e PLACE OF INJURY—At home, farm, street, factory, office building, etc. (Specify)		34f LOCATION (Street and Number or Rural Route Number, City or Town, State)	

34g DATE PRONOUNCED DEAD (Month, Day, Year)	34h MOTOR VEHICLE ACCIDENT? (Yes or no) If yes, specify driver, passenger, pedestrian, etc.

SDH06-004   State Form 10110 (R4/3-93) Deathcer/PD 1

Ruth (Ervin) Hilgendorf – Death Certificate

This is a copy of Ruth (Ervin) Hilgendorf's death certificate. She died on 18 December 2000. The cause of death is noted as Acute Myocardial Infarction (heart attack).

Hilgendorf

The Fourth Generation:

Clarence John Hilgendorf (1910-1990)

Family Chart

Arthur Hilgendorf Jr. – b. 27 May 1908, d. 1908?

Lawrence Arthur Hilgendorf – b. 25 July 1909, d. 21 April 1999
    Spouse: Anna B. Dick – b. 19 May 1911, d. 26 February 2006
    Children: None

Clarence John Hilgendorf – b. 30 October 1910, d. 24 July 1990
    Spouse: Leatha Cecelia Haag – b. 1 February 1916, d. 3 December 1961
    Children:
        Sally Joan Hilgendorf – b. 23 November 1941
        Kenneth Richard Hilgendorf – b. 17 June 1943
        Mary Jane Hilgendorf – b. 3 August 1946
        Martha Ann Hilgendorf – b. 6 April 1951
        Clarence John Hilgendorf Jr. - b. 14 February 1956

Roy A. Hilgendorf – b. 7 October 1912, d. 9 April 1970
    Spouse: Dorothy Marie Edwards – b. 21 March 1914, d. 15 July 1992
    Children:
        James Hilgendorf – b. 12 January 1940
        John Thomas Hilgendorf – b. 25 June 1951, d. 29 April 2014

Wilbur C. Hilgendorf – b. 21 October 1914, d. 1 May 1943
    Spouse: Never married

Raymond J. Hilgendorf – b. 5 July 1916, d. 7 June 1981
    Spouse: Jean Cormick, b. 11 July 1915, d. 29 April 1997
    Children:
        Christine Hilgendorf – b.
    Spouse: Helen Louise Gray – b. 23 December 1912, d. 29 August 1996

Arthur Hilgendorf Jr. – b. 15 March 1919, d. 10 December 1922

Marie Elizabeth Hilgendorf – b. 1 April 1922, d. 1 April 2009
    Spouse: George Raymond Wineholt – b. 16 February 1918, d. 16 November 1976
    Children:
        Dan Wineholt – b.
        Thomas Wineholt – b.

Doris Hilgendorf – b. 9 July 1924, d. 22 August 2016
    Spouse: Richard K. Bowman – b. 23 July 1924, d. 30 June 1912
    Children:
        Larry Bowman – b.
        Patrick Bowman – b.

ARTHUR HILGENDORF JR. (1908-1908?)

Arthur Hilgendorf Jr. was born on 27 May 1908, making him the first child of Arthur and Mary Hilgendorf. The birth certificate notes that this is the first child of Mary, and there are no other children. We might assume that he died soon after birth, but no death record has been located. There is no indication of any complications at birth. Added to this, however, is the fact that he was born about six months after Arthur and Mary were married. So, perhaps he was premature and did not live long. But, again, there are no indications of this on the birth record. There is also a place on the birth record to check whether the child was born alive or not, but nothing is checked in this location.

Arthur Hilgendorf Jr. – Birth Certificate

This is a copy of Arthur Hilgendorf Jr.'s birth certificate. He was the "first" Arthur Jr. born to Arthur and Mary. A "second" Arthur Jr. was born in 1919. This first Arthur Jr. was born on 27 May 1908 in La Porte, Indiana, and likely died shortly thereafter.

LAWRENCE ARTHUR HILGENDORF (1909-1999)

In 1920, Lawrence was ten years old living with his family on 1116 Ridge Street in La Porte. In the 1930 census, Lawrence, now 20, is single and working as a pressman at the La Porte Press Inc. He is at home with his family on Ridge Street.

Lawrence married Anna B. Dick on 16 December 1933. We see them in the 1940 census living at Rural Route 4 in Scipio Township in La Porte County. Lawrence is 30, and Anna is 28. Lawrence is still working in the printing business, as he would be for the remainder of his life.

Lawrence enlisted in the Navy on 18 December 1943. He served until 3 December 1945. He and Anna continued to live at Route 4 in La Porte. They enjoyed raising pigs on their small farm south of town.

Lawrence died on 21 April 1999, and Anna passed on 26 February 2006. They had no children. They are buried in the North Dewberry Hill section of Pine Lake Cemetery in La Porte.

PLACE OF BIRTH

INDIANA STATE BOARD OF HEALTH
DIVISION OF VITAL STATISTICS.

CERTIFICATE OF BIRTH. 25615

County of _La Porte_

Township of _Center_

Village of
or
City of _Laporte_ (No. _107_ _Ludlow St_, St.; _3_ Ward) Registered No. _336_

FULL NAME OF CHILD _Lawrence Arthur Hilgendorf_ { Born Alive } { Yes No }

If child is not named, make supplemental report.

| Sex of Child | _Male_ | Twin, Triplet, or Other | and { Number in order of birth } | Legiti- mate? | _Yes_ | Date of Birth | _July_ | _25_ | 190 _9_ |

FATHER		MOTHER	
Full Name	_Arthur Hilgendorf_	Full Maiden Name	_Marie Kramer_
Residence	_107 Ludlow_	Residence	_107 Ludlow St_
Color or Race	_W_	Age at last Birthday _24_	Color or Race	_W_	Age at last Birthday _25_
Birthplace	_Laporte_	Birthplace	_Laporte Co_
Occupation	_Moulder_	Occupation	_Housewife_

Number of child of this mother _2_ | Number of children, of this mother, now living _1_ | Were precautions taken against Ophthalmia neonatorum? _Yes_

CERTIFICATE OF ATTENDING PHYSICIAN OR MIDWIFE*

I hereby certify that I attended the birth of above child; and that it occurred on _July 25_, 190 _9_, at _8_ _P._ M.

{ *When there is no attending physician or midwife, then the householder should make this return. See instructions on back. } (Signature) _H H Long_

Attending physician, midwife, householder.*

Given or christian name added from a supplemental report _____ 190___

Dated _July 28_ 190 _9_ Address _Laporte_

Filed _July 31_ 190 _9_. _Harry B Darling_

HEALTH OFFICER. | HEALTH OFFICER.

Lawrence Arthur Hilgendorf – Birth Certificate

This is a copy of Lawrence Arthur Hilgendorf's birth certificate. He was born on 25 July 1909 in La Porte, Indiana.

ATTENTION ESTATE: Disclosure of the SS# we need to pursue our responsibilities is voluntary and there will be no penalty for refusal.

Local No. ...1603...........

INDIANA STATE DEPARTMENT OF HEALTH

CERTIFICATE OF DEATH

State No. 014862

THE RECORDS IN THIS SERIES ARE CONFIDENTIAL PER IC 16-1-19-3

TYPE/PRINT IN PERMANENT BLACK INK	1 DECEASED—NAME (First, Middle, Last) LAWRENCE A. HILGENDORF		2 SEX MALE	3a TIME OF DEATH 4:23 A. M	3b DATE OF DEATH (Month, Day, Yr) April 21, 1999

5a AGE—Last Birthday (Years) **89** | 5b UNDER 1 YEAR Months Days | 5c UNDER 1 DAY Hours Minutes | 6 DATE OF BIRTH (Mo. Day, Yr) July 25, 1909 | 7 BIRTHPLACE (City and State or Foreign Country) LaPorte, Indiana

DECEDENT

8a WAS DECEDENT A U.S. VETERAN? YES | 8b YEAR LAST SERVED IN U.S. ARMED FORCES? 1945 | 8a PLACE OF DEATH (Check only one. See instructions) HOSPITAL ☒ Inpatient ☐ ER/Outpatient ☐ DOA   OTHER ☐ Nursing Home ☐ Other (Specify) ☐ Residence

9b FACILITY NAME (If not institution, give street and number) LaPorte Hospital | 9c CITY TOWN OR LOCATION OF DEATH LaPorte | 9d COUNTY OF DEATH LaPorte

10 MARITAL STATUS (Specify) Married | 11 SURVIVING SPOUSE (If wife, give maiden name) Anna Dick | 12a DECEDENT'S USUAL OCCUPATION (Give kind of work done during most of working life. Do not use retired) Printing Superintendant | 12b KIND OF BUSINESS/INDUSTRY Printing Industry

13a RESIDENCE—STATE IN | 13b COUNTY LaPorte | 13c CITY TOWN, OR LOCATION LaPorte | 13d STREET AND NUMBER 3674 S. U.S. Highway 35

13e ZIP CODE 46350 | 13f INSIDE CITY LIMITS ☒ No ☐ Yes   13g ON A FARM? ☐ No ☒ Yes | 14 CITIZEN OF WHAT COUNTRY? USA | 15 WAS DECEDENT OF HISPANIC ORIGIN? ☒ No ☐ Yes (If yes specify Cuban. Mexican, Puerto Rican, etc) | 16 RACE—American Indian, Black, White, etc (Specify) White | 17 DECEDENT'S EDUCATION (Specify only highest grade completed) Elementary/Secondary (0-12) 12   College (1-4 or 5+) 2

PARENTS

18 FATHER'S NAME (First, Middle, Last) Arthur Hilgendorf | 19 MOTHER'S NAME (First, Middle, Maiden Surname) Mary Kramer

INFORMANT

20a INFORMANT'S NAME (Type/Print) Anna Hilgendorf | 20b MAILING ADDRESS (Street and Number or Rural Route Number, City or Town, State, Zip Code) 3674 S. U.S. Hwy. 35, LaPorte, IN 46350 | 20c Relationship WIFE

DISPOSITION

21a METHOD OF DISPOSITION ☒ Burial ☒ Cremation ☐ Donation ☐ Embalment ☐ Removal from State ☐ Other (Specify) | 21b DATE AND PLACE OF DISPOSITION (Name of cemetery, crematory, other place) April 23,1999/April 24,1999 Calvary Crematory/Pine Lake Cemetery | 21c LOCATION—City or Town, State Portage, Indiana LaPorte, Indiana

22a EMBALMER'S NAME NOT EMBALMED | 22b EMBALMER'S LICENSE NO n/a | 23 WAS DEATH REPORTED TO CORONER? ☒ No ☐ Yes

24a SIGNATURE OF FUNERAL DIRECTOR *Mark E. Essling* | 24b LICENSE NUMBER (If Licensed) FD01001104 | 25 NAME, ADDRESS, AND LICENSE NUMBER OF FUNERAL HOME Essling Funeral Home FH3004049 1117 Indiana Ave., LaPorte, IN 46350

CAUSE OF DEATH

26 PART I   Enter the diseases, injuries, or complications that caused the death. Do not enter nonspecific terms, such as cardiac or respiratory arrest, shock, or heart failure. List only one cause on each line.

IMMEDIATE CAUSE (Final disease or condition resulting in death) a. *heart attack*   DUE TO (OR AS A CONSEQUENCE OF)

Conditions, if any, which gave rise to the immediate cause, stating the underlying cause last b. ___   DUE TO (OR AS A CONSEQUENCE OF)

c. ___   DUE TO (OR AS A CONSEQUENCE OF)

d. ___

Approximate Interval Between Onset and Death *16 hours*

PART II Other significant conditions · Conditions contributing to death but not previously stated in Part I

27 WAS DECEDENT PREGNANT OR 90 DAYS POSTPARTUM (Yes or no) NO | 28a WAS AN AUTOPSY PERFORMED? (Yes or no) NO | 28b WERE AUTOPSY FINDINGS AVAILABLE PRIOR TO COMPLETION OF CAUSE OF DEATH? (Yes or no) NO

CERTIFIER

29a CERTIFIER (Check only one) ☒ CERTIFYING PHYSICIAN To the best of my knowledge death occurred at the time, date, and place and due to the cause(s) as stated ☐ HEALTH OFFICER On the basis of examination and/or investigation, in my opinion, death occurred at the time, date, and place, and due to the cause(s) as stated ☐ CORONER On the basis of examination and/or investigation in my opinion, death occurred at the time, date, and place, and due to the cause(s) and manner as stated

29b SIGNATURE AND TITLE OF CERTIFIER *Christopher Powers MD* | 29c MEDICAL LICENSE NO 01045491 | 29d DATE SIGNED (Month, Day, Year) 4-23-1999

30 NAME AND ADDRESS OF PERSON WHO COMPLETED CAUSE OF DEATH (ITEM 26) (Type/Print) Christopher D. Powers, M.D. 1300 State Street, Ste. 2G, LaPorte, IN 46350

HEALTH OFFICER local+IVA

31 HEALTH OFFICER'S SIGNATURE *Edwin C. Mueller MD* | 32 DATE FILED (Month, Day, Year) APR 23 1999

R ✓

33 MANNER OF DEATH ☐ Natural ☐ Accident ☐ Suicide ☐ Homicide ☐ Pending Investigation ☐ Could not be Determined | 34a DATE OF INJURY (Month, Day, Year) | 34b TIME OF INJURY | 34c INJURY AT WORK? (Yes or no) | 34d DESCRIBE HOW INJURY OCCURRED

34e PLACE OF INJURY—At home, farm, street, factory, office building, etc (Specify) | 34f LOCATION (Street and Number or Rural Route Number, City or Town, State)

34g DATE PRONOUNCED DEAD (Month, Day, Year) | 34h MOTOR VEHICLE ACCIDENT? (Yes or no) If yes, specify driver, passenger, pedestrian, etc

SDH06-004   State Form 10110 (R4/3-93) Deathcer/PD 1

Lawrence A. Hilgendorf – Death Certificate

This is a copy of Lawrence A. Hilgendorf's death certificate. He died on 21 April 1999. His death was due to a heart attack.

Lawrence A. Hilgendorf – U.S. Navy Portrait

CLARENCE JOHN HILGENDORF (1910-1990)

Clarence was the second son of Arthur and Mary Hilgendorf born in 1910. In the 1920 census, he is nine years old and at home with the family at 1116 Ridge Street in La Porte. He is still at home in the 1930 census. Somewhere along the line, he obtained the nickname "Dutch." From high school yearbook photos, we know that he was known by this nickname in high school, and would use it for the rest of his life.

In 1940, now 29, Dutch is at home with his parents. He is single and working as a stockman and clerk at an automobile brake factory, Bendix Corporation in South Bend, Indiana.

Dutch was apparently shopping for a dress for his younger sister Marie when he was taken by the sales clerk, Leatha Haag. Clarence and Leatha were married on 14 September 1940 in La Porte. This is the point of the Hilgendorf-Haag connection. The couple is now living at 1212 Weller Avenue.

Leatha remained a housewife while Dutch maintained a career at Bendix, driving from La Porte to South Bend every day. They were a social couple with many friends. Dutch liked to meet with friends regularly on Saturday afternoons at the local Elks club where they would play cards. The couple was also active in the Catholic Church.

Dutch continued to work at Bendix until his retirement. Dutch and Leatha had five children: Sally, Ken, Jane, Marti and CJ (Clarence Jr.).

Leatha passed too soon on 3 December 1961. Dutch remarried to Mary (Allen) Watson in March of 1964. After his retirement, they moved to Bradenton, Florida. Dutch died on 24 July 1990 in Bradenton. Mary passed in Bradenton on 12 February 2005. Dutch and Leatha are interred together in the North Dewberry Hill section of Pine Lake Cemetery in La Porte.

KENNETH YOUNG—Junior
[Forward]
This little half-pint forward was certainly a full measure when he got upon the basketball floor. Kenny was a thorn in the side of the other team's defense. Besides being high scorer of the Slicer team, he was also chosen on the second all-Conference team.

CLARENCE HILGENDORF—Junior
[Forward]
Dutch's ability to intercept passes baffled the other team's offense considerably. Some uncanny intuition always kept Dutch wherever the ball was. He always managed to get points, no matter what the opposition might be.

HAROLD WEGNER—Senior
[Guard]
Harold was the coach's "right hand man" and as acting captain for the season, showed a remarkable ability for handling the other players, and for good all-around basketball. Wegner and Young were the only players who saw action in every game.

RUDOLPH GNATT—Fres[h]
[Guard]
Rudy had the distinction of being the only Freshman on the varsity. He was speed and cleverness personified. La-Porte High school expects much from him in the next three years.

ERNEST PEASE—Junior
[Center]
Although Ernie was listed on the score book as a guard, he ran center all season. He always instilled the pepper in the team, for his Pease spirit was not lacking. An injury to his hand kept Ernie out of several games; nevertheless, he was third high as scorer for the season.

"B" TEAM
Top Row—Alfred Pease, Lester Gierke, Victor Bell. Bottom Row—Earl Ramp, Wilbur Hahn, Charles Weller, Clarence Hilgendorf, Wilbur Itkowitsch.

Clarence (Dutch) Hilgendorf – Basketball

Dutch had obviously obtained his nickname at least as early as high school. The above two pages are from the *La Porte High School El-Pe* yearbook, 1928 (full page) and 1929 (team photo).

Clarence (Dutch) Hilgendorf – Basketball & Football

Dutch's athletic skills were displayed in football as well as basketball, although it seemed basketball was his first choice. He played on La Porte High School's very successful 1930 basketball team. La Porte made a deep playoff run but fell one win short of advancing to the Final Four. Eventual state runner-up Muncie Central handed the Slicers a 43-25 defeat.

The school officials select from the student body boys who are sixteen years of age or older, who are interested in such a training scheme and who would profit by it. The schools in consultation with industry set up a course of study for the students which will meet the demands of the boy and industry, and at the same time enable the boys to complete the work of the high school.

TOP ROW—Joe Luber, Robert Heider, John Kowaski, Arthur Giesler.
BOTTOM ROW—Clarence Hilgendorf, Fred Cory, Bowen Bowell, M. E. Hyde, C. A. Abbott, James Bowell, Joe Thomas.

CLARENCE HILGENDORF

"He has the combined qualities of a gentleman and an athlete."

Basketball "B" 2
Basketball 3-4
Baseball 3
Football 4
Interclass Sports 1-2-3-4
Industrial Arts Club 4

Clarence (Dutch) Hilgendorf – High School

Dutch appears in the top photo of the Industrial Arts Club. His senior portrait from the 1930 *La Porte High School El-Pe* notes his interests as well as his fine qualities.

Clarence (Dutch) Hilgendorf – Bendix Corporation, South Bend

Dutch appears seated second from the right in an undated photo of workers at the Bendix Corporation in South Bend, Indiana. Dutch spent his career at Bendix and subsequently retired from there.

Dutch and Leatha (Haag) Hilgendorf

These are two early photos of Dutch and Leatha. Both photos are from 1940.

Clarence (Dutch) Hilgendorf and Leatha Haag Wedding
14 September 1940

In this wedding photo from left to right are: Kathleen Deacon, unknown (maybe Nicholas Maschek), John Parker, Clarence (Dutch) Hilgendorf, Leatha (Haag) Hilgendorf, Helen (Haag) Parker, Richard Cloutier and Kenny Young.

Mr. and Mrs. Harry J. Haag

request the honor of your presence

at the marriage of their daughter

Leatha Cecelia

to

Clarence J. Hilgendorf

on

Saturday Morning, September Fourteenth

Nineteen Hundred and Forty

at Nine o'Clock

St. Peter's Church

La Porte, Indiana

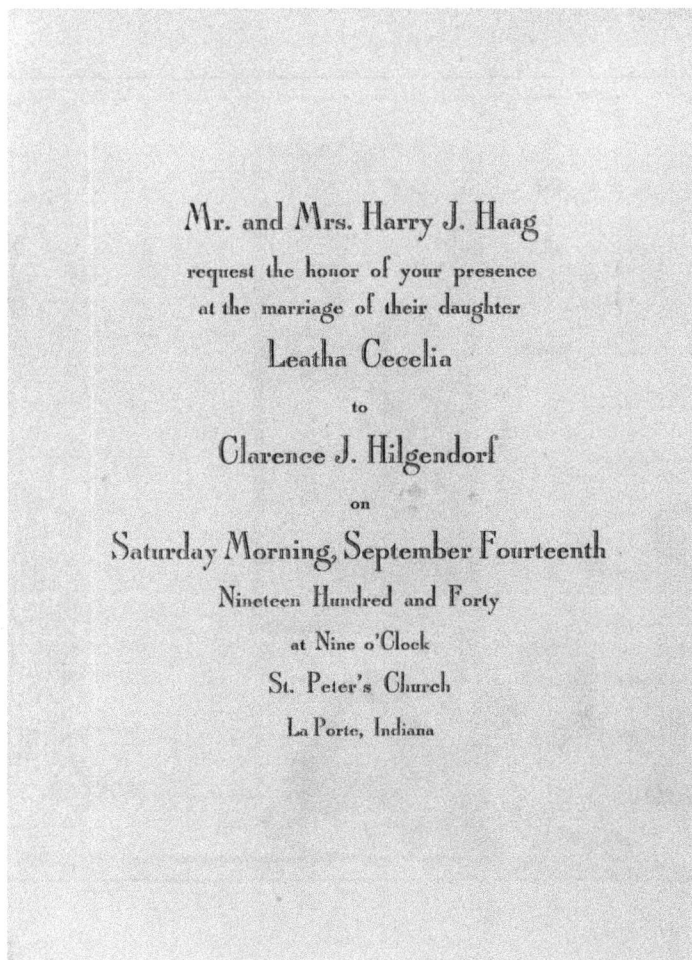

Clarence (Dutch) Hilgendorf and Leatha Haag Wedding Invitation

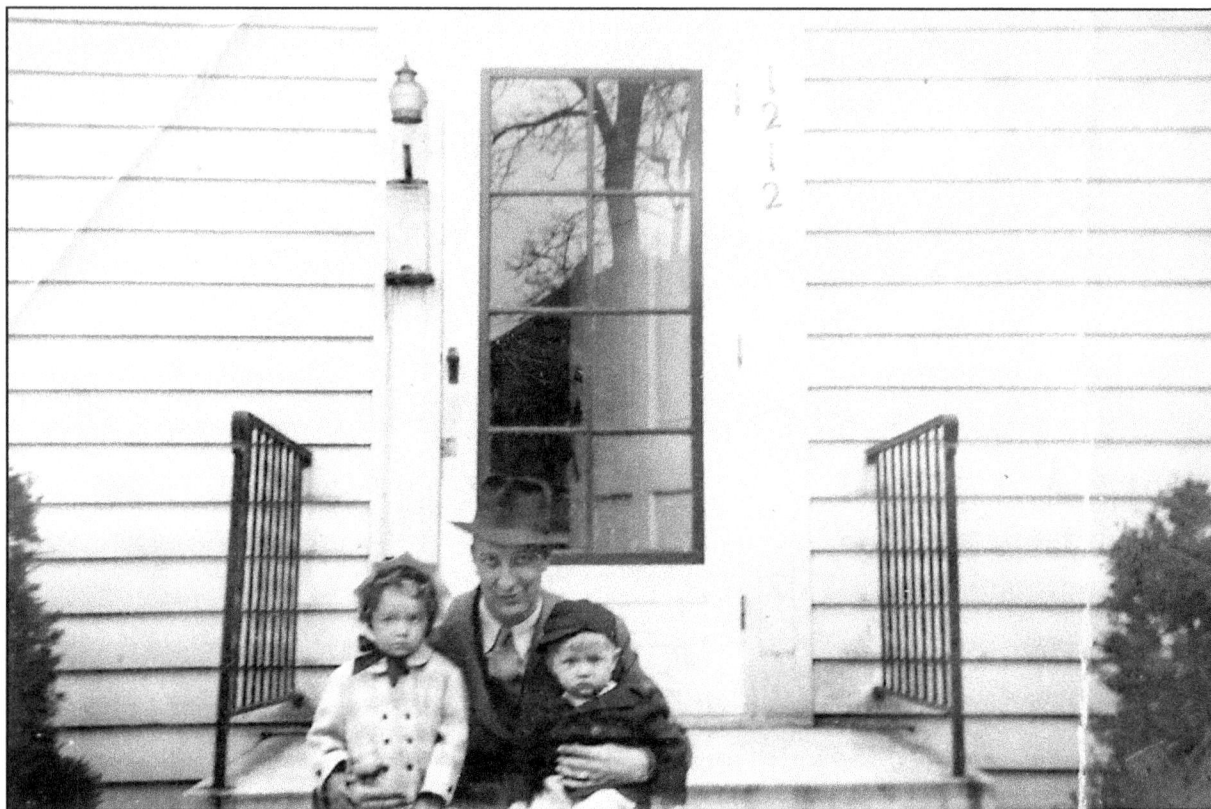

Dutch Hilgendorf with Sally and Kenny

This undated photo of Dutch with children Sally and Kenny at their 1212 Weller Avenue home may be from about 1944/1945.

Dutch Hilgendorf and Children

Dutch with children Sally, Jane and Ken about 1947.

Dutch and Leatha Hilgendorf with Marti

This photo of Dutch and Leatha with daughter Marti in the yard of their home at 1212 Weller Avenue is from about 1960.

Dutch with CJ (Clarence Jr.)

This photo of Dutch with son CJ (Clarence Jr.) in the yard of their home at 1212 Weller Avenue is from about 1964.

Dutch Hilgendorf with his brother Lornie (Lawrence)

The above photo of Lornie (Lawrence) Hilgendorf, his wife Ann and Dutch (Clarence) Hilgendorf is from Christmas 1977.

ROY A. HILGENDORF (1912-1970)

In 1920, Roy is a seven-year-old living with his parents at 1116 Ridge Street in La Porte. At home are his four brothers. In 1930, now 17, he is at home, and his two sisters have been added to the family. One year later, Roy is working as a chauffeur at the Nehi Beverage Company.

Roy married Dorothy Edwards on 13 November 1936. In 1938 they are living at 102 Boston Street, and Roy is working at Metal Door & Trim. His father-in-law is also employed at a "metal door factory," and they also live on Boston Street. The 1940 census lists Roy and Dorothy at 314 Boston Street, while a city directory for that year shows them at 115 ½ Oberreich Street. The census shows Roy as a tractor operator at a farm machine manufacturer (most likely Allis-Chalmers). Also with them in the 1940 census is five-month-old James. In 1951, a second son, John, was born.

A 1943 directory notes a position with the police for Roy. In 1947 he is working at Modine Manufacturing Co., where it appears he worked in several positions through at least 1960. The 1960 city directory shows the family living at 410 Allen Street in La Porte.

Roy died in La Porte on 9 April 1970. Dorothy died in Santa Monica, California, on 15 July 1992. Roy is buried in Pine Lake Cemetery in La Porte.

Roy Hilgendorf – Birth Certificate

This is a copy of Roy Hilgendorf's birth certificate. He was born on 7 October 1912 in La Porte, Indiana. Note that the name appears to be Ray rather than Roy, but this is the date that Roy was born. Ray was born in 1916, and his birth certificate appears several pages forward.

Roy A. Hilgendorf – Death Certificate

This is a copy of Roy A. Hilgendorf's death certificate. He died on 9 April 1970. His death was due to an Aneurysm (rupture) of the Abdominal Aorta.

Roy Hilgendorf

The above two photos are of Roy Hilgendorf. The photo on the left is a school photo from 1928. The photo on the right is Roy's senior photo in the 1930 La Porte High School yearbook.

WILBUR C. HILGENDORF (1914-1943)

Wilbur was born in 1914 and thus first appears in the 1920 census. He is five years old and living with his parents and four brothers at 1116 Ridge Street in La Porte. In the 1930 census he is 15 and now has two sisters as well.

A 1938 city directory notes that Wilbur is employed by Modine Manufacturing Company. Then, the 1940 census finds the 25-year-old working at an automobile radiator company.

On 21 March 1942, Wilbur enlisted in the U.S. Army at Fort Benjamin Harrison, Indiana. His enlistment notes that he is single.

Wilbur participated in the Tunisia Campaign in North Africa in WWII. This particular campaign in North Africa began in late 1942, and the final battle ended with the German surrender on 13 May 1943. Unfortunately, Wilbur was one of 2,715 United States losses in this campaign. He died on 1 May 1943, just days before the end of the campaign.

Allied leaders decided in mid-1942 that an offensive in North Africa would set the stage to enter Europe from the south, as well as the planned English Channel invasion. On November 8, 1942, Operation TORCH began. Three Allied naval task forces put U.S. and British forces ashore near Casablanca, Oran, and Algiers.

From December 1942 through February 1943, winter rains, strong German forces and air superiority stalled Allied advances into Tunisia. After a brief retreat, U.S. forces regained the advantage in heavy fighting. The Germans withdrew toward Tunis.

In April and May, U.S. infantry forces broke through German defenses. The enemy retreated into a small area of northeast Tunisia. By May 13, the enemy forces surrendered. The conclusion of the campaign in North Africa set the stage for next steps in the Mediterranean: the invasion of Sicily and onward into Italy.

Notes on Wilbur's interment indicate that he was part of the 802nd Military Police Battalion. I could find no history on an 802nd MP Battalion. However, I did find a 202nd MP Battalion that served in the Tunisia Campaign. The information notes that these were "strictly combat MPs." Activated in May 1942, they were responsible for traffic control and security. They were often on the forward lines directing troop movements, or they were left in the rear to clean-up after the rest of the units had moved on. This would leave them vulnerable without any additional support.

Allied forces lost about 80,000 troops in the Tunisian campaign. American casualties in Tunisia alone totaled more than 18,500. The Allied victory in North Africa destroyed or neutralized nearly 900,000 German and Italian troops, opened a second front against the Axis, permitted the invasion of Sicily and the Italian mainland in the summer of 1943, and removed the Axis threat to the oilfields of the Middle East and to British supply lines to Asia and Africa. It was critically important to the course of World War II.

Wilbur's death was reported in the *La Porte Herald-Argus* in May 1943:

> *Another blue service star here had turned to gold today with receipt of the death*

overseas of Pvt. Wilbur C. Hilgendorf, 27, son of Mr. and Mrs. Arthur Hilgendorf, 1116 Ridge Street.

A telegram from the war department was received by Private Hilgendorf's parents. It said he died on May 1. A letter, the telegram said, would follow. Three weeks ago the Hilgendorfs were notified by the adjutant general of the army that their son, who was in the middle eastern war theater, was seriously ill.

Born in La Porte on Oct. 22, 1915, Private Hilgendorf graduated from La Porte High School in the class of 1933 and had been an assembler at the Modine plant here before joining the service almost 14 months ago, on March 21, 1942. After training at Camp Claiborne, La., he went overseas last August. He was in the military police force of the army.

Survivors include his parents, who operate a confectionery store at 111 Clement Street; four brothers, Roy, Clarence, Raymond and Lawrence; and two sisters, Marie and Doris, all of La Porte.

Wilbur is interred at the North Africa American Cemetery in Carthage, Tunisia. He is located in Plot A, Row 11, Grave 8. The cemetery lies between the Mediterranean Sea and the Bay of Tunis, atop part of ancient Roman Carthage. It was established in 1948 to consolidate temporary cemeteries in North Africa. The government of Tunisia granted its free use as a permanent burial ground in perpetuity without charge or taxation.

PLACE OF BIRTH

INDIANA STATE BOARD OF HEALTH

DIVISION OF VITAL STATISTICS

County of *Laporte*

Township of *Center*

CERTIFICATE OF BIRTH

Town of
or
City of *Laporte* No. *1116 Ridge* St.; *3rd* Ward;

Registered No.

FULL NAME OF CHILD *Wilbur Hilgendorf*
if child is not named, make supplemental report.

| Sex of Child *M* | Twin, Triplet, or other? | and Number in order of birth (To be answered only in event of plural birth) | Legiti-mate? *yes* | Date of Birth *Oct 21* 19 *14* (Month) (Day) (Year) |

FATHER	**MOTHER**
Full Name *Arthur Hilgendorf*	Full Maiden Name *Marie Kramer*
Residence *1116 Ridge St*	Residence *1116 Ridge*
Color or Race *W*	Age at last Birthday *30* (Years)	Color or Race *W*	Age at last Birthday *30* (Years)
Birthplace *Ind*	Birthplace *Ind*
Occupation *Piano maker*	Occupation *Housewife*

| Number of children born to this mother, including present birth *5* | Number of children, of this mother, now living, including present birth *4* | Were precautions taken against ophthalmia neonatorum? *yes* |

CERTIFICATE OF ATTENDING PHYSICIAN OR MIDWIFE

I hereby certify that I attended the birth of this child, who was *born* at *8* P. M
on the date above stated. (Born alive or Stillborn)

When there was no attending physician or midwife, then the father, householder, etc., should make this return. A stillborn child is one that neither breathes nor shows other evidence of life after birth.

(Signature) *N. H. Long*

Given name added from a supplemental
report _____, 19___

Address *La Porte Ind*

Filed *11-1-*, 19 *14*

H. G. Thompson

HEALTH OFFICER

HEALTH OFFICER

Wilbur Hilgendorf – Birth Certificate

This is a copy of Wilbur Hilgendorf's birth certificate. He was born on 21 October 1914 in La Porte, Indiana.

LD-ARGUS, LA PORTE, INDIANA, FRIDAY, MA

LaPorte Soldier, Wilbur C. Hilgendorf, Dead Overseas

Succumbs in Middle Eastern Area to Serious Illness, Parents Are Informed

IN ARMY OVER A YEAR

Another blue service star here had turned to gold today with receipt of word of the death overseas of Pvt. Wilbur C. Hilgendorf, 27, son of Mr. and Mrs. Arthur Hilgendorf, 1116 Ridge street.

A telegram from the war department was received by Private Hilgendorf's parents. It said he died on May 1. A letter, the telegram said, would follow. Three weeks ago the Hilgendorfs were notified by the adjutant general of the army that their son, who was in the middle eastern war theater, was seriously ill.

Born in LaPorte on Oct. 22, 1915, Private Hilgendorf graduated from LaPorte High school in the class of 1933 and had been an assembler at the Modine plant here before joining the service almost 14 months ago, on March 21, 1942. After training at Camp Claiborne. La., he went overseas

PRIVATE HILGENDORF

last August. He was in the military police force of the army.

Survivors include his parents, who operate a confectionery store at 111 Clement street; four brothers, Roy, Clarence, Raymond and Lawrence, and two sisters, Marie and Doris, all of LaPorte.

Wilbur Hilgendorf – Death Notice

This is a copy of Wilbur Hilgendorf's death notice from the *La Porte Herald-Argus*.

IN MEMORY OF

★ ★ ★ ★ ★

WILBUR C. HILGENDORF

RANK

PRIVATE, U.S. ARMY

UNIT

802ND MILITARY POLICE BATTALION

DATE OF DEATH

MAY 1, 1943

COMMEMORATED IN PERPETUITY AT

NORTH AFRICA AMERICAN CEMETERY

TUNIS, TUNISIA

"Time will not dim the glory of their deeds."
— GENERAL JOHN J. PERSHING

This is a copy of a certificate commemorating the service of Wilbur Hilgendorf in North Africa. The certificate was obtained from the North Africa American Cemetery website provided by the American Battle Monuments Commission.

This is a photo from the 27-acre North Africa American Cemetery and Memorial in Carthage, Tunisia, Africa, where 2,841 of our military dead, including Wilbur Hilgendorf, are buried.

RAYMOND J. HILGENDORF (1916-1981)

Born in 1917, Raymond first appears in the 1920 census at four years of age. He is living with his parents and four brothers at 1116 Ridge Street. In the 1930 census thirteen-year-old Ray now also has two sisters.

Ray married Jean Cormick in La Porte on 21 December 1936, and in 1938 Ray is working at Metal Door & Trim Company. They are living at 101 D Street. 1940 and 1943 city directories show Ray working at a service station at 103 McCollum Street and living at 511 E. Jefferson Avenue. The 1943 directory also shows Jean working as a clerk at the high school. Ray and Jean had one daughter, Christine.

The 1947 city directory does not contain a listing for Ray, but it does show Jean now working at the county treasurer's office. She is living at 1416 Pennsylvania Avenue, the home of her parents. Apparently, Ray and Jean had divorced about this time.

1949 lists Ray under a heading for "Cigars and Tobacco – Retail" at 403 Lincolnway East.

In 1954 Ray is now married to Helen Gray, and they are living at 825 ½ East Lincolnway. This is the second marriage for each of them, Helen having been previously married to Thomas Bales. Ray is working as a grocer at 107 Clement Street. This would have been at his father's store.

1956 and 1960 city directories find Ray as an assembler at Coleman Co., and he and Helen are living at 1020 Ridge Street.

Ray died in 1981 and is buried in Pine Lake Cemetery. His first wife Jean died in 1997 in Michigan City, and his second wife Helen died in 1996 and is buried in Pine Lake Cemetery in La Porte.

Raymond Hilgendorf – Birth Certificate

This is a copy of Raymond Hilgendorf's birth certificate. He was born on 5 July 1916 in La Porte, Indiana.

Raymond Hilgendorf

The above photo of Raymond Hilgendorf was taken from a 1933 La Porte High School yearbook when Raymond was in his junior year of high school.

Jean (Cormick) Hilgendorf

The above photo of is of Jean Cormick, Raymond Hilgendorf's first wife. This photo was taken from a 1933 La Porte High School yearbook.

Raymond Hilgendorf – Death Certificate

This is a copy of Raymond Hilgendorf's death certificate. He died on 7 June 1981. His death was due to "Carcinoma of the lung with metastases" (lung cancer that has spread to other parts of the body.)

INDIANA STATE DEPARTMENT OF HEALTH

CERTIFICATE OF DEATH

State No. 016233

* ATTENTION ESTATE: Disclosure of the SS# we need to pursue our responsibilities is voluntary and there will be no penalty for refusal. *

Local No. 143

THE RECORDS IN THIS SERIES ARE CONFIDENTIAL PER IC 16-1-19-3

1. DECEASED—NAME (First Middle Last)	Jean Hilgendorf Anderson
2. SEX	Female
3a. TIME OF DEATH	7:05PM
3b. DATE OF DEATH (Month Day Yr)	April 29, 1997
5a. AGE - Last Birthday (Years)	81
6. DATE OF BIRTH (Mo Day Yr)	Jul 11, 1915
7. BIRTHPLACE (City and State or Foreign Country)	Gary, IN 46400
8a. WAS DECEDENT A U.S. VETERAN?	No
8b. YEAR LAST SERVED IN U.S. ARMED FORCES	N/A
9a. PLACE OF DEATH	OTHER ☒ Nursing Home
9b. FACILITY NAME	Michigan City Health Care Cen.
9c. CITY TOWN OR LOCATION OF DEATH	Michigan City
9d. COUNTY OF DEATH	LaPorte
10. MARITAL STATUS	Married
11. SURVIVING SPOUSE	Richard Anderson
12a. DECEDENT'S USUAL OCCUPATION	Director
12b. KIND OF BUSINESS INDUSTRY	Red Cross
13a. RESIDENCE - STATE	IN
13b. COUNTY	LaPorte
13c. CITY TOWN OR LOCATION	Michigan City
13d. STREET AND NUMBER	405 Hendricks Street
13e. ZIP CODE	46360
13f. INSIDE CITY LIMITS	☒ Yes
13g. ON A FARM?	☒ No
14. CITIZEN OF WHAT COUNTRY?	USA
15. WAS DECEDENT OF HISPANIC ORIGIN?	☒ No
16. RACE	White
17. DECEDENT'S EDUCATION Elementary/Secondary (0-12)	12
18. FATHER'S NAME (First, Middle, Last)	Stephen Cormick
19. MOTHER'S NAME (First, Middle, Maiden Surname)	Hedwig Annay
20a. INFORMANT'S NAME (Type/Print)	Christine Denman
20b. MAILING ADDRESS	P.O. Box 3707 M/S 2H-96, Seattle, WA
20c. Relationship	Daughter
21a. METHOD OF DISPOSITION	☒ Cremation
21b. DATE AND PLACE OF DISPOSITION	May 2, 1997 Calvary Crematory
21c. LOCATION - City or Town State	Portage, IN
22a. EMBALMER'S NAME	not embalmed
23. WAS DEATH REPORTED TO CORONER?	☒ No
24a. SIGNATURE OF FUNERAL DIRECTOR	*Mark E. Essling*
24b. LICENSE NO.	FDO1001104
25. NAME ADDRESS AND LICENSE NUMBER OF FUNERAL HOME	FH63004049 Essling Funeral Home, Inc. 1117 Indiana Avenue , LaPorte, IN 46350

26. CAUSE OF DEATH

PART I. Enter the diseases injuries or complications that caused the death. Do not enter nonspecific terms such as cardiac or respiratory arrest, shock, or heart failure. List only one cause on each line.

		Approximate Interval Between Onset and Death
IMMEDIATE CAUSE (Final disease or condition resulting in death)	a. *Cardiac Registry failure*	MONTHS
Conditions if any which gave rise to the immediate cause stating the underlying cause last	b. *Chronic Cardiomyopathy*	1 YR
	c.	
	d.	

PART II. Other significant conditions - Conditions contributing to death but not previously stated in Part I.

OREYNAUDS PHENOMENON

27. WAS DECEDENT PREGNANT OR 90 DAYS POSTPARTUM?	28a. WAS AN AUTOPSY PERFORMED?	28b. WERE AUTOPSY FINDINGS AVAILABLE PRIOR TO COMPLETION OF CAUSE OF DEATH?
No	No	No

29a. CERTIFIER (Check only one) ☒ CERTIFYING PHYSICIAN

29b. SIGNATURE AND TITLE OF CERTIFIER	29c. MEDICAL LICENSE NO	29d. DATE SIGNED (Month Day Year)
	I26880	5-1-97

30. NAME AND ADDRESS OF PERSON WHO COMPLETED CAUSE OF DEATH (ITEM 26) (Type/Print)

Charles T. Janovsky, M.D., 1225 E. Coolspring Ave., Michigan City, IN 46360

31. HEALTH OFFICER'S SIGNATURE *Aggarwal MD*

32. DATE FILED (Month Day Year) MAY 0 1 1997

33. MANNER OF DEATH: ☒ Natural

34a. DATE OF INJURY	34b. TIME OF INJURY	34c. INJURY AT WORK?	34d. DESCRIBE HOW INJURY OCCURRED
		No	

34e. PLACE OF INJURY 34f. LOCATION

34g. DATE PRONOUNCED DEAD 34h. MOTOR VEHICLE ACCIDENT? (Yes or no) No

SDH06-004   State Form 10110-04   (R4 / 3-93)   DEATHCER/PO t

Jean (Cormick) Hilgendorf Anderson – Death Certificate

This is a copy of Jean (Cormick) Hilgendorf Anderson's death certificate. She died on 29 April 1997. Her death was due to cardiac failure.

* ATTENTION ESTATE: Disclosure of the SS# we need to pursue our responsibilities is voluntary and there will be no penalty for refusal. *

Local No. 330

INDIANA STATE DEPARTMENT OF HEALTH
CERTIFICATE OF DEATH

State No. 029109

THE RECORDS IN THIS SERIES ARE CONFIDENTIAL PER IC 16-1-19-3

TYPE/PRINT IN PERMANENT BLACK INK	1. DECEASED–NAME (First Middle Last) Helen L. Hilgendorf	2. SEX Female	3a. TIME OF DEATH 8:09PM / 3b. DATE OF DEATH (Month Day Yr) August 29, 1996

| 5a. AGE - Last Birthday (Years) 83 | 5b. UNDER 1 YEAR Months Days | 5c. UNDER 1 DAY Hours Minutes | 6. DATE OF BIRTH (Mo Day Yr) Dec 23, 1912 | 7. BIRTHPLACE (City and State or Foreign Country) Garber, OK |

| 8a. WAS DECEDENT A U.S. VETERAN? No | 8b. YEAR LAST SERVED IN U.S. ARMED FORCES N/A | 9a. PLACE OF DEATH (Check only one. See Instructions) HOSPITAL ☐ Inpatient ☐ ER/Outpatient ☐ DOA / OTHER ☒ Nursing Home ☐ Other (Specify) ☐ Residence |

DECEDENT

| 9b. FACILITY NAME (If not institution, give street and number) Fountainview Terrace N.H. | 9c. CITY TOWN OR LOCATION OF DEATH LaPorte | 9d. COUNTY OF DEATH LaPorte |

| 10. MARITAL STATUS (Specify) Widowed | 11. SURVIVING SPOUSE (If wife, give maiden name) NONE | 12a. DECEDENT'S USUAL OCCUPATION (Give kind of work done during most of working life. Do not use retired) Homemaker | 12b. KIND OF BUSINESS/INDUSTRY Home Owner |

| 13a. RESIDENCE - STATE IN | 13b. COUNTY LaPorte | 13c. CITY TOWN OR LOCATION LaPorte | 13d. STREET AND NUMBER 1900 Andrew Avenue |

| 13e. ZIP CODE 46350 | 13f. INSIDE CITY LIMITS ☐ No ☒ Yes / 13g. ON A FARM? ☒ No ☐ Yes | 14. CITIZEN OF WHAT COUNTRY? USA | 15. WAS DECEDENT OF HISPANIC ORIGIN? ☒ No ☐ Yes (If yes specify Cuban, Mexican, Puerto Rican, etc.) | 16. RACE - American Indian Black, White, etc. (Specify) White | 17. DECEDENT'S EDUCATION (Specify only highest grade completed) Elementary/Secondary (0-12) 12 / College (1-4 or 5+) |

PARENTS

| 18. FATHER'S NAME (First, Middle, Last) Duane Gray | 19. MOTHER'S NAME (First, Middle, Maiden Surname) Esther Brown |

INFORMANT

| 20a. INFORMANT'S NAME (Type/Print) Natalie Yeater | 20b. MAILING ADDRESS (Street and Number or Rural Route Number, City or Town, State, Zip Code) 7738 N. 200 E., LaPorte, IN 46350 | 20c. Relationship Daughter |

DISPOSITION

| 21a. METHOD OF DISPOSITION ☐ Burial ☒ Cremation ☐ Donation ☐ Entombment ☐ Other (Specify) ☐ Removal from State | 21b. DATE AND PLACE OF DISPOSITION (Name of cemetery, crematory or August 31, 1996 Calvary Crematory | 21c. LOCATION - City or Town State Portage, IN |

| 22a. EMBALMER'S NAME not embalmed | 22b. EMBALMER'S LICENSE NO. n/a | 23. WAS DEATH REPORTED TO CORONER? ☒ No ☐ Yes |

| 24a. SIGNATURE OF FUNERAL DIRECTOR *Mark E. Essl* | 24b. LICENSE NUMBER (of Licensee) FDO1001104 | 25. NAME ADDRESS AND LICENSE NUMBER OF FUNERAL HOME FH83004049 Essling Funeral Home, Inc. 1117 Indiana Avenue, LaPorte, IN 46350 |

CAUSE OF DEATH

26. PART I Enter the diseases, injuries or complications that caused the death. Do not enter nonspecific terms such as cardiac or respiratory arrest, shock, or heart failure. List only one cause on each line.

		Approximate Interval Between Onset and Death
IMMEDIATE CAUSE (Final disease or condition resulting in death)	a. Cardiac Ischemia	Minutes
	DUE TO (OR AS A CONSEQUENCE OF)	
Conditions if any which gave rise to the immediate cause stating the underlying cause last	b. Diabetes mellitus	Years
	DUE TO (OR AS A CONSEQUENCE OF)	
	c.	
	DUE TO (OR AS A CONSEQUENCE OF)	

| PART II. Other significant conditions - Conditions contributing to death but not previously stated in Part I. | 27. WAS DECEDENT PREGNANT or 90 DAYS POSTPARTUM? (Yes or no) No | 28a. WAS AN AUTOPSY PERFORMED? (Yes or no) No | 28b. WERE AUTOPSY FINDINGS AVAILABLE PRIOR TO COMPLETION OF CAUSE OF DEATH? (Yes or no) No |

CERTIFIER

| 29a. CERTIFIER (Check only one) ☒ CERTIFYING PHYSICIAN To the best of my knowledge, death occurred at the time, date, and place and due to the cause(s) as stated. ☐ HEALTH OFFICER On the basis of examination and/or investigation in my opinion death occurred at the time, date and place and due to the cause(s) as stated. ☐ CORONER On the basis of examination and/or investigation in my opinion death occurred at the time, date, and place and due to the cause(s) and manner as stated. |

| 29b. SIGNATURE AND TITLE OF CERTIFIER *Michael D. Howard* | 29c. MEDICAL LICENSE NO 1030220 | 29d. DATE SIGNED (Month Day Year) 8/30/96 |

| 30. NAME AND ADDRESS OF PERSON WHO COMPLETED CAUSE OF DEATH (ITEM 26) (Type/Print) Michael D. Howard, 900 "I" Street, LaPorte, Indiana 46350 |

HEALTH OFFICER

2 cm

| 31. HEALTH OFFICER'S SIGNATURE *Aggarwal MD* | 32. DATE FILED (Month Day Year) AUG 30 1996 |

| 33. MANNER OF DEATH ☒ Natural ☐ Accident ☐ Suicide ☐ Homicide ☐ Pending Investigation ☐ Could not be Determined | 34a. DATE OF INJURY (Month Day Year) | 34b. TIME OF INJURY | 34c. INJURY AT WORK? (Yes or no) No | 34d. DESCRIBE HOW INJURY OCCURRED |

| 34e. PLACE OF INJURY - At home, farm, street, factory, office building, etc. (Specify) | 34f. LOCATION (Street and Number or Rural Route Number City or Town State) |

| 34g. DATE PRONOUNCED DEAD (Month, Day, Year) | 34h. MOTOR VEHICLE ACCIDENT? (Yes or no) If yes specify driver, passenger, pedestrian, etc. No |

SDH06-004   State Form 10110-04 (R4 / 3-93) DEATHCER/PD 1

Helen Louise (Gray) Hilgendorf – Death Certificate

This is a copy of Helen Louise (Gray) Hilgendorf's death certificate. Helen was Raymond's second wife. She died on 29 August 1996. Her death was due to Cardiac Ischemia (a severe blockage of a coronary artery leading to a heart attack).

ARTHUR HILGENDORF JR. (1919-1922)

This "second" Arthur Jr. was born 15 May 1919, placing him between between Ray and Marie. His death record has been found, but no birth record.

Strangely, the 1920 census does not show Arthur Jr., even though he did not die until 1922. Perhaps he was ill from birth and living under some type of care. Unfortunately, with the lack of information available, we may never know the answer.

His death certificate notes the cause of death as "lobar pneumonia – both lungs" and a secondary factor of "Measles." He is buried in Pine Lake Cemetery.

Now, note in the obituary following for Doris Hilgendorf that one Arthur Jr. is mentioned. In addition, that obituary refers to a brother named Charles. No records have been found for a Charles Hilgendorf. Perhaps one of the two Arthurs went by the name Charles, perhaps a middle name. None of the very few records for the two Arthurs notes a middle name, however.

Arthur Hilgendorf Jr. – Death Certificate

This is a copy of Arthur Hilgendorf Jr.'s death certificate. This is the "second" Arthur Jr. born to Arthur and Mary Hilgendorf. He was born 15 March 1919 and died on 10 December 1922. His death was caused by Lobar Pneumonia of both lungs with a contributory cause of Measles.

MARIE ELIZABETH HILGENDORF (1922-2009)

Following seven boys, Marie was the first daughter born to and Mary Hilgendorf. She appears with the family in the 1930 and 1940 census records at 1116 Ridge Street. She also appears in the 1940 La Porte city directory as a student.

Most records, including her death certificate, show her with a middle initial of J; however, her birth certificate clearly shows her middle name to be Elizabeth.

In a 1947 La Porte city directory, Marie is a spooler at La Porte Bachmann Woolen Mills. This woolen mill was located at the corner of Fox and Webber Streets in La Porte. (An apartment building was constructed in this area about 1965.) That same year, 1947, Marie married George Wineholt. George had been the secretary for the Chamber of Commerce Office, and he was working as a cost account at Hoosier Industries in 1947. Marie and George had two sons, Dan and Tom.

In 1952 Marie and George are living at 206 Ohio Street. Directories through 1960 have them at that same address. George works as purchasing agent for Coleman Co. George was also a World War II veteran having enlisted on 21 February 1942.

Marie's birth certificate notes that at the time of her birth that she was the eighth child to be born to her parents and that seven children were living. Regarding the number of children, this would agree with the first Arthur Jr. having already passed and with the second Arthur Jr. still living, as he would pass in December of the year of Marie's birth.

George died in November of 1976, and Marie passed in April of 2009. They are buried in Kingsbury Cemetery in Kingsbury, Indiana.

PLACE OF BIRTH

INDIANA STATE BOARD OF HEALTH
DIVISION OF VITAL STATISTICS

County of *La Porte*

Township of *Center*

CERTIFICATE OF BIRTH 19174

Town of

or

City of *La Porte* (No. *1116 Ridge* St.; Ward)

Registered No. *99*

FULL NAME OF CHILD *Marie Elizabeth Hilgendorf*

If child is not named, make supplemental report.

| Sex of Child *J* | Twins, Triplets, or others? (To be answered only in event of plural births) | and | Number in order of birth | Legitimate? *Yes* | Date of Birth *April 1, 1922* (Month) (Day) (Year) |

	FATHER		**MOTHER**
Full Name	*Arthur Hilgendorf*	Full Maiden Name	*Mary Kramer*
Post office Address	*1116 Ridge Street La Porte*	Post office Address	*1116 Ridge Street*
Color or Race *White*	Age at last Birthday *38* (Years)	Color or Race *White*	Age at last Birthday *38* (Years)
Birthplace *Wis.*		Birthplace *Ind.*	
Occupation *Core Maker*		Occupation *Hwf.*	

Number of children born to this mother, including present birth *8*

Number of children, of this mother, now living, including present birth *7*

Were precautions taken against ophthalmia neonatorum? *Yes.*

CERTIFICATE OF ATTENDING PHYSICIAN OR MIDWIFE *

I hereby certify that I attended the birth of this child, who was *alive* at *2* P. M.

(Born alive or Stillborn)

on the date above stated.

* When there was no attending physician or midwife, then the father, householder, etc., should make this return. A stillborn child is one that neither breathes nor shows other evidence of life after birth.

(Signature) *W W Ross*

(Attending physician, midwife, householder *)

Given name added from a supplemental

Address *La Porte Ind.*

report , 19

Filed *April 3*, 19 *22* *Neil E Funk*

HEALTH OFFICER

HEALTH OFFICER

Marie Elizabeth Hilgendorf – Birth Certificate

This is a copy of Marie Elizabeth Hilgendorf's birth certificate. Marie was born on 1 April 1922 in La Porte, Indiana.

Marie Elizabeth Hilgendorf

Marie Hilgendorf with nephew Ken Hilgendorf and niece Sally Hilgendorf about 1945/46.

INDIANA STATE DEPARTMENT OF HEALTH
CERTIFICATE OF DEATH

Local No. OGO281

State No. OO8629

1 Decedent's Legal Name (First, Middle, Last)	1a Maiden Last Name (if Female)	2 Sex	3 Time of Death	4 Date of Death (Month Day Year)
Marie J. Wineholt	Hilgendorf	F	2:10 PM	04/01/2009

5 Social Security Number	6a Age Years	6b Under 1 Year Months	6c Under 1 Month Days	6d Under 1 Day Hours	6e Under 1 Hour Minutes	7 Date of Birth (Month/Day/Year)	8 Birthplace (City, State Or Foreign Country)
	87					04/01/1922	LaPorte, IN

9 Ever In US Armed Forces	10 If Death Occurred In Hospital	10a If Death Occurred Somewhere Other Than Hospital
Yes X No Unknown	X Inpatient Emergency Dept Outpatient Dead on Arrival	Hospice Facility Decedent's Home Nursing/Long Term Care Facility Other (Specify)

LaPorte Hospital

11 Facility Name (If Not Institution, Give Street And Number)
LaPorte Hospital

12 City Or Town, State And Zip Code	13 County of Death	14 Marital Status At Time of Death
La Porte IN 46350	La Porte	Married Married, But Separated Divorced X Widowed Never Married Unknown

15 Surviving Spouses Name	15a (If Wife) Give Maiden Last Name	16 Decedent's Usual Occupation	17 Kind of Business/Industry
None		Homemaker	Home Owner

18 Residence - State	18a County	18b City or Town
IN	La Porte	LaPorte

18c Street And Number	18d Apt. No.	18e Zip Code	18f Inside City Limits
3754 S. US 35		46350	Yes X No

19 Decedent's Education	20 Decedent Of Hispanic Origin	21 Decedent's Race
High School Graduate or GED Completed	No, Not Spanish/Hispanic/Latino	White

22 Father's Name (First, Middle, Last)	23 Mother's Name (First, Middle, Last)	23a Mother's Maiden Last Name
Arthur Hilgendorf	Mary Kramer Hilgendorf	Kramer

24 Informant's Name	24a Relationship To Decedent	24b Mailing Address (Street, Number, City, State, Zip Code)
Tom Wineholt	Son	3772 S. US 35 LaPorte, IN 46350

25a Method of Disposition	25 Place Of Disposition	
Burial X Cremation Donation Entombment Removal From State Other (Specify)	25b Place Of Disposition (Name of Cemetery, Crematory, Other Place) La Porte Crematory	25c Location City, Town And State La Porte, IN

26 Was Coroner Contacted	27 Name And Complete Address Of Funeral Facility	27a Funeral Home License Number
Yes X No	Essling Funeral Home 1117 Indiana Avenue LaPorte, Indiana 46350	FH83004049

27b Signature Of Indiana Funeral Service Licensee
Mark E. Essling

27c License Number (Of Licensee)
FD01001104

Cause Of Death (See Instructions And Examples)

		Approximate Interval Onset To Death
28 Part 1. Enter the Chain Of Events - Diseases, Injuries, Or Complications - That directly caused the Death. Do Not Enter Terminal Events Such As Cardiac Arrest, Respiratory Arrest, Or Ventricular Fibrillation Without Showing The Etiology. Do Not Abbreviate. Enter Only On Cause On A Line. Add Additional Lines If Necessary	A CEREBRAL INFARCTION	37 DAYS
Immediate Cause (Final Disease Or Condition Resulting In Death)	B ATEROSCLEROTIC CARDIOVASCULAR DISEASE	YEARS
Sequentially List Conditions, If Any, Leading To The Cause Listed On Line A. Enter The Underlying Cause (Disease Or Injury That Initiated The Events Resulting In Death) Last	C	
	D	

Part II. Enter Other Significant Conditions Contributing To Death But Not Resulting To The Underlying Cause Given In Part I	29 Was An Autopsy Performed Yes X No
ESSENTIAL HYPERTENSION - TYPE II DIABETES MELLITUS	30 Were Autopsy Findings Available To Complete Cause Of Death Yes No

31 Did Tobacco Use Contribute To Death	32 If Female	33 Manner Of Death
Yes Probably No Unknown	Not Pregnant Within Last Year Pregnant At Time Of Death Not Pregnant But Pregnant within 42 Days Of Death Not Pregnant But Pregnant 43 Days To 1 year Before Death Unknown If Pregnant Within The Past Year	X Natural Homicide Accident Pending Investigation Suicide Could Not Be Determined

34 Date Of Injury (Month/Day/Year)	35 Time Of Injury	36 Place Of Injury (E.G. Decedent's Home, Construction Site, Restaurant, Wooded Area)	37 Injury At Work Yes No

38 Location Of Injury - State	38a City Or Town	38b Street And Number	38c Apt. No.	38d Zip Code

39 Describe How Injury Occurred

40 If Transportation Injury, Specify Driver/Operator   Passenger   Pedestrian   Other (Specify)

41 Signature Of Person Certifying Cause Of Death
Murphy Martin M.D.

42 Certifier (Check Only One) X Certifying Physician   Coroner   Health Officer

43 Name, Address And Zip Code Of Person Certifying Cause Of Death	44 License Number	45 Date Certified
Murphy Martin 300 Wile St Ste 6, LaPorte, IN 46350	01038063	4-2-09

46 Additional Funeral Service Provider

48 Signature Of Local Health Officer

49 For Registrar Only - Date Filed (Month/Day/Year)
APR 0 3 2009

Marie Hilgendorf Wineholt – Death Certificate

This is a copy of Marie Hilgendorf Wineholt's death certificate. She died on 1 April 2009. The cause of death is noted as Cerebral Infarction (a stroke resulting from a blockage in the arteries supplying blood and oxygen to the brain).

DORIS HILGENDORF (1924-2016)

Doris was the youngest child, the second daughter, of Arthur and Mary Hilgendorf born in 1925. She appears at home with her family on 1116 Ridge Street in the 1930 and 1940 census records.

In 1947 Doris is working as a bookkeeper at La Porte Savings Bank. She is still living at home with her parents. On 19 June 1948 she married Richard Bowman in La Porte.

In the 1949 city directory, they are living at 207 I Street in La Porte, and Dick is working in the factory at Studebaker Corporation in South Bend. In 1954 through 1956 they live on East State Road 2 in La Porte, and Dick is an insurance adjuster.

Dick died on 30 June 2012 in Palatine, Illinois, where they made their home. Dick was a decorated World War II veteran. Dick and Doris have two children, Larry and Patrick.

Doris' Obituary:

> *Doris Mae Bowman, 92, of Palatine, Illinois, formerly of La Porte, Indiana, passed at home on Monday, Aug. 22, 2016.*

> *Born July 9, 1924, in La Porte, Indiana, she was the beloved daughter of Arthur and Mary (Kramer) Hilgendorf. United in marriage on June 19, 1948, Doris was the cherished wife of Richard (Dick) K. Bowman. He preceded her in death on June 30, 2012. They were married for 64 wonderful years and members of St. Theresa Catholic Church in Palatine since 1956.*

> *Doris graduated from La Porte High School in 1942, and as a young woman worked at the La Porte Savings Bank. She also worked at Carson Pirie Scott for several years after relocating to Palatine, Illinois.*

> *Doris was a loving mother and is survived by her children, Lawrence (Carolyn) Bowman of Kildeer, Illinois, and Patrick (Vickie) Bowman of Palatine, Illinois. She was the proud grandmother of six grandchildren, Sarah, Paul Brent, Tracy, Kacie and Ryan. Doris was a devoted Aunt to many nieces and nephews and a cherished friend to many.*

> *In retirement Dick and Doris had a summer home built in Cornucopia, Wisconsin, on the beautiful shores of Lake Superior, as a legacy to their family. Even today 'Corny Cabin' is enjoyed and shared with family and friends.*

> *In addition to her husband, Doris was preceded in death by her seven brothers, Arthur Jr., Charles, Lawrence, Clarence, Wilbur, Raymond and Roy Hilgendorf, and sister Marie (Wineholt).*

> *A memorial mass celebrating Doris's life will be held on Saturday, Sept. 17, 2016, at 10 a.m. at St. Theresa Catholic Church, 455 N. Benton St., Palatine, Illinois, followed by a private interment at Saint Michael The Archangel in Palatine. In lieu of flowers memorial donations may be made to St. Theresa Catholic church, or to the American Cancer Society.*

PLACE OF BIRTH

INDIANA STATE BOARD OF HEALTH
DIVISION OF VITAL STATISTICS

Local No. *2 71*

nty of *La Porte*

CERTIFICATE OF BIRTH

wnship of *Center*

State Registered No. *37665*

wn of
or of *La Porte* (No. *1116*, *Ridge* St., *4* Ward)

LL NAME OF CHILD *Doris Hilgendorf*

:hild is not named, make supplemental report.

| x of ild *female* | ⁴Twins, Triplets, or others? and Number in order of birth (To be answered only in event of plural births) | ⁶Legitimate? *yes* | ⁷Date of Birth *July* 9 19*24* (Month) (Day) (Year) |

FATHER		MOTHER	
l ne *Arthur J Hilgendorf*		¹⁴Full Maiden Name *Mary Kramer*	
:office Address *La Porte Ind.*		¹⁵Postoffice Address *La Porte Indiana*	
or :ace *White*	¹¹Age at last Birthday *39* (Years)	¹⁶Color or Race *white*	¹⁷Age at last Birthday *40* (Years)
bplace *Indiana*		¹⁸Birthplace *Indiana*	
upation *Core Maker*		¹⁹Occupation *Housewife*	

| nber of children born to this her, including present birth *9* | ²¹Number of children, of this mother, now living, including present birth *7* | ²²Were precautions taken against ophthalmia neonatorum? *yes* |

CERTIFICATE OF ATTENDING PHYSICIAN OR MIDWIFE*

I hereby certify that I attended the birth of this child, who was *alive* at *10 P* M.
the date above stated. (Born alive or Stillborn)

*When there was no attending physician or midwife, then the father, householder, etc., should make this return. A stillborn child is one that neither breathes nor shows other evidence of life after birth.

(Signature) *Dr Bo Bowell*
attending physician
(Attending physician, midwife, householder*)

Given name added from a supplemental

Address *La Porte, Indiana*

ort _____, 19 ____

Filed *July 11*, 19*24*   *Neil E Funk*

HEALTH OFFICER   HEALTH OFFICER

Doris Hilgendorf – Birth Certificate

This is a copy of Doris Hilgendorf's birth certificate. Doris was born on 9 July 1924 in La Porte, Indiana.

Doris (Hilgendorf) Bowman

This photo of Doris (Hilgendorf) Bowman is from about 2008.

HAAG

THE FIRST GENERATION:

HANS MARTIN HAG
(1647-1690)

FAMILY CHART

<u>Hans Martin Hag</u> – b. 1647, d. 1690
      Spouse: Catherina Sauerman – b. 8 August 1651, d. 28 July 1731
      Children:
            Johanna Elisabetha Hag – b. May 1675, d. unknown
            Anna Maria Hag – b. November 1679, d. unknown
            Hans Martin Hag – b. April 1687, d. July 1761
            <u>Jacob Haag</u> – b. February 1689, d. 7 February 1762

Note 1: The names in **<u>underlined bold</u>** above, and at each generation similarly, represent the descendant line that will be followed ultimately leading to the Hilgendorf-Haag union. Each chapter represents one family generation. Only the family that is **<u>underlined bold</u>** is followed at each generation, or chapter. Thus, detail is provided for the underlined individual and that person's siblings in each chapter. So, this first chapter is about Hans Martin Haag and the next chapter will be about Jacob Haag. Siblings will be studied in the order of birth in each chapter.
Note 2: As noted in the opening paragraph of this chapter which follows, one particular family tree from Ancestry.com has been utilized as the base for the first four generations of the Haag family contained in this book. This tree was created by kimberly0326 and is known as the "Endres Family Tree" at Ancestry.com.

LOOKING BACKWARDS TO GERMAN ROOTS THROUGH MICHAEL HAAG (1813-1890)

Michael Haag, the fifth generation of the Haag family, is the first of the Haags to appear in the United States. He was born in Walsheim, Saarland, Germany, in 1813. Using this location as a starting point to find the location of his parents, there was one particular set of international family trees that included Michael and that showed his father coming from Auerbach, Karlsruhe, Baden-Wuerttemberg, Germany, and his mother from Walsheim. Michael's parents were married in Walsheim, the town where Michael was born.

The town of Walsheim in the German state of Saarland is only about 50-55 miles west and a bit north of the district of Karlsruhe in the state of Baden-Wuerttemberg. The Karlsruhe location continues back through several generations of Haags to Hans Martin Hag.

Further strength is added to the argument for using the connection to Walsheim by the fact that Michael Haag's first and second wives were from Alsace, France. Walsheim is within about ten miles of the nearest border of Alsace, France. Alsace is located on France's eastern border and on the west bank of the upper Rhine River. Bordering Germany and Switzerland, it has alternated between German and French control over the centuries and reflects a mix of those cultures. Further, Karlsruhe is only about five miles from the border of Alsace, and the town of Auerbach is about ten miles from the border. So, there seems to be a likely possibility that Michael Haag knew the women prior to immigrating to America.

So, using the family tree thus selected, we begin the first generation of the Haag family with Hans Martin Hag, born in 1647 in Durlach, Stadt Karlsruhe, Baden-Wuerttemberg, Germany. Note the spelling as "Hag" which becomes "Haag" with son Jacob.

A BRIEF HISTORY OF KARLSRUHE, GERMANY

The Karlsruhe district is the second-largest city in the state of Baden-Wuerttemberg, in southwest Germany, near the French-German border. Durlach is a borough of the German city of Karlsruhe. In 1938 Durlach was incorporated into Karlsruhe, which had grown bigger than Durlach.

According to legend, the name Karlsruhe, which translates as "Charles' repose," was given to the new city after a hunting trip when Margrave Charles III William of Baden-Durlach, woke from a dream in which he dreamt of founding his new city. A variation of this story claims that he built the new palace in order to find peace from his wife.

Charles William founded the city on June 17, 1715, after a dispute with the citizens of his previous capital, Durlach. The founding of the city is closely linked to the construction of the palace. Karlsruhe became the capital of Baden until 1945.

Karlsruhe was visited by Thomas Jefferson during his time as the American envoy to France. When Pierre Charles L'Enfant was planning the layout of Washington, D.C., Jefferson passed to him maps of twelve European towns to consult, one of which was a sketch he had made of Karlsruhe during his visit.

Much of the central area, including the palace, was reduced to rubble by Allied bombing during World War II but was rebuilt after the war. Located in the American zone of the post-war Allied occupation, Karlsruhe was home to an American military base, established in 1945. In 1995, the bases closed, and their facilities were turned over to the city of Karlsruhe.

HANS MARTIN HAG (1647-1690)

Utilizing the process previously outlined, the ancestry of the Haag family begins with Hans Martin Hag born in 1647 in Durlach, Stadt Karlsruhe, Baden-Wuerttemberg, Germany

Part of the reasoning for selecting this particular set of early German ancestors is based upon Michael Haag's father's birthplace in Karlsruhe. This seems to be a good indicator of the possible location of his ancestors, in this case Hans Martin Hag and his wife Catherina Sauerman who was born 8 Aug 1651 also in Durlach, Stadt Karlsruhe, Baden-Wuerttemberg, Germany. With some bit of confidence utilizing this type of pattern and dates, a particular list of early ancestors was selected for this study. Hopefully, this process has provided a better than 50/50 chance that this is the actual lineage of this Haag family.

Hans Martin Hag married Catherina Sauerman in 1671. She was also from Durlach. The known children of Hans and Catherina as shown in the chart at the opening of this chapter include Johanna Elisabetha Hag, Anna Maria Hag, Hans Martin Hag, and Jacob Haag.

Hans Martin Hag died in 1690 not long after the birth of his son Jacob. Hans' wife, Catherina, died in 1767. The line of the Haag family that we will follow in this book continues with son Jacob Haag born in Auerbach, Durlach, Baden, Germany, in February of 1689.

HAAG

THE SECOND GENERATION:

JACOB HAAG (1689-1762)

FAMILY CHART

Johanna Elisabetha Hag – b. May 1675, d. unknown

Anna Maria Hag – b. November 1679, d. unknown

Hans Martin Hag – b. April 1687, d. July 1761

Jacob Haag – b. February 1689, d. 7 February 1762
    Spouse: Anna Maria Leonhardt – b. 11 June 1700, d. 7 August 1767
    Children:
        Maria Christina Haag – b. 27 May 1718, d. 7 August 1761
        Anna Barbara Haag – b. August 1720, d. 16 June 1754
        Anna Catharina Haag – b. 5 March 1722, d. 1778
        Phillip Haag – b. 31 March 1726, d. 17 August 1763
        Hans Jacob Haag – b. 16 June 1729, d. 1732
        Matthias Haag – b. March 1730, d. unknown
        Johannes Jacob Haag – b. 14 September 1732, d. 2 Jun 1797

INTRODUCTION

There is very little additional information to provide through the second, third and fourth generations of the Haag families. The family continued to reside in the Auerbach and Karlsruhe areas in the German state of Baden-Wuerttemberg. Auerbach is a smaller town about eight or nine miles southeast of Karlsruhe.

There was not a lot of movement of the family members in this second generation of Haags. They all remained in the German state of Karlsruhe in either Durlach or Auerbach. Four children have been located in the Hans Martin Hag family. Considering that families were generally large at this time, there certainly may be other children that have not yet been found.

JOHANNA ELISABETHA HAG (1675 – UNKNOWN)

Johanna is the first known child of Has Martin and Catherina Haag. She was born in Durlach, Stadt Karlsruhe, Baden-Wuerttemberg, Germany, in May 1675.

ANNA MARIA HAG (1679 – UNKNOWN)

The second known child was Ann Maria born in November of 1679 in Durlach, Stadt Karlsruhe, Baden-Wuerttemberg, Germany.

HANS MARTIN HAG (1687 – 1761)

Third known child, named after his father, was born April 1687 in Durlach, Stadt Karlsruhe, Baden-Wuerttemberg, Germany. Hans died in Nottingen, Enzkreis, Baden-Wuerttemberg, Germany, in July 1671. Nottingen is about nine miles southeast of Durlach.

JACOB HAAG (1689 – 1762)

Jacob Haag, the last known son of Hans Martin Hag was born in Auerbach, Durlach, Baden, Germany, in February of 1689. It is with Jacob that we see the change in the spelling of the family name. Jacob married Anna Maria Leonhardt, born 11 June 1700 in Heiningen, Germany. Together they had seven known children. It is their last known child, Johannes Jacob, that will continue our line of Haags.

Jacob died 7 Feb 1762, in the location of his birth, and his wife Anna Maria died five years later on 7 August 1767 in Auerbach.

HAAG

THE THIRD GENERATION:
JOHANNES JACOB HAAG (1732-1797)

FAMILY CHART

Maria Christina Haag – b. 27 May 1718, d. 7 August 1761

Anna Barbara Haag – b. August 1720, d. 16 June 1754

Anna Catharina Haag – b. 5 March 1722, d. 1778

Phillip Haag – b. 31 March 1726, d. 17 August 1763

Hans Jacob Haag – b. 16 June 1729, d. 1732

Matthias Haag – b. March 1730, d. unknown

<u>Johannes Jacob Haag</u> – b. 14 September 1732, d. 2 Jun 1797
    Spouse: unknown
    Children:
        Catharina Haag – b. 14 August 1757, d. unknown
        Friederich Haag – b. 14 September 1760, d. 29 October 1760
        Christina Haag – b. 2 March 1762, d. 13 May 1828
        Johann Jacob Haag – b. 8 March 1765, d. 23 June 1765

Johann Jacob Frederick Haag – b. 20 November 1766, d. 6 July 1839
Phillip Haag – b. 13 October 1769, d. 1770
Johann Martin Haag – b. 3 November 1771, d. 20 February 1772
Michael Haag – b. 27 January 1774, d. 1839
Phillip Haag – b. 22 March 1780, d. 15 May 1846

MARIA CHRISTINA HAAG (1718 – 1761)

The first child of Jacob and Anna Maria Haag is Maria Christina born 27 May 1718 in Auerbach, Karlsruhe, Baden-Wuerttemberg, Germany. She died 7 August 1761 in the town of her birth.

ANNA BARBARA HAAG (1720 – 1754)

Anna Barbara Haag was born August 1720 in Auerbach, Karlsruhe, Baden-Wuerttemberg, Germany. She died on 16 June 1754 in Obermutchelbach, Baden-Wuerttemberg, Germany. Obermutchelbach is only a couple of miles north of Auerbach.

ANNA CATHARINA HAAG (1722 – 1778)

Anna Catharina Haag was born 5 March 1722 in Auerbach, Karlsruhe, Baden-Wuerttemberg, Germany. She died in 1778.

PHILLIP HAAG (1726 – 1763)

Phillip Haag was born 31 March 1726 in Untermutschelbach, Karlsruhe, Baden-Wuerttemberg, Germany. Untermutschelbach is about 10 miles northeast of Auerbach. Phillip died 17 August 1763 in Auerbach.

HANS JACOB HAAG (1729 – 1732)

Hans Jacob Haag was born in Auerbach, Karlsruhe, Baden-Wuerttemberg, Germany, on 16 June 1729. He died within about three years in 1732.

MATTHIAS HAAG (1730 – UNKNOWN)

Matthias Haag was born in March 1730 in Auerbach, Karlsruhe, Baden-Wuerttemberg, Germany. The date of his death is unknown.

JOHANNES JACOB HAAG (1732 – 1797)

Johannes Jacob Haag, was born on 4 September 1732 in Durlach, Stadt Karlsruhe, Baden-Wuerttemberg, Germany. His wife is unknown. Nine children were located for this family. As can be seen by the birth and death dates in the family chart, four of the children – Friederich, Johann Jacob, Phillip, and Johann Martin – died as infants. Most of the family continued to remain in the German state of Karlsruhe. Three of them moved to other nearby towns, and Johann Jacob Frederick Haag moved to Walsheim in the bordering state of Saarland.

Johannes Jacob died in Durlach, Stadt Karlsruhe, Baden-Wuerttemberg, Germany, on 2 June 1797. His fifth child, Johann Jacob Frederick Haag, was born in 1766 in Auerbach and married Elizabeth Kramer in Walsheim, Saar-Pfatz Kreis, Saarland, Germany. It is the lineage of Johann Jacob Frederick and Elizabeth that we will follow in the next chapter as we follow the Haag family to Saarland, Germany.

HAAG

THE FOURTH GENERATION:

JOHANN JACOB FREDERICK HAAG (1766-1839)

FAMILY CHART

Catharina Haag – b. 14 August 1757, d. unknown

Friederich Haag – b. 14 September 1760, d. 29 October 1760

Christina Haag – b. 2 March 1762, d. 13 May 1828

Johann Jacob Haag – b. 8 March 1765, d. 23 June 1765

Johann Jacob Frederick Haag – b. 20 November 1766, d. 6 July 1839
    Spouse: Elizabeth Kramer – b. 13 November 1780, d. 9 December 1837
    Children:
        Johannes Daniel Haag – b. 10 December 1806, d. 1851
        Michael Haag – b. 6 March 1813, d. 8 May 1890
        Maria Anna Haag – b. 9 June 1815, d. 8 October 1876
        Johann Peter Haag – b. unknown, 20 November 1834
        Nikolaus Haag – b. unknown, d. unknown

Phillip Haag – b. 13 October 1769, d. 1770

Johann Martin Haag – b. 3 November 1771, d. 20 February 1772

Michael Haag – b. 27 January 1774, d. 1839

Phillip Haag – b. 22 March 1780, d. 15 May 1846

CATHARINA HAAG (1757 – UNKNOWN)

Catharina Haag, the first known child of Johannes Jacob Haag and Anna Maria (Leonhardt) Haag, was born 14 August 1757 in Auerbach, Karlsruhe, Baden-Wuerttemberg, Germany. Her date of death is not known.

FRIEDERICH HAAG (1760 – 1760)

Friederich Haag was the first of four children who died in their infancy. Friederich was born 14 September 1760 in Auerbach, Karlsruhe, Baden-Wuerttemberg, Germany, and died about two weeks later on 29 September 1760.

CHRISTINA HAAG (1762 – 1828)

Christina Haag, the third child, was born 2 March 1762 in Auerbach, Karlsruhe, Baden-Wuerttemberg, Germany. She died 13 May 1828.

JOHANN JACOB HAAG (1765 – 1765)

Fourth child Johann Jacob Haag was born 8 March 1765 and lived just about four months, passing on 23 June 1765 in Auerbach, Karlsruhe, Baden-Wuerttemberg, Germany.

JOHANN JACOB FREDERICK HAAG (1766 – 1839)

Johann Jacob Frederick Haag was born 20 November 1766 in Auerbach, Stadt Karlsruhe, Baden-Wuerttemberg, Germany. Auerbach is about 7-8 miles away from Durlach, Stadt Karlsruhe, Baden-Wuerttemberg, Germany, where his parents had lived. Johann Jacob Frederick moved to Walsheim, Saar-Pfatz Kreis, Saarland, Germany, by 1797 as that is where he and his wife Elizabeth were married. Elizabeth Kramer was born in Walsheim on 13 November 1780. Walsheim is about 60 miles northwest of Auerbach.

The couple had five known children: Johannes Daniel, Michael, Maria Anna, Nikolaus, and Johann Peter. Two of the children are known to have come to the United States. Daughter Maria Anna is known to have died in Louisiana in 1876. Then there is Michael who ends up in southern Indiana.

Johann Jacob Frederick Haag died in Walsheim on 6 July 1839. His wife Elizabeth preceded him on 9 December 1837, also in Walsheim. The previous generations of the Haag family lead us to son Michael Haag, the first-known member of this Haag family line to be found in America. Michael's story is seen in the next chapter.

PHILLIP HAAG (1769 – 1770)

As with the other children, Phillip was also born in Auerbach, Karlsruhe, Baden-Wuerttemberg, Germany. He was born 13 October 1769, and, unfortunately, he passed in 1770.

JOHANN MARTIN HAAG (1771 – 1772)

As his brother before him, Johann Martin Haag passed early. He was born 2 November 1771 in Auerbach, Karlsruhe, Baden-Wuerttemberg, Germany, and died months later in 20 February 1772.

MICHAEL HAAG (1774 – 1839)

Michael Haag was born in Auerbach, Karlsruhe, Baden-Wuerttemberg, Germany, on 27 January 1774. He died there in 1839. He would be an uncle to Johann Jacob Frederick Haag's son Michael who we will be following in the next chapter.

PHILLIP HAAG (1780 – 1846)

Phillip is the last known child, born 22 March 1780 in Auerbach, Karlsruhe, Baden-Wuerttemberg, Germany. He died on 15 May 1846 in Auerbach.

HAAG

THE FIFTH GENERATION:

MICHAEL HAAG
(1813-1890)

FAMILY CHART

Johannes Daniel Haag – b. 10 December 1806, d. 1851

Michael Haag – b. 6 March 1813, d. 8 May 1890
    Spouse: Julian Guthneck – b. 1816, d. 18 April 1868
    Children:
        Louis August Haag – b. 29 August 1842, d. 27 January 1922
        John Haag – b. 16 October 1845, d. 23 July 1893
        George Haag – b. 1847, d. likely before 1860
        Catherine Haag – b. 1849, d. 30 May 1874
        Hubert Charles Haag – b. 16 July 1851, d. 28 May 1919
    Spouse: Mary Magdalene Balzar – b. May 1821, d. 10 December 1903

Maria Anna Haag – b. 9 June 1815, d. 8 October 1876
    Spouse: Charles Lauer – b. 24 June 1817, d. 13 December 1874
    Children:
        Louisa Lauer – b. 1844, d. 1930
        Charles Lauer Jr. – b. 28 December 1845, d. 17 September 1874
        Gustav Lauer – b. about 1851, d. unknown
        Therese Lauer – b. 3 October 1852, d. 15 January 1887
        Henrietta Lauer – b. about 1856, d. unknown

Johann Peter Haag – b. unknown, 20 November 1834

Nikolaus Haag – b. unknown, d. unknown

JOHANNES DANIEL HAAG (1806 – 1851)

Johannes Daniel Haag was born 10 December 1806 in Reinheim, Saar-Pfatz Kreis, Saarland, Germany. He died in 1851 in Wittersheim, Saarpfalz-Kreis, Saarland, Germany. Reinheim is only about three miles to the southwest of Walsheim. Wittersheim, where Johannes Daniel died, is only about four miles to the northwest of Walsheim. Recall from the previous chapter that his mother Elizabeth was born in Walsheim, and his parents likely moved there after marriage. It is also where his parents both died.

MICHAEL HAAG (1813 – 1890)

In the opening chapter, *The German Connection*, we looked at a brief history of Saarland, Germany and the connection of the Haags to this area. There are a couple reasons to look at this history. The first of these is to understand the French-German ties of this region. And, specifically, the connection between coal mining in Saarland and the iron ore deposits of Alsace-Lorraine in France. This connection to Alsace, France, shows up in Michael Haag's two marriages; both of his wives were from this region of France.

The second reason to look at this area is the coal mining industry itself. It is not known if Michael or any of the Haags were involved in coal mining in Saarland. In fact, when Michael appears in the 1850 U.S. Census, he is a tailor. However, the Haag family later relocated to the coal mining area of southwestern Indiana, and there they engaged in the coal industry for several generations.

Fortunately, we have much more information on Michael than we have had for his aunts, uncles and siblings so far. Born in 1813 in Walsheim, Saarland, Germany, Michael Haag was the first known generation of the family to immigrate to America. It is not known when this occurred. Search of ship passenger lists did not locate a Michael Haag that quite fit with his age and location. Based upon other information, he may have come to America about 1841. Michael was the first known generation of the Haag family to immigrate to America. It was in that year that Michael married his first wife, Juliana Guthneck. Juliana had come to America from Alsace, France.

The first we find of Michael in America is in the 1850 United States Federal Census. As was stated, the date of his entry to the country is unknown, but we do know that the second large wave of German immigrants occurred between 1820 and 1871. This wave of emigration from Germany was caused chiefly by economic hardships, including unemployment and crop failures. Many Germans also left to avoid wars and military service. In some cases, government entities encouraged poor citizens to emigrate. It is further known that many Germans either lived in Alsace-Lorraine or passed through it to emigrate.

In 1850, Michael and his family are living in Hinds County, Mississippi. Michael is 38 years old at the time of the 1850 census and is working as a tailor. By 1860, the family moved to Sugar Creek Township in Vigo County, Indiana. This township includes today's West Terre Haute.

Michael, now 47 years old, is working as a farmer. The census for 1860 also notes that his wife, Juliana Guthneck (or Guthnick) was born in France. A marriage index indicates that Michael and Juliana were married in Jasper County, Illinois, in 1841. It may be possible that Michael and Juliana came to America together and married shortly thereafter. Jasper County is a sparsely populated area within about 40-45 miles of West Terre Haute, Indiana.

Children at home in 1860 were: Lewis, 18, born in Indiana; John, 15, born in Mississippi; Catherine, 11, born in Mississippi; and, Hubert, 9, born in Indiana. There is also a 2-year-old girl by the name of Mary Bazar (or, perhaps Balzar – see following information on Michael's second wife) living with them. The census notes that Catherine is deaf and dumb.

When looking at the children above, it should be noted that 18-year-old Lewis was born in Indiana. Lewis having been born in August 1842 seems to indicate that the family was in Illinois for a short time after Michael and Juliana married and subsequently moved to Indiana where Lewis was born. The next oldest child, John, was born in Mississippi in 1845. So, we know that sometime between 1842 and 1845, the family relocated to Mississippi. Their stay in Mississippi was brief as son Hubert was born in Indiana in1851.

Juliana died on 18 April 1868. In October of 1868, Michael married Mary Magdalene Balzar. Mary was also from Alsace, France. (Perhaps the 2-year-old girl living with Michael and Juliana in 1860 was related to Mary, perhaps a daughter?) It is interesting to note that both Michael's first wife and his second wife were born in Alsace, France. Perhaps the two women were friends, or even relatives? One source seems to indicate that they were cousins.

The marriage record for Michael and Mary lists her name as Mary Smith, not much of a French name for sure. Other records, however, do list her name as Balzar. A 1900 census seems to indicate that Mary Balzar had a previous marriage to a Mr. Smith. The census for Sugar Creek Township for that year shows Mary M. Haag living with a son by the name of Henry Smith. This record also notes that Mary and her parents were born in France. Additionally, it notes that she immigrated to the United States in 1841 … perhaps along with Michael and Juliana?

In the 1870 census, the family is still living in Sugar Creek Township. Children at home are: Catherine, 20; Lewis, 27; Elizabeth, 22; Joseph, 8 months; and Hubert, 19, working as a miner. Actually, Elizabeth is Lewis' wife, and Joseph is their child. With Hubert, we have the first indication of the Haag family working in the coal mining industry in Indiana.

Daughter Catherine Haag disappears after the 1870 census. Interestingly, there is a column in that year's census with the heading "Whether deaf and dumb, blind, insane, or idiotic." This column contains an entry for Catherine with the notation "Idiot." It is likely that Catherine was mentally and/or physically disabled in some extreme manner, and recall the 1860 census noted that she was deaf and dumb.

By 1880, Michael works as a gardener for Leamond Smith, one of Mary's sons, in Sugar Creek Township. He and Mary are apparently living with the family according to the 1880 census. An 1887 directory for Vigo County notes that Michael lives in Mackville, Indiana, which was later renamed to today's West Terre Haute.

It does not appear that Michael and Mary had any children. All the other children are noted in the detailed family tree of this book.

Michael died on 8 May 1890, in Terre Haute, Vigo County, Indiana. A record for the burial of his second wife Mary locates her grave in Saint Joseph Cemetery in Terre Haute. No records were found for Michael or Juliana, but several sources note that they are also buried in Saint Joseph Cemetery in Terre Haute.

It is Michael and Juliana's fifth of five children, Hubert Charles Haag, that we will next follow in the Haag family line.

SCHEDULE I.—Free Inhabitants in ___ in the County of Hinds State of Mississippi enumerated by me, on the 10th day of Sept 1850. Geo M. Barne Ass't Marshal.

	Dwelling-houses numbered in the order of visitation	Families numbered in the order of visitation	The Name of every Person whose usual place of abode on the first day of June, 1850, was in this family	Age	Sex	Color	Profession, Occupation, or Trade of each Male Person over 15 years of age	Value of Real Estate owned	Place of Birth, Naming the State, Territory, or Country	Married within the year	Attended School within the year	Persons over 20 y'rs of age who cannot read & write	Whether deaf and dumb, blind, insane, idiotic, pauper, or convict
	1	2	3	4	5	6	7	8	9	10	11	12	13
1			Agnus Jock	5	m				Mi				
2			Wm "	1	m				"				
3			Wm Summerville	36	m		Cabinet maker		Scotland				
4			E B Mosely	35	m		Clk		Va				
5	276	276	A Hutchinson	52	m		Atty	2000	"				
6			Mary A "	36	F				NC				
7	277	277	Ann E Mitchel	40	F	B	Washer		Va				
8			Kelly A "	18	F	B			"				
9			James E "	5	m	B			Mi				
10			Clara "	1	F	B			"				
11			Ellen "	6	F	B			"				
12			Cornelius Holden	36	m		Carpenter		Ohio				
13	278	278	Geo Bufed	52	m		Gardner		Germany				
15			Michael Hagg	38	m		Taylor		Germany				
16			Louisa "	32	F				"				
18			John "	7	m				Mi				
19			George "	3	m				"				
21			Catherine "	9/12	F				"				
22			Isrusch McBrannin	32	m		Keeps Sw. Stable		Ky.				
23	280	280	Nancy Alston	26	F	B	Washer	600	"				
24	281	281	Michael Hagg	38	m		Taylor		Germany				
25			Louisa "	32	F				"				
26			John "	7	m				Mi				
27			George "	3	m				"				
28			Catherine "	9/12	F				"				
29			Isrusch McBrannin	32	m		Keeps Sw. Stable		Ky.				
30	282	282	Wm J. Holland	26	m		"	2000	"				
31	283	283	Wyatt Hardy	11	m				Mi				
32			Meas "	13	m				"				
33			John S Cooke	44	m		Planter	4000	Ky				
34	284	284	Sarah "	55	F				SC				
35			Ruth "	50	F				"				
36			Mary M Buckner	17	F				Mi				
37			Mary E Lound	16	F				"				
38			Thomas C "	19	m				"				
39			Louisa Hagg	[illegible]	F				Mi				
40	285	285	Thomas Gordon	[illegible]	m		[illegible]	[illegible]	NC				
41			Julia "	[illegible]	F				Ala				
42			Gilbert [illegible]	[illegible]					Mi		1		

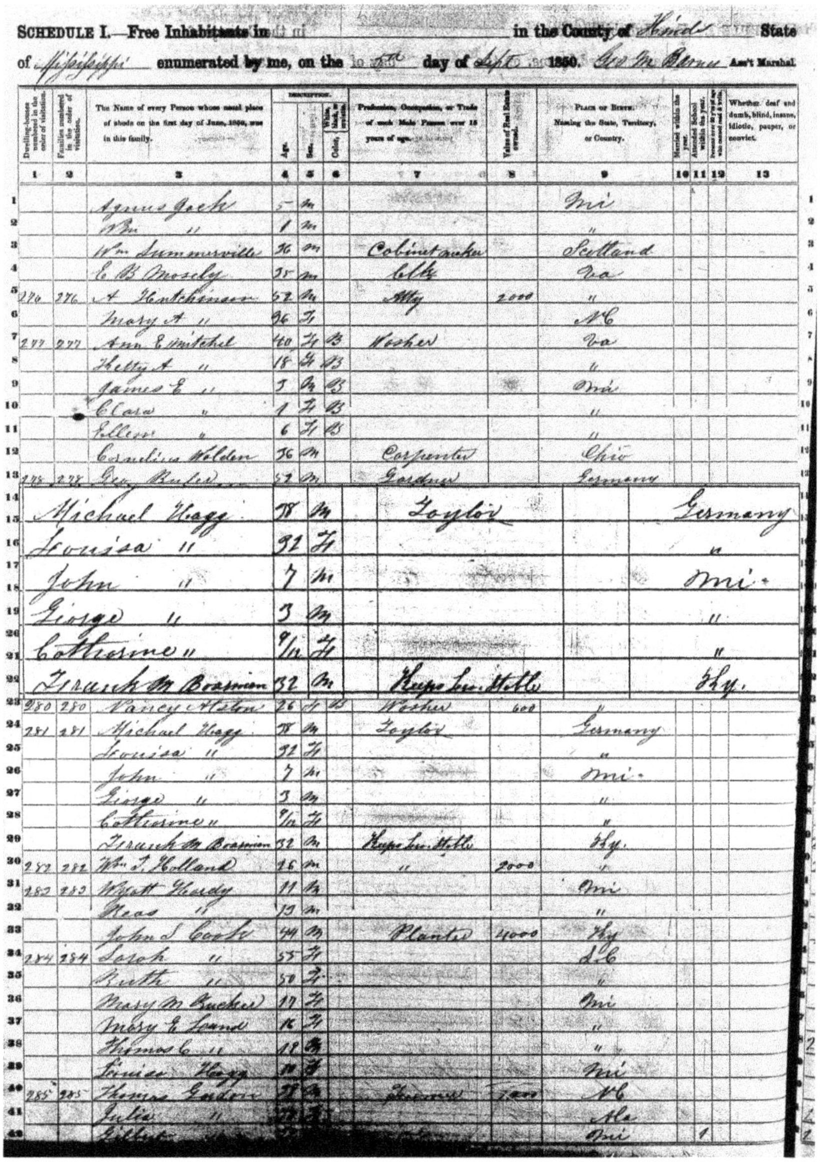

Michael Haag – 1850 Federal Census for Hinds Co., Mississippi

The above image shows a page from the 1850 census. The highlighted area shows Michael Haag, his wife Louisa (Juliana), and children John, George and Catherine. It is not known why oldest son Louis is not shown.

Page No. 27 273

SCHEDULE 1.—Free Inhabitants in Sugar Creek Township in the County of Vigo State of Indiana enumerated by me, on the 19th day of June 1860. W Ousick Ass't Marshal.

Post Office Terre Haute.

Dwelling-houses numbered in the order of visitation	Families numbered in the order of visitation	The name of every person whose usual place of abode on the first day of June, 1860, was in this family	Age	Sex	Color	Profession, Occupation, or Trade of each person, male and female, over 15 years of age	Value of Real Estate	Value of Personal Estate	Place of Birth, Naming the State, Territory, or Country	Married within the year	Attended School within the year	Persons over 20 y'rs of age who cannot read & write	Whether deaf and dumb, blind, insane, idiotic, pauper, or convict
1	2	3	4	5	6	7	8	9	10	11	12	13	14
		July Nelson	11	F					Vt		/		
		William "	21	M		Domestic			New Hampshire				
		Nelson Rosworth	30	M		Plasterer			Eng				
188	188	Christian Kelley	54	F		Farmer	900	150	Ireland			/	
		John "	20	M		"			Ohio			/	
		Charles "	12	M		"			Ind				
189	189	Mechial Hagg	47	M		Farmer	600	120	Bavaria				
		July "	44	F		"			France			/	
		Luis "	18	M		"			Ind				
		John "	15	M		"			Mississippi		/		
		Catherine "	11	F					do				deaf & dumb
		Hubert "	9	M					Ind		/		
		Mary Eagar	2	F					do				
190	190	John [illegible]	32	M		Coal Miner			[illegible]				
		James [illegible]	18	M		Day Labo			unknown		/		
192	192	Vensel Novotine	48	M		Day Lab		40	Bohemia				
		Catharine "	46	F		" "			do				
		Franklin "	19	M		" "			do		/		
		John "	14	M					do		/		
		Mary "	11	F					do				
		Annie "	9	F					do				
		Varonia "	6	F					do				
		Elizabeth "	3	F					Ind				
193	191	James Scher	29	M		Coal Miner		200	Delaware				
		Rebecca "	26	F		" "			Ind				
		Indiana "	4	F					do				
		Mary "	3	F					do				

No. white males, 21 No. colored males, No. foreign born, 15 No. blind, 3364 746 No. idiotic, No. convicts,
No. white females, 18 No. colored females, No. deaf and dumb, 1 No. insane, No. paupers,

Mechial Hagg 47 M Farmer 600 120 Bavaria
July " 44 F " France
Luis " 18 M " Ind
John " 15 M " Mississippi
Catherine " 11 F do
Hubert " 9 M Ind
Mary Eagar 2 F do

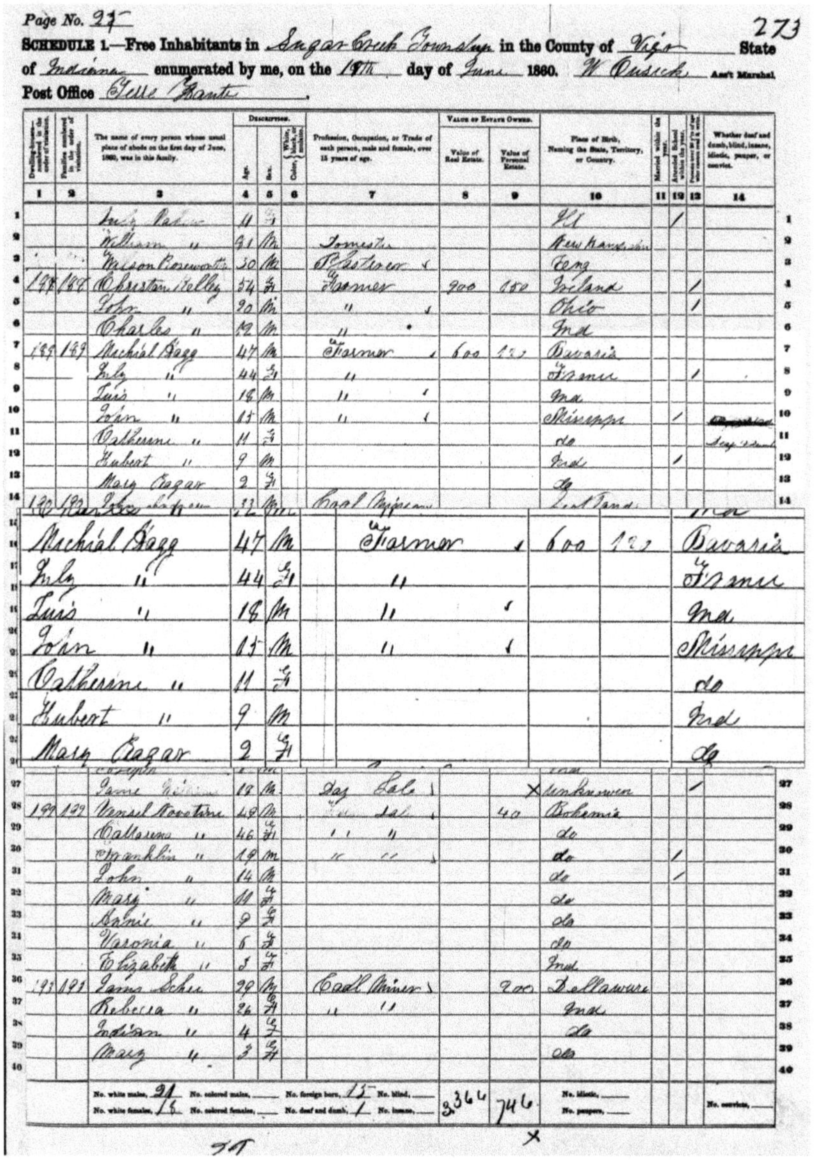

Michael Haag – 1860 Federal Census for Sugar Creek Township, Vigo Co., Indiana

The above image shows a page from the 1860 census. The highlighted area shows Michael Haag, his wife July (Juliana), and children Luis, John, Catherine and Hubert, as well as 2-year-old Mary Bazar (Balzar). Note that the far right column indicates that Catherine is deaf and dumb.

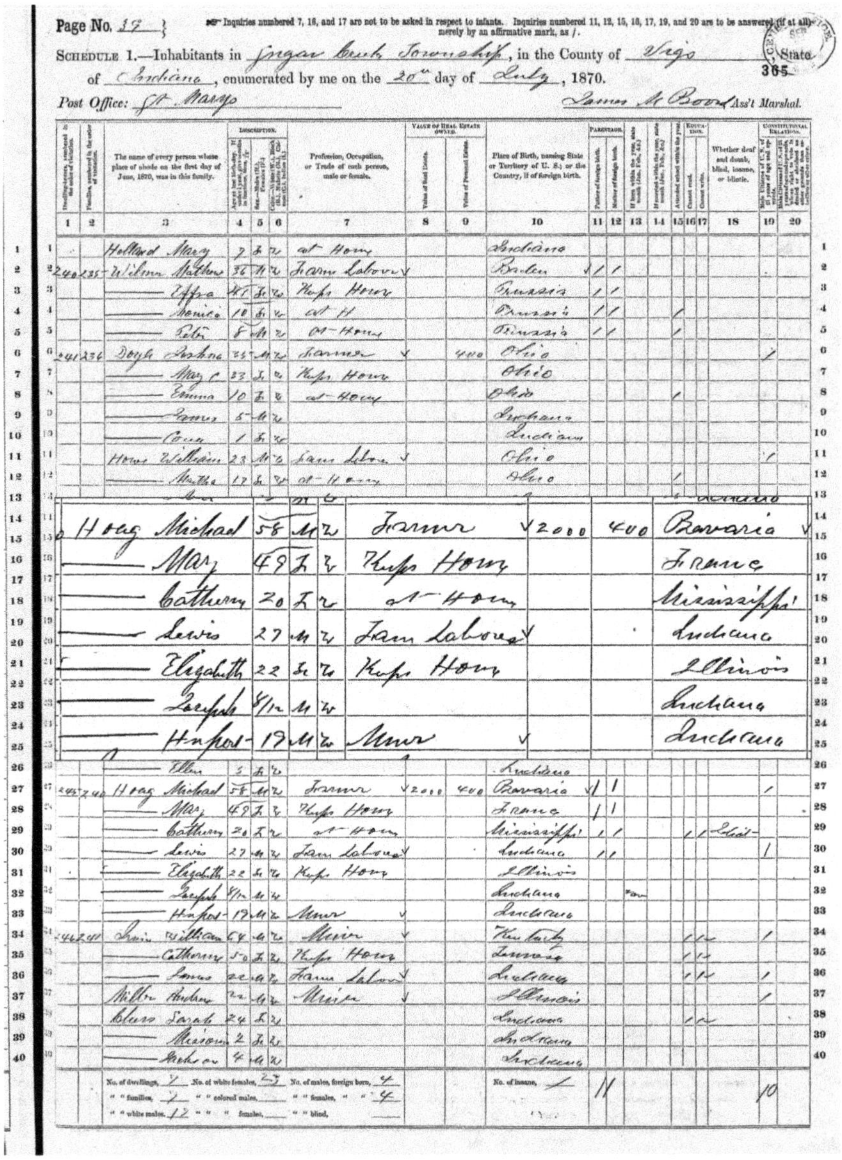

Michael Haag – 1870 Federal Census for Sugar Creek Township, Vigo Co., Indiana

The above image shows a page from the 1870 census. The highlighted area shows Michael Haag, his second wife Mary, and his children Catherine, Lewis and Hubert. Also with them are Lewis' wife Elizabeth and their son Joseph.

Michael Haag – 1880 Federal Census for Sugar Creek Township, Vigo Co., Indiana

From the 1880 census, the highlighted area shows the Leamond Smith family. Michael and Mary (the names are not recorded as such, but the evidence makes clear the circumstances) are living with Mary's son's family at this time, and Michael is working as a gardener.

Mary M. Haag – 1900 Federal Census for Sugar Creek Township, Vigo Co., Indiana

The above image shows a page from the 1900 census. The highlighted area shows the Henry Smith family. Living with widower Henry are his 14-year-old son and his mother Mary. This census record notes that Mary immigrated into the U.S. from France in 1841.

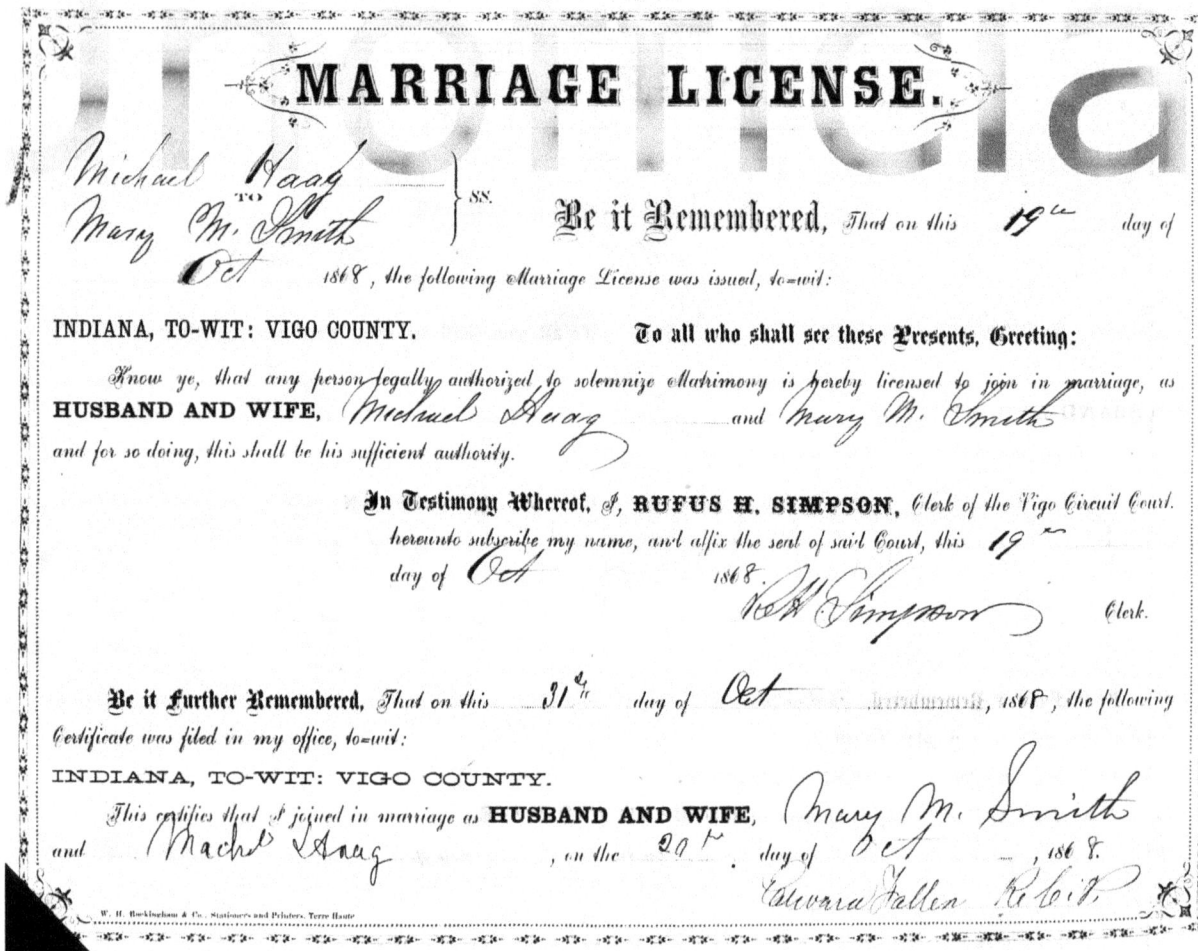

Michael Haag and Mary M. (Balzar) Smith – Marriage License

Above is a copy of the marriage license for Michael and Mary. They were married on 20 October 1868 in Vigo County.

Michael Haag – Last Will and Testament

This is a copy of the complete last will and testament of Michael Haag. It was completed 25 January 1890. Michael died on 8 May 1890. The next page shows detail that is more easily readable.

I, Michael Haag, of Vigo County, in the State of Indiana, being of Sound mind, do hereby make and publish, this my last Will and Testament; that is to Say,

Item 1st. I give and devise, to my Wife, Mary Magdalena Haag, the following described Real Estate, in Vigo County, in the State of Indiana, to-wit: The (West half 1⁄2) of the South West Quarter (1⁄4), of Section eighteen (18), township Twelve (12) North Range nine (9) West, Containing Sixty and Twenty two hundreths (60 22⁄100) acres, More or less, to have and to hold the Same in fee Simple.

Item 2nd: I give and bequeath to my Said Wife, Mary Magdalena Haag, all personal property, rights, credits, Moneys, and choses in action, if any, that I may hold, and own at the time of my death.

Item 3d: I Nominate, and appoint, my Said Wife Executrix of this my last Will and Testament.

Item 4th: I hereby revoke, all former wills by me made.

In testimony whereof, I hereunto Set my hand, and Seal, this 25" day of January 1890.

Michael Haag (Seal)

Michael Haag – Last Will and Testament (Detail)

This image displays the details from Michael Haag's will.

Mary M. (Balzar) Haag – Death Certificate

This is a copy of Mary M. (Balzar) Haag's death certificate. She died on 10 December 1903, it seems at a nursing home (Little Sisters of the Poor) in Indianapolis, Indiana. The cause of death is listed as senility. Senility is an older term used to describe a decline in an older adult's physical and cognitive health. Like dementia, senility can cause changes in mental health.

MARIA ANNA HAAG (1815 – 1876)

Maria Anna Haag was born in Zweibrucken, Germany, on 9 June 1815. Zweibrucken is about 35 miles east of Walsheim. Maria was the other member of the family who seems to have immigrated to America.

Maria married Charles Lauer, from Hasslach, Ortenaukreis, Baden-Wuerttemberg, Germany, and their first child is recorded as Louisa Lauer born in Louisiana in 1844.

The 1870 census finds the family in New Orleans where Charles works as a wholesale merchant. At this time he is 52 and Maria is 55. Living with them are: Charles Jr., 24; Gustav, 19; Therese, 17; and Henrietta, 14.

No marriage record was located for Maria and Charles, and no other census records were located. Maria died 8 October 1876 in New Orleans, Orleans Parish, Louisiana, while Charles had preceded her in December of 1874. They are buried in Lafayette Cemetery No. 1 in New Orleans.

Page No. 46

Inquiries numbered 7, 16, and 17 are not to be asked in respect to infants. Inquiries numbered 11, 12, 15, 16, 17, 19, and 20 are to be answered (if at all) merely by an affirmative mark, as /.

Schedule 1.—Inhabitants in New Orleans, in the County of Orleans, State of Louisiana, enumerated by me on the 16th day of June, 1870.

Post Office: New Orleans La — John Shuler, Ass't Marshal.

Name	Age	Sex	Color	Occupation	Real Estate	Personal Estate	Place of Birth
Lauer, Charles	52	M	W	Ret. Merchant	16000	700	Bavaria
—— Maria	55	F	W				do
—— Charles	24	M	W	Clerk in Store			Louisiana
—— Gustav	19	M	W	do			do
—— Therese	17	F	W				do
—— Henrietta	14	F	W				do
Semmes, Rachel	30	F	B	Servant			do

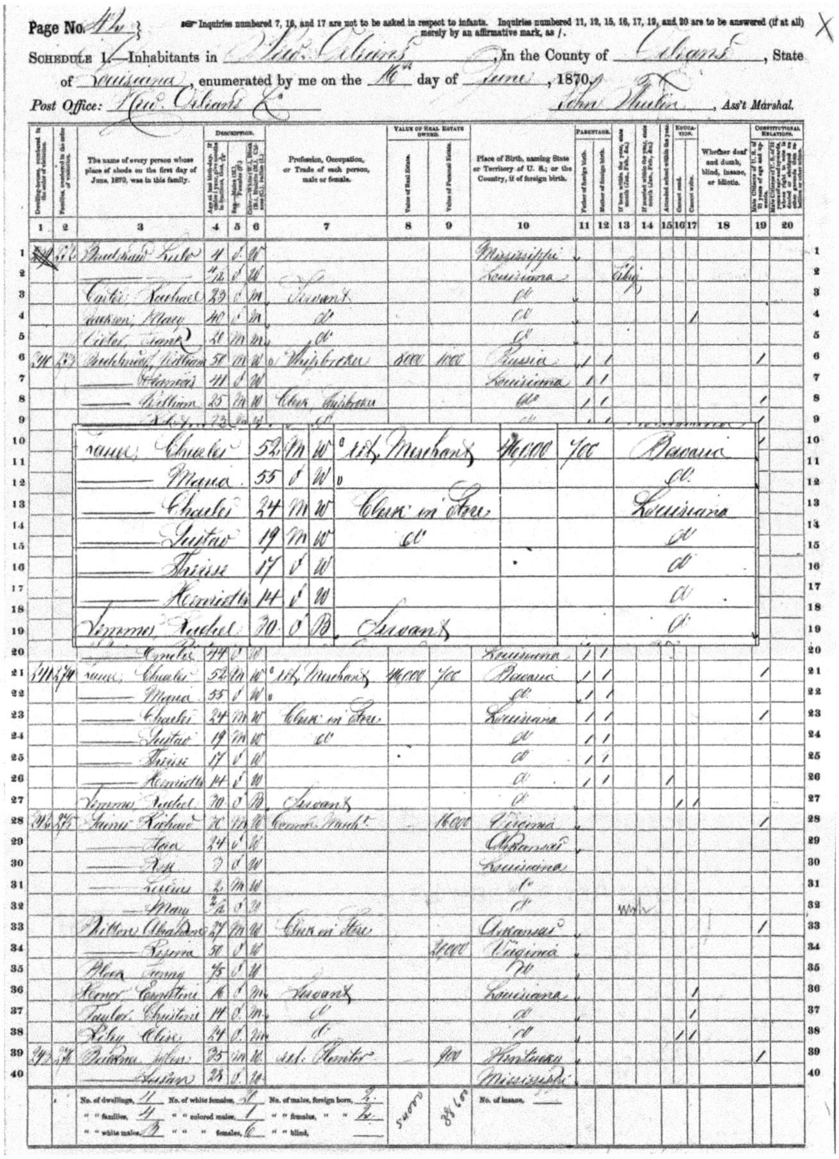

Maria Anna Haag Lauer – 1870 Federal Census for New Orleans, Louisiana

The above image shows a page from the 1870 census. The highlighted area shows Charles Lauer, his 55-year-old wife Maria (Haag), and their children Charlie, Gustav, Therese and Henrietta. Also with them is Rachel Semmes, a 30-year-old black servant.

LAUER—On Sunday, October 8, 1876, at 6 a. m., Mrs. Maria Anna Haag, relict of the late Charles Lauer, Esq., aged 61 years and 4 months.

The friends and relatives of the family, as also those of her son Gustave and her brother-in-law Francis Lauer, are respectfully invited to attend the funeral, which will take place from her late residence No. 518 St. Charles Avenue, corner Josephine street, on Monday, October 9, at 3 o'clock p. m.

Terre Haute, Ind., papers please copy.

Maria Anna Haag Lauer – Death Notice

This is a death notice for Maria Anna Haag Lauer published in the *New Orleans Times* 9 October 1876. We see that they lived at 518 St. Charles Avenue, at the corner of Josephine Street, in New Orleans. Note that a notice was to be copied to the Terre Haute, Indiana, newspapers, the area where much of her family was located.

Maria Anna (Haag) Lauer – Grave Marker

This is a photo of the Lauer family grave marker located in Lafayette Cemetery Number 1, New Orleans, Louisiana. Note that three of their children are also buried there: Charles, Theresa and Louisa, as well as the husbands of the daughters.

JOHANN PETER HAAG (UNKNOWN – 1834)

Johann Peter Haag was born in Walsheim, Saarpfalz-Kreis, Saarland, Germany. The date of his birth is not known. He died there on 20 November 1834.

NIKOLAUS HAAG (UNKNOWN – UNKNOWN)

There is one other known child, and that is Nikolaus Haag. However, we do not know anything other than that he was born in Walsheim, Saarpfalz-Kreis, Saarland, Germany.

HAAG

THE SIXTH GENERATION:
HUBERT CHARLES HAAG
(1851-1919)

FAMILY CHART

Louis August Haag – b. 29 August 1842, d. 27 January 1922
    Spouse: Elizabeth Shirley – b. 1847, d. 1924
    Children:
        Joseph Haag – b. about 1869, d. unknown
        John Haag – b. about 1872, d. 22 June 1936
        Mary E. Haag – b. about 1876, d. unknown
        William H. Haag – b. about 1879, d. unknown
        Ola V. Haag – b. 1881, d. unknown
        Anna Haag – b. 1882, d. unknown

John Haag – b. 16 October 1845, d. 23 July 1893
    Spouse: Elizabeth – b. 17 February 1847, d. 18 June 1923
    Children:
        Mary Haag – b. September 1870, d. unknown
        Josephine Haag – b. November 1873, d. unknown
        Emma Haag – b. 30 April 1876, d. 2 February 1950
        Catherine Haag – b. January 1880, d. unknown
        Leo Haag – b. February 1886, d. unknown

George Haag – b. 1847, d. likely before 1860

Catherine Haag – b. 1849, d. possibly 1874

<u>Hubert Charles Haag</u> – b. 16 July 1851, d. 28 May 1919
      Spouse: Mariah J. Satterfield – b. 2 January 1851, d. 15 August 1880
      Children:
            Julia A. Haag – b. about 1870, d. unknown
            <u>John Edward Haag</u> – b. 1874, d. 1956
            George Francis Haag – b. 2 February 1875, d. 22 June 1943
            Nancy E. Haag – b. 1 March 1878, d. 18 March 1879
            Charles Hubert Haag – b. 14 April 1880, d. August 1963
      Spouse: Mary H. Shirley – b. 3 September 1861, d. 14 March 1930
      Children:
            James Albert Haag – b. 1881, d. 1898
            Oscar Eugene Haag – b. 1883, d. 1947
            Alodia F. Haag – b. December 1886, d. 1929
            Terrence Vincent Haag – b. January 1889, d. 1967
            Herman L. Haag – b. April 1891, d. 1956
            Kevin Michael Haag – b. August 1894, d. 1917
            Ralph J. Haag – b. March 1897, d. 1935
            Mary Rosa Haag – b. 1899, d. 1903
            Dolah Marie Haag – b. 5 December 1903, d. 1986

LOUIS AUGUST HAAG (1842 – 1922)

The first child of Michael and Juliana Haag, Louis was born in Madison, Jefferson County, Indiana, on 29 August 1842. In the 1860 census Louis (spelled Luis) is 18 years old and working with his father as a farmer in Sugar Creek Township, Vigo County, Indiana. Ten years later, now 27, Louis (spelled Lewis) is still at home working on the farm.

It seems that in the intervening years, Louis served in the Union army. In June of 1863, he registered for the draft in Indiana. According to one source, Louis was a 20-year-old farmer when he volunteered for Civil War duty on January 12, 1864 at Matoon, Illinois. He became a private in Company E, 54th Regiment of the Illinois Infantry Volunteers and was trained at Camp Butler, Illinois. His term of enlistment was for three years, and he was paid a bounty of $60. He was 5'5" tall and had black eyes, black hair and a dark complexion. He was stationed at Devalls Bluff, Arkansas, a city of strategic importance along the White River, in July and August of 1864 and at Hickory Station, Arkansas, for the remainder of the year. During 21 months of service he spent 65 days in the regimental hospital fighting fever, dysentery and diarrhea.

In 1880, Louis and his wife Elizabeth are in Barr Township, Daviess County, Indiana, where Louis is a night engineer. This job is most likely a mining position. Some of Indiana's highest quality coal mines are found in Barr Township, and later census records specifically note his occupation as a coal miner. In this 1880 census, there are four children at home: Joseph, 10; John, 8; Mary E., 4; and William H., 1. Also living with them is Elizabeth's sister, Mary Shirley.

Census records for 1900 through 1920 find them in Cannelburg, Indiana, a town in Barr Township. In each of these census records, Louis works as a coal miner. In 1900, the children at home are William, 21; Ola V., 18; and Anna, 17. At that time son William is also working as a coal miner.

Louis died in Cannelburg on 27 January 1922, and Elizabeth passed in 1924. They are buried in St. Peter's Cemetery in Montgomery, Daviess County, Indiana.

Louis Haag – Civil War Draft Registration

This is a copy of the Civil War draft registration for the Seventh District of Indiana from July 12, 1863. The lower part of the page contains entries for Sugar Creek Township in Vigo County, Indiana. The highlighted section shows the entry for 20-year-old, unmarried Louis Haag. Louis served in Company E, 54th Regiment of the Illinois Infantry Volunteers.

(3-H-3)

NAME OF SOLDIER:	Haag Lewis			

| NAME OF DEPENDENT: | Widow, | Haag Elizbeath | | | |
| | Minor, | | | | |

| SERVICE: | E 54 Ill Inf | | | |

DATE OF FILING.	CLASS.	APPLICATION NO.	CERTIFICATE NO.	STATE FROM WHICH FILED.
1886 Mch 4	Invalid,	564,533	486,870	
1922 Feb 2	Widow,	1185286	921059	Ind.
	Minor,			

| ATTORNEY: | | | | |
| REMARKS: | | | | |

Louis Haag – Civil War Pension Index

This is a copy of the Civil War pension index for Louis Haag noting his widow Elizabeth Haag.

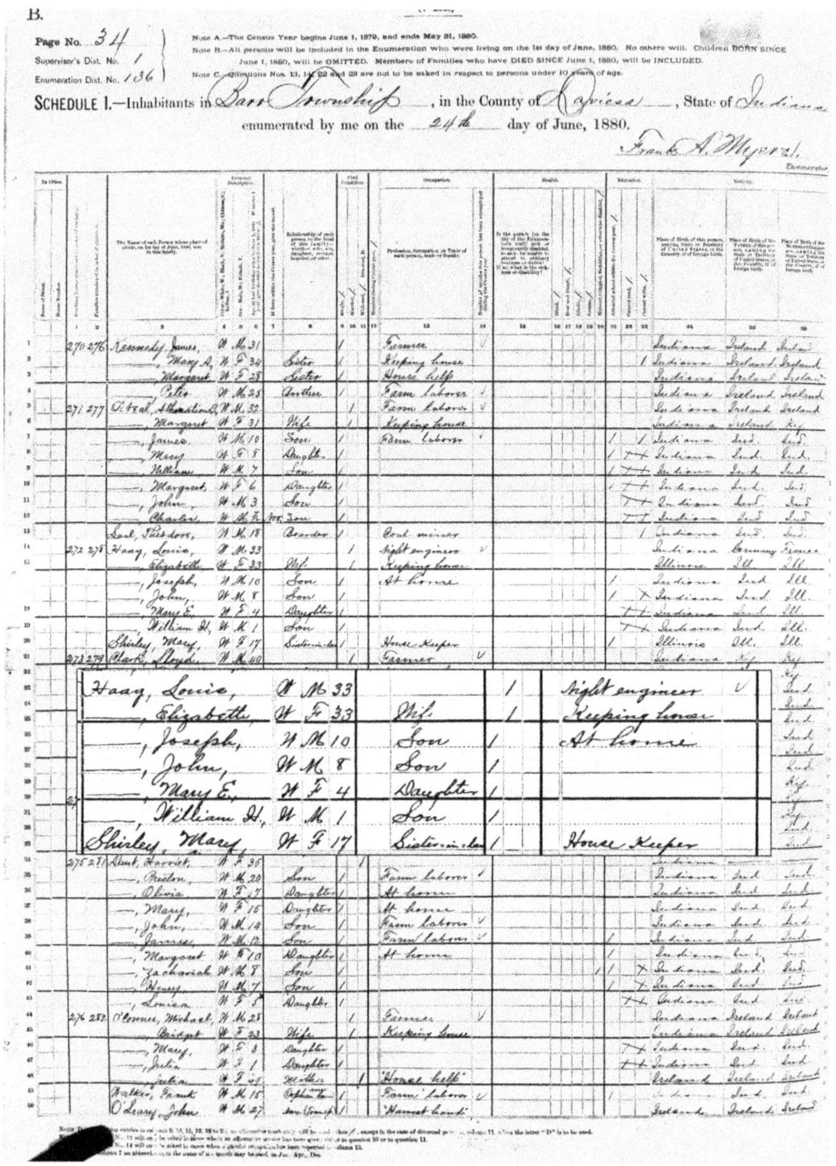

Louis Haag – 1880 Federal Census for Barr Township, Daviess Co., Indiana

The above image shows a page from the 1880 census. The highlighted area shows Louis Haag, his wife Elizabeth and children Joseph, John, Mary E., and William H. Also living with them is Elizabeth's sister Mary. Louis is listed as a shift engineer which would be a position at a mine.

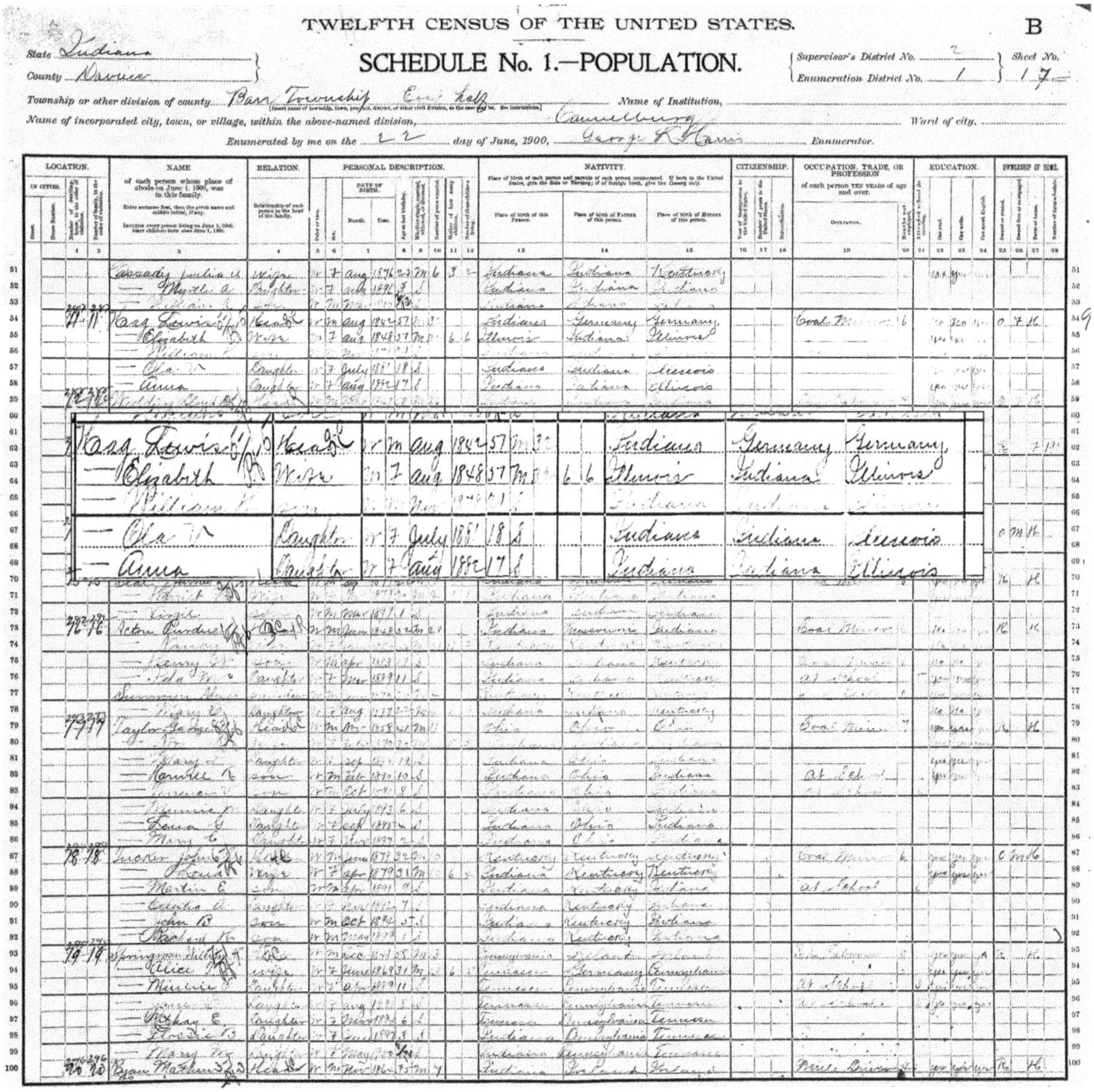

Louis Haag – 1900 Federal Census for Cannelburg, Daviess Co., Indiana

The above image shows a page from the 1900 census. The highlighted area shows Louis (Lewis) Haag, his wife Elizabeth and children William H., Ola V. and Anna. L. At this time, Louis is working as a coal miner as well as is his son William.

Louis Haag – 1910 Federal Census for Cannelburg, Daviess Co., Indiana

The above image shows a page from the 1910 census. The highlighted area shows Louis Haag and his wife Elizabeth, both now age 66. This confirms that they had six children and that six are still living. Note that Louis is still working as a coal miner.

Louis Haag – 1920 Federal Census for Cannelburg, Daviess Co., Indiana

The above image shows a page from the 1920 census. The highlighted area shows Louis Haag and his wife Elizabeth. Note that in this census, Louis has noted that both parents were from France and spoke French. Recall that Louis' father Michael was from that area of Germany that had been tossed back and forth between Germany and France. He may very likely have spoken both languages.

Louis Haag and Elizabeth Haag – Grave Marker

This is a photo of the grave marker for Louis/Lewis and Elizabeth Hilgendorf. This is located in St. Peter's Cemetery in Montgomery, Daviess County, Indiana.

JOHN HAAG (1845 – 1893)

John Haag was born on 16 October 1845 while the family was living in Hinds County, Mississippi. By the time of the 1860 census, the family has moved to Sugar Creek Township (West Terre Haute) in Vigo County, Indiana.

1870 finds John married to Elizabeth Forbeck and living in Anderson Township, Clark County, Illinois, about 20 miles southwest of Terre Haute. John is working as a farmer.

By 1880, they have moved to Kuttawa, Lyon County, Kentucky, about 175 miles southeast of Terre Haute. John is working in a hub factory. Children at this time are Mary, 9; Josephine, 6; Emily, 4; and Catherine, 5 months. Josephine was born in Illinois, and Emily was born in Kentucky. This would place the family's move to Kentucky between 1874 and 1876. At some point prior to 1900, the family relocated to Paducah, McCracken County, Kentucky, about 30 miles to the west of Kuttawa.

John passed on 23 July 1893. Elizabeth continued to live in Paducah, eventually living with son Leo until she passed in 1923. John and Elizabeth are buried in Mount Carmel Cemetery in Paducah.

John Haag

This is an undated photo of John Haag. It was shared on Ancestry.com by Julie Perhacs. There was no documentation to confirm the photo.

Elizabeth (Forbeck) Haag

This is an undated photo of John Haag's wife Elizabeth (Forbeck) Haag. It was shared on Ancestry.com by Julie Perhacs. There was no documentation to confirm the photo.

GEORGE HAAG (1847 – LIKELY BEFORE 1860)

Unfortunately, little is known about George. He was born about 1847 while the family was living in Mississippi. He appears as a three-year-old in the 1850 census for Hinds County, Mississippi. In the next census for 1860, George no longer appears with the family. It seems most likely he died sometime before 1860.

CATHERINE HAAG (1849 – 1874)

Catherine was born in 1849 in Hinds County, Mississippi, and appears as a nine-month old in the 1850 census. In the 1860 census while the family is in Sugar Creek Township, Vigo County, Indiana, it is noted in the census that Catherine is deaf and dumb. In the 1870 census, Catherine is now 20 years old. Interestingly, there is a column in that year's census with the heading "Whether deaf and dumb, blind, insane, or idiotic." This column contains an entry for Catherine with the notation "Idiot."

An article from Wikipedia relates the following regarding the use of the term:

> In 19th- and early 20th-century medicine and psychology, an "idiot" was a person with a very profound intellectual disability. In the early 1900s, Dr. Henry H. Goddard proposed a classification system for intellectual disability based on the Binet-Simon concept of mental age. Individuals with the lowest mental age level (less than three years) were identified as idiots; imbeciles had a mental age of three to seven years, and morons had a mental age of seven to ten years. The term "idiot" was used to refer to people having an IQ below 30[citation needed].

It is likely that Catherine was mentally and/or physically disabled in some extreme manner, and recall the 1860 census noted her as deaf and dumb. At least one source seems to indicate that Catherine died after giving birth. This source records an infant born to Catherine on 11 May 1874, and records the death on the same day. Catherine died shortly thereafter on 30 May 1874. She is buried in St. Joseph Cemetery, Terre Haute, Vigo Co., Indiana, USA.

HUBERT CHARLES HAAG (1851 – 1919)

Hubert Charles Haag was born 16 July 1851 in West Terre Haute, Vigo County, Indiana, the fifth of five children of Michael Haag and Juliana Guthneck. As his father before him, Hubert was also a coal miner. His time as a coal miner began about the time that the industry was just beginning to grow in this area.

Hubert was married twice. His first wife Mariah J. Satterfield died 15 August 1880. In 1881, Hubert married Mary H. Shirley. Mary and Hubert had nine more children together.

Hubert makes his first appearance in the 1860 census as a nine-year-old living with his parents in Sugar Creek Township in Vigo County, Indiana. The family had moved to this location from Missouri. Hubert's father is working as a farmer at this time.

In 1870 Hubert is living at home with his parents, still in Sugar Creek, and is now age 19 years. At that time, it is noted that he is working as a miner. As best as could be determined, there were very few mines in Vigo County in the 1870s, and even the early 1880s; although, the coal deposits in Indiana begin in this area and grow throughout southwestern Indiana.

The Coal Industry in Indiana

The first discovery of coal in North America was in Illinois by Jacques Marquette and Louis Joliet, recorded in 1673. Bituminous coal was first discovered in Indiana along the Wabash River in 1736. Coal mining began in Indiana in the mid-1800s using the underground mining method. Today, abandoned underground coal mines underlay extensive areas of Indiana.

Before 1850, Indiana coal was used principally as fuel for steamboats on the Ohio River, for heating, and for blacksmiths' forges. The first Indiana coal company to be incorporated was the American Coal Company of Cannelton in Perry County in 1837. Perry County had the first of many "company towns" whose existence depended on coal. Miners employed by the American Cannelton Coal Company – and their families – lived in cabins owned by the boss and did all their shopping at a company-owned store.

The first underground mine shaft in Indiana was developed in 1850 in Newburgh, Indiana. The construction of railroads in Indiana, beginning in the late 1850s, opened Indiana coal fields to urban and industrial use throughout Indiana and the Chicago region. The railroads themselves became major consumers of coal.

By the early 1900s, with the development of steam-powered equipment, surface mining soon became the dominant method of coal removal in Indiana. The Illinois Coal Basin, of which Indiana is a part, is one of the largest coal fields in the United States. Most of the coal deposits in Indiana are located in the eighteen counties in the southwestern part of the state.

The United States holds the largest recoverable coal reserves in the world, about 9.7 billion tons. At our current rate of consumption, these coal reserves would last more than 275 years. Coal provides about 50% of the total amount of electricity used in the U.S. and 94% in Indiana.

Historically, Indiana has been one of the top ten states in national coal production with about 34 million tons mined annually. In recent years, Warrick, Sullivan, Pike, Daviess and Greene have been the top coal producing counties in Indiana, followed closely by Clay, Knox and Gibson counties.

Hubert and Mariah J. Satterfield

Hubert and Mariah J. Satterfield were married on 26 August 1870 in Daviess County. 1880 finds Hubert and Mariah living in Cannelburg, Daviess County, Indiana, just under 30 miles due east of Vincennes. This is definitely coal mining country by this time. Nearby towns are Montgomery (about 2.5 miles to the west) and Washington (about 9 miles to the west). Hubert works as an engineer at a coal mining company in the area. Mariah and Hubert have been married about ten years at this time. They have four children: Julia, 10; John, 6; George, 4; and Charles, 2 months. Another child, Nancy, had died in 1879. Unfortunately, Mariah passed away in 1880.

Hubert and Mary H. Shirley

On 12 January 1881 Hubert married Mary H. Shirley. They had nine children together. Some of the children died at young ages. The 1900 census notes that Hubert is a hoisting engineer at the coal mine. Son Oscar, 16, also works at the coal mine. Other children are: Alodia, 13; Terrence, 11; Herman, 9; Kevin, 5; Ralph, 3; and Mary, 7 months.

The 1910 census finds the family still in Cannelburg where Hubert remains an engineer at a coal mine. Daughter Alodia is 23 and working as a postmistress at a post office. Sons Herman, 19, and Kevin, 15, are coal miners. Other children at that time are Ralph and Dolah. It would be likely for the male children to follow their parents into the coal mining industry at this time.

Hubert's Death in a Mining Accident

In 1919 Hubert was tragically killed in a mine accident at the Oak Grove #1 Mine just north of Montgomery, Indiana. Records note that the Oak Grove Coal Company operated Oak Grove #1 Mine from 1918 to 1923.

Hubert's obituary from the *Daviess County Democrat* of June 6, 1919, describes the accident:

> *Mr. Haag was assisting in removing some slate from the main entry of the coal mine when a large piece unexpectedly fell, catching Mr. Haag underneath it. His left side was crushed, his back hurt, and his left arm and left leg were broken. He died in half an hour's time. Mr. Haag was the second tragic death to occur in his family, he having been the father of Kevin Haag who was killed in the Baltimore & Ohio railroad yards in this city.*

So, we also discover that one of his children, Kevin, was also killed in a tragic accident. The obituary continues:

> *Mr. Haag was 67 years old and had been employed in coal mines practically all his life working himself up to the position of mine boss. He served in this capacity in several mines in Barr Township. Mr. Haag was a good citizen. Plain, honest and industrious he was respected by all who knew him, and his acquaintances were many. The community in which Mr. Haag lived has lost one of its most valuable residents in his death.*

While Hubert's death certificate indicates that he was born in 1851, his grave maker has the date as 1852. It was his son Oscar who provided the information for the death certificate. Based upon the age noted in the census records, the year 1851 does seem to be the correct date.

Hubert and both of his wives are buried in St. Peter's Cemetery in Montgomery, Indiana. Mary died in 1930. Research of the Haag family in this area of Indiana uncovered numerous Haags. St. Peter's Cemetery in Montgomery, Indiana, the burial site of Hubert Haag, contains at least 47 Haag graves.

There are five known children of Hubert's first wife, Mariah, and nine known children of Hubert's second wife, Mary. The complete family is shown in the detailed family tree of this book. It is John Edward Haag, the second child of Mariah and Hubert, that continues the family line in the next chapter.

Hubert Charles Haag – 1880 Federal Census for Cannelburg, Daviess Co., Indiana

The above image shows a page from the 1880 census. The highlighted area shows Hubert Haag, his first wife Mariah, and their children Julia A., John E., George F., and Charles H. The census lists Hubert's job as an engineer; this would be a coal mining position.

Hubert Charles Haag – 1900 Federal Census for Cannelburg, Daviess Co., Indiana

The above image shows a page from the 1900 census. The highlighted area shows Hubert Haag, 2nd wife Mary, and children Oscar E., Alodia F., Terrence V., Herman L., Kevin M., Ralph, and Mary R. Note son Oscar is also working in the coal mine where Hubert is a Hoisting Engineer.

Hubert Charles Haag – 1910 Federal Census for Cannelburg, Daviess Co., Indiana

The above image shows a page from the 1910 census. The highlighted area shows Hubert Haag, his wife Mary, and children Alodia, Herman, Kevin, Ralph, and Dola. Note in this census that sons Herman and Kevin are coal miners while Hubert is still listed as an engineer at a coal mine.

HAAG'S 1917
Back row L to R; John, Charlie, Oscar, Terrance, Ralph, Firman (holding Hubert), Kevin, Harry and Bernie (John's boys).
Front row L to R; Carl (Oscar's boy), James (Charlie's boy), Hubert and Louis Haag

Haag Photo – 1917

The above photo was shared on Ancestry.com by someone known as STARITE. Hubert is in the front row (with the mustache), and his older brother Louis (with the beard) is seated next to him. Fortunately, all of the individuals in the photo have been identified. Note that Harry Haag is second from the right in the back row, and his father John is standing on the far left.

Haag Family Photo – Daviess County, 1917

The above photo was shared on Ancestry.com by someone known as STARITE. Hubert and Louis are in the center row, easily identified from the photo on the previous page. The caption that was provided with this picture reads: *Hubert Charles & Lewis August Haag Families. 3 generations: Hubert Charles Haag, Charles Hubert Haag, James Alvin Haag*. Unfortunately, individuals are not identified.

American Coal Mining Company, Bicknell, Indiana

This is an undated photo of the American Coal Mining Company in Bicknell, Indiana during its operation. The American Coal Company had six mines operating in Bicknell between 1914 and 1922.

HAAG FUNERAL FRIDAY MORNING

Prominent Barr Township Resident Dies Within Half Hour After Being Hurt.

The funeral services over the body of Hubert Haag, one of Barr township's most respected residents, who was killed Wednesday afternoon by a fall of slate in the Oak Grove mine north of Montgomery, was held Saturday morning at 9 o'clock at St. Peter's church at Cannelburg.

Mr. Haag was assisting in removing some slate from the main entry of the coal mine when a large piece unexpectedly fell, catching Mr. Haag underneath it. His left side was crushed, his back hurt, and his left arm and left leg were broken. He died in half an hour's time. The death of Mr. Haag was the second tragic death to occur in his family, he having been the father of Kevin Haag, who was killed in the Baltimore & Ohio railroad yards in this city.

Mr. Haag was 67 years old and had been employed in coal mines practically all his life working himself up to the position of mine boss. He served in this capacity in several mines in Barr township. Mr. Haag was a good citizen. Plain, honest and industrious he was respected by all who knew him, and his acquaintances were many. The community in which Mr. Haag lived has lost one of its most valuable residents in his death.

Hubert Charles Haag – Obituary

Hubert Haag's obituary from the *Daviess County Democrat* 6 June 1919.

Hubert Charles Haag – Death Certificate

This is a copy of Hubert Charles Haag's death certificate. He died on 28 May 1919 in Cannelburg. The cause of death is listed as Accidental with a contributory factor of Falling Slate in Cole (*sic*) in Mine.

Hubert Charles Haag – Grave Marker

This is a photo of the grave marker for Hubert Haag and his second wife Mary. They are buried in St. Peter's Cemetery in Montgomery, Indiana. His first wife, Mariah, is also buried there.

HAAG

THE SEVENTH GENERATION:

JOHN EDWARD HAAG
(1874-1956)

FAMILY CHART

Julia A. Haag – b. about 1870, d. unknown
    Spouse: Lawrence McGee – b. unknown, d. unknown
    Children: unknown

John Edward Haag – b. 1874, d. 1956
    Spouse: Gertrude S. Carrico – b. February 1872, d. 19 July 1908
    Children:
        Cleophas F. Haag – b. March, 1894, d. before 1935
        Harry Joseph Haag – b. 4 September 1895, d. 1 August 1963
        John LeRoy Haag – b. March 1900, d. 29 July 1916
        Michael Bernard Haag – b. 19 October 1902, d. 29 July 1980
        Vincent Bartholomew Haag – b. 14 January 1906, d. 8 March 1970
        Mary Agnes Haag – b. 27 June 1908, d. 2 August 1908
    Spouse: Francis A McAtee – b. 3 October 1861, d. 13 October 1920
    Children:
        Mary A. Haag – b. about 1909, d. unknown
        Charles Haag – b. about 1922, d. unknown
        Margaret Haag – b. 3 April 1922, d. 1 December 1992
    Spouse: Jean McArthur – b. 2 June 1901, d. 27 May 1964
    Children:

John Robert Haag – b. 29 November 1927, d. 8 March 1991
Francis G. Haag – b. 24 September 1929, d. 18 April 1995
Mary Jean Haag – b. 20 November 1930, d. 29 August 2008
James William Haag – b. 3 November 1932, d. 6 August 2008
Martha Rose Haag – b. 23 September 1934, d. 2 February 1935
Thomas Adrian Haag – b. 14 September 1935, d. 7 June 1936

George Francis Haag – b. 2 February1875, d. 22 June 1943
    Spouse: Addie L. Graves – b. 1873, d. 1960
    Children:
        Leo F. Haag – b. 1897, d. 1956
        Raymond Haag – b. 1901, d. 1956
        Earl A. Haag – b. about 1906, d. unknown

Nancy E. Haag – b. 1 March 1878, d. 18 March 1879

Charles Hubert Haag – b. 14 April 1880, d. August 1963
    Spouse: Lillie Victoria Wilson – b. 1882, d. 1968
    Children:
        Frances Haag – b. 28 August 1899, d. 8 January 1919
        May Haag – b, 1902, d. unknown
        Gertrude Calesta Haag – b. 3 March 1905, d. 11 February 1998
        Lucile Haag – b. 28 September 1909, d. unknown
        James Alvin Haag – b. 6 April 1911, d. 16 March 1944
        Mary Haag – b. 26 June 1913, d. 13 October 1921
        Loretta V. Haag – b. 21 January 1915, d. 19 October 1916
        Joseph R. Haag – b. 27 October 1920, 17 February 2004

JULIA A. HAAG (ABOUT 1870 – UNKNOWN)

Little is known about Julia. Appearing in the 1880 census for Cannelburg, Daviess County, Indiana, she was born about 1870 in Indiana. She married Lawrence McGee in Daviess County on 1 June 1886. No record of children or her death has been located.

JOHN EDWARD HAAG (1874 – 1956)

John Edward Haag was the second son of Charles Hubert Haag and Mariah J. Satterfield. John would marry three times upon the deaths of his first two wives. The line that follows the Hilgendorf-Haag lineage is through John's son Harry Joseph Haag. Harry was John's second son born to his first wife Gertrude S. Carrico in 1895. John had a total of 15 children from his three wives beginning with the first child born in 1894 through the last child born in 1935. John died in 1956.

John followed in the footsteps of his father as a coal miner. John lived and worked in Indiana, Illinois and Missouri. By 1916, John and his family returned to Indiana where they remained in the area of Bicknell.

John Edward Haag first appears in the 1880 census as a six-year-old living with his parents Hubert and Mariah in Cannelburg, Indiana. Brothers George and Charles, as well as sister Julia, are also present. At this time, John's father is working as an engineer in the coal mines in the area.

John was born between 1872 and 1874. Several different sources display different ages. While most census records simply show the age at the time of the census, the 1900 census shows the date of birth. The date of birth for John in this 1900 census is January 1872. The first census in which John appears in 1880 lists his age as six; this would make his birth about 1874. Other records also seem to indicate a birth around 1874. So, the exact date of John's birth is not easy to determine in the absence of a birth record.

On the 27th of January in 1891 in Daviess County, John was married to Gertrude S. Carrico. We do not see them again until the 1900 census. John and Gertrude are living in La Salle, Illinois, at that time. John is a coal miner, following in the business of his father. They have three children at this time, ages 6, 4, and 3 months. The two youngest, Harry and Roy were born in Illinois. Their sister Cleophas was born in March of 1894 in Indiana, and Harry was born in September of 1895 in Illinois. Those dates place the family's move to Illinois between these dates in 1894-1895.

Coal mining was a key in La Salle's development. During the Panic of 1893 (when the economy went into a depression), there were large strikes by the union miners and much fighting. The aftermath may have opened mining jobs in the area. A Peru, Illinois, city directory has a listing for John and Gertrude in 1898. The cities of Peru and La Salle are adjacent to one another, Peru to the west and La Salle to the east.

Gertrude died in 1908 when she would have been about 36 years old. Gertrude had given birth to a daughter, Mary Agnes, on 27 June 1908. Gertrude died on the 19th of July, and Mary Agnes died on the 2nd of August. There may have been some complications that resulted from the birth. A copy of Gertrude's death certificate does contain the cause of death, but it is difficult to read. It seems to note that the immediate cause of death was pneumonia, and the chief cause *possibly* says peripheral occlusion. Mary's death certificate says that she died from malnutrition and notes toxemia from the mother.

About 1909 John remarried to Francis A. Patterson. This was her second marriage as she had lost her husband in 1893. Francis's maiden name was McAtee.

The 1910 census finds the new family in St. Louis, Missouri, and John continues to work as a coal miner. Children at home at this time are: Julie Patterson, 26; Cleo, 17, and working as a seamstress; Joseph H. (known later as Harry), 15, and working as a laborer at a coffin factory; John LeRoy, 12; Michael B. (known later as Bernard), 8; and Vincent B., 4. Vincent, the youngest, was born in January 1906 in La Salle, Illinois. This means that the family moved to St. Louis some time after that date.

John Leroy, known as LeRoy and Roy, died in 1916. His death was caused by pneumonia and peritonitis. It is possible that he may have been a victim of the influenza epidemic that peaked in 1917-1918. It was also noted on his death certificate that he was a coal miner.

By 1920, the family had returned to Indiana and was now living in Bicknell, Indiana, in Knox County, about 12 miles northeast of Vincennes. This is also about 15 miles northwest of Montgomery, Indiana. So, the family is back in the area where John's parents had lived. Recalling that John's father was killed in the Oak Grove Coal mine near Montgomery in 1919, perhaps he moved back at the time of his father's death. John is still working as a coal miner at this time.

The family is living at 312 W. 5th Street in Bicknell 1920. A 1924 city directory for Vincennes lists John at 521 S. 5th Street in that city, so they had moved. That city directory also indicates that sons Harry (Joseph H.) and Bernard (Michael B.) are running a grocery and billiards business known as Haag Brothers at 103-5 N. 15th Street.

On October 13, 1926, Francis died at the age of 62. John was about 54 at this time. On August 5, 1927, John married Jean McArthur in La Porte, Indiana. It is unknown why they were married in La Porte, unless Jean's family had ties to La Porte. Jean was 27 years old at the time of their marriage. Jean was born in June of 1901 in Scotland, and she had entered America with her family in 1902. Jean's father was also a coal miner, and the family was living in Washington Township, Knox County, in 1920.

We know that John and Jean did not remain in La Porte as the 1930 census finds the family in Ragsdale, Washington Township, Knox County, Indiana. Ragsdale is an unincorporated town about two miles outside of Bicknell. John is fire boss at a coal mine.

At home with the family in 1930 are: Margaret, 7; Charles, 7, adopted; John R., 2 ½; and Francis G., 7 months. At least two other children died very young. A death certificate was located for Martha Rose, born in September of 1934, and died in February of 1935. Also, a death certificate was found for Thomas Adrian, born in September of 1935, and died in June of 1936.

The 1940 census shows the family living in Bicknell, where John, now 66, is still employed as a coal miner. Jean is now 38. Children at home are: Margaret O., 18; Charles, 17; John, 13; Francis, 10; and Billy, 7.

John died in 1956 and is buried in St. Peter's Cemetery in Montgomery, Indiana, the resting place of his father. Jean died in 1964 in Vincennes, and she is also buried in St. Peter's Cemetery.

Name: John Eduard Hagg
Gender:Male
Event Type: Christening
Event Date: 13 Apr 1874
Event Place: SAINT PETER, MONTGOMERY, DAVIESS, INDIANA
Father's Name: Hubert Hagg
Mother's Name:Maria Saterfield
Indexing Project (Batch) Number: C53823-1
System Origin: Indiana-ODM
GS Film number: 1433375

Citing this Record:
"Indiana Births and Christenings, 1773-1933," database, FamilySearch (https://familysearch.org/ark:/61903/1:1:V2XT-TLP: 6 December 2014), John Eduard Hagg, 13 Apr 1874; Christening, citing SAINT PETER, MONT-GOMERY, DAVIESS, INDIANA; FHL microfilm 1,433,375.

John Edward Haag – Record of Christening

While the actual document is not available, this is a citation of the Christening of John Edward Haag on 13 April 1874 at Saint Peter's Catholic Church in Montgomery, Daviess County, Indiana. As with many old records, there are some spelling errors recorded.

John Edward Haag – 1900 Federal Census for LaSalle, LaSalle Co., Illinois

The above image shows a page from the 1900 census. The highlighted area shows John E. Haag, his wife Gertrude, and their first three children Cleophas, Harry and Roy (John LeRoy). John is working as a coal miner in Illinois.

John Edward Haag – 1910 Federal Census for St. Louis, Missouri

The above image shows a page from the 1910 census. The highlighted area shows John E. Haag, his second wife Francis, and their children: Julie Patterson (Francis' daughter from her first marriage); and the children from John's first wife (Gertrude), Cleo, Joseph H. (Harry), John LeRoy, Michael B., and Vincent B. In St. Louis, John continues working as a coal miner.

John Edward Haag – 1920 Federal Census for Bicknell, Knox Co., Indiana

The above image shows a page from the 1920 census. The highlighted area shows John E. Haag, his second wife Francis, and the children at home, Michael B. and Vincent B., children of Gertrude, and Mary A., daughter of John and Francis. John and son Michael are working as coal miners.

John Edward Haag – 1930 Federal Census for Ragsdale, Knox Co., Indiana

The above image shows a page from the 1930 census. The highlighted area shows John Haag, his third wife Jean, and the children at home, Margaret, Charles, John R. and Francis G. Margaret and Charles are children of Francis. John R. and Francis G. are children of Jean. John's work is noted as a Fire Boss at the coal mine.

John Edward Haag – 1940 Federal Census for Bicknell, Knox Co., Indiana

The above image shows a page from the 1940 census. The highlighted area shows John Haag, his third wife Jean, and the children at home, Margaret, Charles, John, Francis, Mary and Bill (James William). Margaret and Charles are children of Francis. John, Francis, Mary and Bill are children of Jean. John continues work as a coal miner.

Haag Brothers – Photo 1940s

The above photo was shared on Ancestry.com by someone known as STARITE. The caption reads as follows:

> *4 Haag Brothers & Their Sons*
> *Ca 1940's*
> *Daviess County, Indiana*
> *From left to right: 1. John Haag (Son #15), 2. James Way (sp. of Gertrude Calesta), 3. Robert Haag (son #6), 4. Harry Haag (son #6), 5. George Haag (son #12), 6. JOHN HAAG, 7. ???, 8. Cecil Haag (son #15), 9. CHARLES HUBERT HAAG, 10. Clarence Haag (son #15), 11. Albert Haag (son #15), 12. OSCAR HAAG, 13. Sam Lannan, 14. Tom Rucker (sp. of Martha), 15. TERRANCE HAAG*

The brothers described in all capitals are sons of Hubert Charles Haag. Note son John (person 6) and his son Harry (person 4), who continue the line of Haags that we are following.

John E. Haag and Gertrude S. Carrico – Marriage Certificate

This is a copy of the Marriage Certificate for John E. Haag and Gertrude S. Carrico. They were married 27 January 1891 in Daviess County, Indiana.

Gertrude S. (Carrico) Haag – Death Certificate

This is a copy of the death certificate for John Haag's first wife Gertrude (Carrico) Haag. She died on 19 July 1908 in Bicknell, Indiana. The cause of death is listed as Peripheral Occlusion (blockage or narrowing of an artery in the legs) and Pneumonia.

Francis (McAtee) Haag – Death Certificate

This is a copy of the death certificate for John Haag's second wife Francis (McAtee) Haag. She died on 13 October 1926 in Washington Township, Knox County, Indiana. The cause of death is listed as Lobar Pneumonia.

Jean (McArthur) Haag – Death Certificate

This is a copy of the death certificate for John Haag's third wife Jean (McArthur) Haag. She died on 27 May 1964 in Vincennes, Indiana. The cause of death is listed as Carcinomatosis (multiple cancer development simultaneously, usually meaning there are multiple secondary cancers in multiple sites.) The secondary cause is Endometrial Carcinoma (cancer of the uterus).

GEORGE FRANCIS HAAG (1875 – 1943)

George was born in Vigo County, Indiana, on 2 February 1875. Vigo County is the location of Terre Haute. George and his wife Addie appear in the 1910 census for Stockton Township in Greene County, Indiana. This is about 35 miles south of Terre Haute, Indiana. George is working as a coal miner. He and Addie have two children at this time, Leo age 12 and Ray age 8. Both children were born in Indiana. The 1920 census still has them in Stockton Township, and George is still working as a coal miner. Leo is still at home and working as an undertaker. This census also shows son Earl, age 14. It is not known why Earl did not appear in the previous census in 1910.

In 1930 the family is still living in the same place. The census notes that George works at a strip mine. Also living with them is Morris, a 5-year-old grandson. The last record of the family in the 1940 census finds George, now 65, working as a manager at a trucking company. He and Addie once again have a grandson living with them – 4-year-old Maurice. They are now listed as living in the town of Linton, a coal mining town located in the heart of Stockton Township.

George died on 22 June 1943, and Addie died in 1960. They are buried in Fairview Cemetery in Linton, Indiana. George's death certificate notes that he worked for the Maumee Colliers Co. This was a coal mining company headquartered in Terre Haute that operated mines in Linton.

George Francis Haag – 1910 Federal Census for Stockton Twp., Greene Co., Indiana

The above image shows a page from the 1910 census. The town of Linton is located in Stockton Township. The highlighted area shows George Haag, his wife Addy, and children Leo, Ray and Earl. George works as a coal miner.

George Francis Haag – 1920 Federal Census for Stockton Twp., Greene Co., Indiana

The above image shows a page from the 1920 census. The highlighted area shows George Haag, his wife Addie, and children Leo and Earl. George continues to work as a coal miner, and oldest son Leo is an embalmer for an undertaker.

George Francis Haag – 1930 Federal Census for Linton, Greene Co., Indiana

The above image shows a page from the 1930 census. The highlighted area shows George Haag, his wife Addie, and grandson Morris. George is still working as a miner.

George Francis Haag – 1940 Federal Census for Linton, Greene Co., Indiana

The above image shows a page from the 1940 census. The highlighted area shows George Haag, his wife Addie, and grandson Maurice (Morris in the 1930 census). George's job is listed as a manager for a truck line.

George Francis Haag – Death Certificate

This is a copy of the death certificate for George Francis Haag. He died on 22 June 1943 in Linton, Indiana. The cause of death is listed as Myocarditis (inflammation of the heart muscle).

NANCY E. HAAG (1878 – 1879)

Born in Daviess County, Indiana, Nancy survived for only one year. Her death is noted as in Cannelburg, Daviess County, Indiana.

CHARLES HUBERT HAAG (1880 – 1963)

Charles Hubert Haag was born in Daviess County, Indiana, on 14 April 1880. In 1900 Charles is living in Barr Township in Davies County with wife Lillie and their daughter Frances. At age 19, Charles is working as a coal miner.

Ten years later, the family is living in Bicknell, about15 miles to the northwest of Barr Township. At this time there are four children at home: Frances, 10; May, 8; Gertrude, 5; and Lucile, 6 months. There is a note in the census that Lillie has had five children, and four are living. Charles is still working as a miner.

In 1920, the children at home are Gertrude, 14; Lucile, 10; James, 8; and Mary, 6. The birth certificate for James notes that he is the sixth of five living children. Charles is now an engineer at the coal mine.

1930 finds a big change for the family. They are now living in Indianapolis where 48-year-old Charles is a millwright at an auto body shop. Two children are at home: Joseph, 9; and Hazel (Lucile), 20. Hazel is married and she, her husband and 2-year-old son are living with Charles and Lillie.

In 1940 they are living in Perry Township in Marion County on Southport Road where Charles is now a farmer. Son Joseph, now 19, is still at home. Charles' draft card in 1944 indicates that he is working at the Stark and Wetzel Packing House in Indianapolis.

Charles died in August of 1963 and is buried at Saint John's Cemetery in Washington, Daviess County, Indiana. Lillie died in July of 1968 and is also buried in Saint John's Cemetery in Washington.

Charles Hubert Haag – 1900 Federal Census for Montgomery, Daviess Co., Indiana

The above image shows a page from the 1900 census. The highlighted area shows Charles H. Haag, his wife Lillie, and new daughter Francis. Charles is employed as a coal miner.

Charles Hubert Haag – 1920 Federal Census for Bicknell, Knox Co., Indiana

The above image shows a page from the 1920 census. The highlighted area shows Charles Haag, his wife Lilla (Lillie), and children Gertrude, Lucile, James and Mary. Charles is listed as an engineer at a coal mine.

Charles Hubert Haag – 1930 Federal Census for Indianapolis, Marion Co., Indiana

The above image shows a page from the 1930 census. The highlighted area shows Charles H. Haag, his wife Lillie, and children Joseph and Hazel (Lucile). Also living there are Hazel's husband Ira and their son Charles A. Charles is now a millwright at an auto body shop.

Charles Hubert Haag – 1940 Federal Census for Perry Twp., Marion Co., Indiana

The above image shows a page from the 1940 census. The highlighted area shows Charles H. Haag, his wife Lilly, and son Joseph. The family is now engaged in farming.

Haag

The Eighth Generation:

Harry Joseph Haag
(1895-1963)

Family Chart

Cleophas F. Haag – b. March 1894, d. before 1935
    Spouse: Walter Friedley Clinton
    Children:
        Grace Leora Clinton – b. 1917, d. 2002
        John Steven Clinton – b. 1919, d. 1923

Harry Joseph Haag – b. 4 September 1895, d. 1 August 1963
    Spouse: Mabel Iselem Boze – b. May 1895, d. July 1969
    Children:
        Leatha Cecelia Haag – b. 1 February 1916, d. 3 December 1961
        Helen Elizabeth Haag – b. 11 March 1918, d. 8 July 2002
        Thelma L. Haag – b. 16 June 1920, d. before 1930

John LeRoy Haag – b. March 1900, d. 29 July 1916
    Spouse: Never married

Michael Bernard Haag – b. 19 October 1902, d. 29 July 1980
    Spouse: Frances G. Dueppe – b. 4 January 1899, d. 23 February 1934
    Children:
        Joseph Haag – b. about 1923, d. unknown

Charles E. Haag – b. 12 December 1933, d. 2 May 2000
Spouse: Mary L. Goodson – b. 12 March 1912, d. 23 September 1995
Children:
> Bernard M. Haag Jr. - b. about 1936, d. unknown
> Judith A. Haag – b. 2 June 1938, d. unknown

Vincent Bartholomew Haag – b. 14 January 1906, d. 8 March 1970
Spouse: Mary Louise Uding- b. 1905, d. 1987
Children:

Mary Agnes Haag – b. 27 June 1908, d. 2 August 1908

CLEOPHAS F. HAAG (1894 – BEFORE 1935)

Cleo first appears in the 1900 census for LaSalle, LaSalle County, Illinois. She was born in March of 1894 in Indiana prior to her parents moving to Illinois. In the next census in 1910, 17-year-old Cleo is working as a seamstress at a pants factory in St. Louis, Missouri, where her family has relocated.

By 1912, the family is back in the Vincennes, Indiana, area as they appear in a city directory. Her father is working as a coal miner.

In the 1920 census, Cleo is married to Walter Friedley Clinton, and the couple has two children. They are living in Edwardsport, Indiana, a small town about 15 miles northeast of Vincennes, and only about four miles from Bicknell, Indiana. Walter is a coal miner.

No other information has been located on Cleo. Walter did remarry in 1935, and the marriage certificate notes that his previous wife had died. So, we can only say that Cleo died before 1935.

Cleophas (Haag) Clinton – 1920 Federal Census for Edwardsport, Vigo Co., Indiana

The above image shows a page from the 1920 census. The highlighted area shows Freedly (Walter Friedley) Clinton, his wife Cleophas and children Leora and John. Also living with them are Walter's brother Roy and sister Ora. Walter and Roy are both coal miners.

HARRY JOSEPH HAAG (1895 – 1963)

It seems most likely that Harry was born as Joseph Harry Haag, the second child of John Edward Haag and his first wife Gertrude S. Carrico, on 4 September 1895. There are two reasons for saying "most likely." First is that most records indicate that Harry was born in 1895. These sources include the 1900 federal census and his World War II draft registration. His death certificate, however, lists his birth as 1896. Then there is his World War I draft registration which indicates 1894. The year of 1894 seems highly unlikely, however, as Harry's older sister was born in March of 1894.

The second reason for saying "most likely" is Harry's name. Most census records list his name as Harry, but the 1910 census lists it as Joseph H. And, while his WWII draft card lists his name as Harry Joseph, his WWI draft card lists his name as Joseph Harry. It appears that his given name was Joseph Harry, but the name he used was Harry.

Harry first appears in the 1900 census at age four with his parents living in La Salle, Illinois. In the 1910 census, his name is listed as Joseph H., now age 15. At this time Harry is working as a laborer at a coffin factory. The family has now moved to St. Louis, Missouri.

By 1912, the family is back in Indiana. In a 1912 Vincennes city directory, Harry is living with his parents and his sister Cleophas at 304 South 9th Street in Vincennes. Now about age 17, Harry is working as a miner at this time.

The following year, on 26 November 1913, Harry married Mabel I. Boze in Knox County, Indiana. The next record for Harry is his 1917 or 1918 World War I draft registration card. He is registered as Joseph Harry Haag living with a wife and one child at 1200 N. Main Street in Bicknell, Indiana. He is a coal miner working at the American Coal Company. Bicknell is located about 12 miles northeast of Vincennes.

The Story of Bicknell, Indiana

From the City of Bicknell website:

> *John Bicknell, born in Knox County, married Eliza Ann Chansler, a neighbor girl, and became a prominent farmer. In 1860 he purchased 240 acres for $13.00 an acre and had part of it laid out in lots. George Fuller, Emison [Township], purchased the first lot in 1868 and built the first store which contained his residence and the Post Office. The area had been called "Stumptown" because of the multitude of tree stumps from the dense forest that had to be removed. After Mr. Fuller built his store people began to call it "Fullertown". In 1869 it was agreed it should be called "Bicknell" in honor of John Bicknell.*
>
> *The town began to grow. The first commercial coal mine was sunk in 1873 and more mines were started. The town was incorporated in 1907 with 4,005 citizens. Main Street was paved six years later and the waterworks was built in 1918. The*

Coal mining industry brought more people, and in 1920 there were almost 8,000 persons living here. There were over 20 shaft mines producing with rail connections, providing employment for 2,000 men.

Daily trains ran from Bicknell to Vincennes, seats and aisles full of commuting miners. In 1927 many of the early mines began to close and according to several citizens, delivered a "death blow" to Bicknell. Today the population is less than 4,000, but the City did not die; it just changed directions from a booming mine town to a great, little City in which people could raise children and retire.

The American Coal Company located in Bicknell was important to the growth of the city. A 1915 history, "Coal Age," talks about the "new American Coal Company" in Bicknell. The American Coal Company had six mines operating in Bicknell between 1914 and 1922.

Harry Joseph Haag Family

The first of three daughters was born to Harry and Mabel on 1 February 1916 when Leatha Cecelia Haag was born in Bicknell. Leatha's birth record confirms Harry's work as a miner. Mable is a housewife.

The second-born daughter was Helen Elizabeth Haag born 11 March 1918. Helen was also born in Bicknell.

The third daughter, Thelma Louise Haag, was born 16 June 1920 in the city of Vincennes where the family was now residing at 409 S. 7th Street. Harry is still working as a miner while living in Vincennes. The birth certificate for Thelma does note that she is the third of three children. Unfortunately, there are no other records of Thelma. She does not appear in the next federal census for 1930, so she did likely die prior to 1930. With little knowledge of Thelma in the family history, it is quite possible that she died not long after her birth.

A 1924 city directory for Vincennes lists Harry working at Haag Brothers in that city. This directory also lists Bernard Haag at Haag Brothers. An entry for Haag Brothers lists the business as "groceries and billiards." It would seem that Harry had gotten out of the mining industry by this time. What is very interesting is that Harry, Mabel and Bernard also appear in a La Porte city directory for that same year, 1924. It is possible that they had moved between the times the two directories were created. In La Porte, Harry is working as a clerk at Northside Grocery. Bernard is living with Harry and Mabel at 311 Jefferson Avenue. He is working at "J C McF Co." Why they moved to La Porte is unknown. No known connection exists other than Harry's father, John, getting married to his third wife in La Porte in 1927.

The 1926 La Porte city directory lists Harry and Mabel at 311 McCollum Street in La Porte, where Harry is a clerk at Northside Grocery and Market. The 1930 census shows the family still on McCollum Street, and Harry working as a salesman at a grocery store. Leatha is now 14 and Helen is 12. Thelma is not listed, and, with no further record of her, she is presumed deceased.

1938 finds the family still on McCollum Street. Harry is a butcher at Kroger's, and Mabel is an alterer at R&H Miller. Leatha is a saleswoman at F. W. Woolworth, and Helen is working as an operator for Indiana Associated Telephone.

In the 1940 census, Harry is still working as a butcher, Mabel is not working, Leatha is a bookkeeper at a ladies' dress shop, and Helen is a saleslady at a retail store. They are still at McCollum Street. Harry and Mabel are age 44, Leatha is 24, and Helen is 22.

At age 46, Harry registered for the World War II draft in 1942. He is registered as Harry Joseph Haag (contrary to Joseph Harry Haag for World War I). They live at 311 McCollum, and Harry is employed at Kroger Grocery and Baking Co. He lists daughter Leatha Hilgendorf at 1212 Weller Avenue as someone who will know of his residence.

In 1949 Harry is listed as a steward of the K of C Club in La Porte. He and Mabel are still at 311 McCollum Street. In 1952 Harry is listed as a club manager, likely at the same place.

La Porte city directories for 1954 through 1956 (only even-year directories were available) do not contain listings for Harry and Mabel. It was during these years that Harry worked at the Soldier's Home in Lafayette, Indiana. Lafayette city directories for those years do not contain Harry and Mabel either. It is possible that because he resided at the Soldier's Home that he was not included in the city directory.

And, finally, the 1958 and 1960 city directories list Harry as a department supervisor at Beatty Memorial Hospital. He and Mabel are now residing at 207 E. 12th Street in La Porte.

Harry died in August of 1963 and is buried at Pine Lake Cemetery in La Porte. Mabel remarried to Wilbur Smith after Harry's passing. Mabel died in July 1969 and is buried in Saint John's Lutheran Cemetery in La Porte.

Harry Joseph Haag – 1920 Federal Census for Vincennes, Knox Co., Indiana

The above image shows a page from the 1920 census. The highlighted area shows Harry Haag, his wife Mabel and daughters Leatha and Helen. At this time Harry is working in the mines as a machine man.

Harry Joseph Haag – 1930 Federal Census for La Porte, La Porte Co., Indiana

The above image shows a page from the 1930 census. Having moved to La Porte about 1924, Harry Haag, his wife Mabel and daughters Leatha and Helen appear in the 1930 census for that city. Harry is now working as a salesman at a grocery store.

Harry Joseph Haag – 1940 Federal Census for La Porte, La Porte Co., Indiana

The above image shows a page from the 1940 census. The highlighted area shows Harry Haag, his wife Mabel and daughters Leatha and Helen. Harry is a butcher at a retail grocer. Leatha is working as a bookkeeper at a ladies dress shop, and her sister Helen is a sales lady at a retail store.

Harry Joseph Hilgendorf – World War I Draft Registration Card

The above image of Harry Haag's Word War I draft registration shows that he used his given name of Joseph Harry Haag. At some point, he apparently preferred to go by Harry Joseph. It can also be seen that Harry worked for the American Coal Company. Note that this document indicates 1894 as Harry's birth year. This seems highly unlikely, however, as Harry's older sister was born in March of 1894.

REGISTRATION CARD—(Men born on or after April 28, 1877 and on or before February 16, 1897)

SERIAL NUMBER	1. NAME (Print)			ORDER NUMBER
U 1995	Harry (First)	Joseph (Middle)	Haag (Last)	

2 PLACE OF RESIDENCE (Print)
311 McCollum (Number and street)   La Porte (Town, township, village, or city)   La Porte (County)   Ind (State)

[THE PLACE OF RESIDENCE GIVEN ON THE LINE ABOVE WILL DETERMINE LOCAL BOARD JURISDICTION; LINE 2 OF REGISTRATION CERTIFICATE WILL BE IDENTICAL]

3. MAILING ADDRESS
Same

[Mailing address if other than place indicated on line 2. If same insert word same]

4. TELEPHONE	5. AGE IN YEARS	6. PLACE OF BIRTH
2080K	46	La Salle
(Exchange) (Number)	Sept DATE OF BIRTH 4 1895 (Mo.) (Day) (Yr.)	Ill. (Town or county) (State or country)

7. NAME AND ADDRESS OF PERSON WHO WILL ALWAYS KNOW YOUR ADDRESS
Mrs. Letha Hilgendorf   1212 Weller Ave   La Porte Ind

8. EMPLOYER'S NAME AND ADDRESS
Kroger Grocery & Baking Co.

9. PLACE OF EMPLOYMENT OR BUSINESS
La Porte Ind
(Number and street or R. F. D. number)   (Town)   (County)   (State)

I AFFIRM THAT I HAVE VERIFIED ABOVE ANSWERS AND THAT THEY ARE TRUE.

Harry J Haag
(Registrant's signature)

D. S. S. Form 1
(Revised 4-1-42)   (over)   16—21630-2

Harry Joseph Hilgendorf – World War II Draft Registration Card

The above image of Harry Haag's Word War II draft registration shows 1895 as Harry's birth year. This seems to be the correct year, not 1894 as shown on his WWI draft registration.

Harry Joseph Haag – Death Certificate

This is a copy of the death certificate for Harry Joseph Haag. He died on 1 August 1963 in La Porte, Indiana. The cause of death is listed as Coronary thrombosis (the formation of a blood clot inside a blood vessel of the heart; a heart attack) and Arteriosclerotic heart disease (hardening of the arteries).

Mabel (Boze) Haag Smith – Death Certificate

This is a copy of the death certificate for Mabel (Boze) Haag Smith. He died on 10 July 1969 in La Porte, Indiana. The cause of death is listed as Atherosclerotic Heart Disease (hardening of the arteries).

Harry and Mabel Haag Portraits

These portraits of Harry and Mabel Haag are from the mid-1930s.

The Harry Haag Family

This photo was taken 30 May 1938 in La Porte, Indiana. Left to right are Harry, Helen, Mabel and Leatha.

LaPorte Central Labor Union

OFFICERS AND TRUSTEES

Left to Right (seated): Walter Rheinholtz, President; H. T. Orcutt, Treasurer; F. A. Kuehne, Secretary; Harry Haag, Vice-President; Russell Herd, Trustee. Standing: Walter Miller, Trustee, and Roy H. Dunifon, Trustee.

La Porte Central Labor Union – Harry Haag, VP

This photo appeared in the *Official 1940-41 Year Book* for La Porte, Indiana. This may have been a publication of the La Porte Central Labor Union. The description of the photo reads:

LA PORTE CENTRAL BODY
Organized 1929

Though there had been AFL union men in the "Maple City" long before, it was not until 1929 that a group of far-seeing La Porte Labor leaders representing Carpenters Local No. 791, Painters Local No. 595, Typographical No. 800, Barbers No.791 and Plasterers No. 438 petitioned the AFL for a Central Body charter for La Porte and vicinity. Granted their charter by the AFL Executive Council on April 22, 1929, and meeting on the third floor of the old City Hall building, the La Porte Central Body has continued to grow and to progress. There are now eight affiliated organizations meeting and sending delegates to the Labor Temple at 613 ½ Michigan Avenue. An integral part of the community, this organization works constantly for the common good and in the best interests of Organized Labor in La Porte.

Harry Haag and Family

This photo was take about 1952-53, likely in Lafayette, Indiana, at the Soldiers Home where Harry worked. In back are Mabel, Leatha and Harry. Leatha's children Jane and Ken Hilgendorf are in front.

Harry Haag and Family

This photo was take about 1953-54 at the Soldiers Home in Lafayette, Indiana. Starting at the lower left around the table are: Sally Hilgendorf, Marti Hilgendorf, Leatha (Haag) Hilgendorf, Dutch Hilgendorf, Bob Parker, Ken Hilgendorf, Mabel Haag, Harry Haag, Dave Parker, Helen (Haag) Parker, John Parker, Sherry Parker, and Jane Hilgendorf.

Harry Haag and Family

This photo was take about 1954-55; the location is unknown. Seated left to right are: Ken Hilgendorf, Dave Parker, Bob Parker, Jane Hilgendorf, Harry Haag, and Marti Hilgendorf. Standing left to right are: John Parker, Sherry Parker, Helen (Haag) Parker, Leatha (Haag) Hilgendorf and Mabel Haag.

Harry and Mabel Haag

This photo of Harry and Mable Haag is undated, but it could be the very early 1960s.

Harry Haag at Work

This photo of Harry Haag was taken in March of 1963. Harry died in August of that year.

JOHN LEROY HAAG (1900 – 1916)

John LeRoy Haag appears with his parents in the 1900 census for LaSalle, Illinois, where he was born, and then in the 1910 census for St. Louis, Missouri. In the June 1900 Census, his age is listed as 3 months, and his birth is noted as March 1900. This fits very well with the census. His death certificate, however, lists his date of birth as 15 Mar 1898. It would seem difficult to mistake the date of birth for a three-month-old during the census, so the March 1900 date is more likely to be correct.

Roy, as he appears to be most often referenced, died in Bicknell, Indiana, on 29 July 1916. His age is listed as 18 based upon the birth date of 1898. Either way, he died at a young age, perhaps an early victim of the influenza epidemic that peaked in 1917-1918. He is buried in Mount Calvary Cemetery, Vincennes, Indiana.

John LeRoy Haag – Death Certificate

This is a copy of the death certificate for John LeRoy Haag. He died on 28 July 1916 in Bicknell, Indiana. The cause of death is noted as Double Lobar Pneumonia with a contributory cause of Peritonitis (inflammation of the lining of the inner wall of the abdomen and cover of the abdominal organs).

MICHAEL BERNARD HAAG (1902 – 1980)

Michael Bernard Haag was born about 1902 in Illinois. We do know that his parents were in La Salle, Illinois, in the 1900 census, so that is likely where he was born. He is with the family in St. Louis, Missouri, in 1910.

In the 1920 census, he is living with his parents in Bicknell, Indiana. He is 19 years old and working as a coal miner. It appears that he was born Michael Bernard, but from this time forward, all references to him are as Bernard M.

Bernard may have been married about 1922, and a first child, Joseph, was born about 1923 to wife Frances G. Dueppe. Interestingly, Frances is working as a clerk in a grocery store in Bicknell in the 1920 census. In 1920, Bernard was working as a coal miner, following in his father's footsteps. Perhaps Bernard met Frances at the store which led to the opening of his own business with his brother.

We see Bernard in a 1924 city directory for Vincennes at Haag Brothers, a grocery and billiards business. It appears as though he and brother Harry were running this business. As with Harry, Bernard also appears in a La Porte city directory for that same year. It is possible that they had moved between the times the two directories were created. In the La Porte directory, Bernard is working as "bench" at "JC McF Co." This appears to have been J C McFarland Co., a steel door manufacturer. He is living at his brother's home at 311 Jefferson Ave. It is still a puzzle as to why they moved to La Porte.

The 1926 La Porte City directory shows Bernard and wife Frances living at 114 Kingsbury Avenue. He is now working at Sunbeam Grocery. He is working at the same place in 1929, but they are now living at 108 B Street.

The 1930 census shows Bernard and Frances with son Joseph, now age 8. Unfortunately, Frances died in February of 1934 not long after the birth of son Charles Edward Haag on 12 December 1933. She had a blood clot in her brain following surgery for gallstones and appendicitis.

That same year in October, Bernard remarried to Mary L. (Gallo) Goodson. Mary was born 12 March 1912 in Wellsboro, a small community near Union Mills, Indiana. While I was able to find a marriage record for Bernard and Mary, I have been able to find little other information on her.

By 1940 Bernard and Mary have two children of their own, Bernard M. Jr., 4; and Judith A., 1; as well as son Charles, now 6. Joseph would have been 18 or 19 at this time, and has likely moved out on his own; however, no record has been found for Joseph after a 1938 La Porte city directory listing. In 1940 the family resides at 507 H Street. At this time Bernard is working at the Haag & Klinedinst Market.

La Porte city directories for 1943-1952 have Bernard at Haag's Meat Market. This was located at 716 Michigan Avenue. The family has moved from H Street to 1509 Michigan Avenue. 1958 finds him as a meat cutter at the Kingsbury Locker Plant. He is still there in 1960, but they are now living at 911 Wright Avenue.

Bernard died in July of 1980 in La Porte and is buried in Pine Lake Cemetery. His first wife Frances is buried in Saint Joseph's Cemetery in La Porte. Mary remarried to Alfred C. Pease in 1981, and she passed in Winter Park, Florida, on 2 May 2000.

Michael Bernard Haag – 1930 Federal Census for La Porte, La Porte Co., Indiana

The above image shows a page from the 1930 census. The highlighted area shows Bernard (born Michael Bernard) Haag, his wife Francis and son Joseph. Bernard works in retail grocery.

Michael Bernard Haag – 1940 Federal Census for La Porte, La Porte Co., Indiana

The above image shows a page from the 1940 census. The highlighted area shows Bernard M. (born Michael Bernard) Haag Sr., his second wife Mary L. and children Charles E., Bernard M. Jr., and Judith A. Charles is the son of his first wife Frances who died in 1934.

Michael Bernard Haag – Death Certificate

This is a copy of the death certificate for Bernard Michael Bernard Haag. (While born Michael Bernard, he used the name Bernard Michael.) He died on 29 July 1980 in La Porte, Indiana. The cause of death is listed as Massive Myocardial Infarction (massive heart attack). There were underlying causes of Arteriosclerotic Cardiovascular Disease (hardening of the arteries), along with Diabetes and Parkinson's Disease.

VINCENT BARTHOLOMEW HAAG (1906 – 1970)

Vincent was born in 1906 when the family was living in La Salle, Illinois. In the 1910 census Vincent is a 4-year-old at home with his parents now in St. Louis, Missouri. In the 1920 census he is 15, and they are living in Bicknell, Indiana. His father and older brother, Michael, are miners.

By the 1930 census, Vincent is a 25-year-old truck driver for a bakery company. Vincent married Mary Louise Ueding at age 19, which would be about 1924; she was 18. At this time, 1930, the couple has one child, Patricia, age 2 ½. They are residing at 1015 Second Street in La Porte.

There is a record of an earlier child's birth. John Vincent Haag was born 15 November 1925, and the birth certificate notes that he is the first child of the mother. There is no further record of John, and it can be surmised that he died very young, perhaps very nearly after his birth.

In 1940, the family is living in Rolling Prairie, Wills Township, in La Porte County. Vincent is a core maker at a radiator manufacturer. Wife Mary is a bus driver for the public schools. They now have three children, Patricia, 12, Margaret, 9, and Vincent L., 5.

In 1943, they are living at 611 Park Street in La Porte. Vincent is a drill press operator at Modine Manufacturing, and Mary is a saleslady at JC Penney. 1947 finds the family living on "15th Street at Lincoln Highway." Vincent is a solderer at Modine, daughter Patricia is a saleswoman at Dee's Fashion, and daughter Margaret is a waiter at Iselman's Dairy Bar.

1954 through 1960 city directories show Vincent and Mary at 412 Oberreich Street, and Vincent continuing employment at Modine.

Vincent died in Sebring Florida, in 1970, and Mary died in 1987 in La Porte.

Vincent Bartholomew Haag – 1930 Federal Census, La Porte, La Porte Co., Indiana

The above image shows a page from the 1930 census. The highlighted area shows Vincent Haag, his wife Mary L., and their daughter Patricia A. Vincent is a truck driver at a bakery company.

Vincent Bartholomew Haag – 1940 Federal Census, La Porte, La Porte Co., Indiana

The above image shows a page from the 1940 census. The highlighted area shows Vincent Haag, his wife Mary L., and their daughters Patricia Ann and Margaret Helen. Vincent is employed as a core baker at a radiator manufacturer.

MARY AGNES HAAG (1908 – 1908)

Mary was born in Bicknell, Knox County, Indiana in 1908. Unfortunately, Mary only survived a little more than a month. She was the ninth of nine children to John Edward and Gertrude. There are no complications noted on her birth certificate. Her death certificate, however, notes that she died of malnutrition as a result of toxemia from the mother.

Haag

The Ninth Generation:

Leatha Cecelia Haag
(1916-1961)

Family

Leatha Cecelia Haag – b. 1 February 1916, d. 3 December 1961
>   Spouse: Clarence John Hilgendorf – b. 30 October 1910, d. 24 July 1990
>   Children:
>>   Sally Joan Hilgendorf – b. 23 November 1941
>>   Kenneth Richard Hilgendorf – b. 17 June 1943
>>   Mary Jane Hilgendorf – b. 3 August 1946
>>   Martha Ann Hilgendorf – b. 6 April 1951
>>   Clarence John Hilgendorf Jr. - b. 14 February 1956

Helen Elizabeth Haag – b. 11 March 1918, d. 8 July 2002
>   Spouse: John Parker Jr. – b. 9 September 1917, d. 3 March 2008
>   Children:
>>   David Lee Parker – b. 19 September 1941
>>   Susan Jeanne Parker – b. 3 January 1944, d. 18 August 1946
>>   Robert Alan Parker – b. 27 October 1948
>>   Sherry Ann Parker – b. 6 November 1951

Thelma L. Haag – b. 16 June 1920, d. before 1930

LEATHA CECELIA HAAG (1916 – 1961)

Leatha was the first-born child of Harry and Mabel (Boze) Haag born in 1916 in Bicknell, Indiana. The family is living at 1200 N. Main Street in Bicknell in 1918. In 1920, there are now two children, Leatha, 3; and Helen, 1. Another sister was born in June of 1920, after the census was taken, but she passed sometime before the next census in 1930. At the time of the 1920 census, the family is living at 409 7th Street in Vincennes, Indiana.

The family moved to La Porte around 1924. The 1930 census finds the family at 311 McCollum Street, and Leatha is now 14 years old.

A 1938 La Porte city directory notes that Leatha is now a saleslady at the F. W. Woolworth store. By 1940, 24-year-old Leatha is a bookkeeper at a ladies' dress shop. It was at a dress shop that Leatha met her husband-to-be, Clarence (Dutch) Hilgendorf. Clarence was shopping for a dress for his younger sister when he met Leatha. On 14 September 1940, Leatha and Clarence were married in La Porte. They made their new home together at 1212 Weller Avenue in La Porte.

Leatha and Clarence had five children: Sally, Ken, Jane, Marti, and CJ (Clarence Jr.). They were a social couple with many friends. They were also active in the Catholic Church. Dutch liked to meet with friends regularly on Saturday afternoons at the local Elks Club where they would play cards. Leatha remained a housewife while Clarence commuted daily to South Bend where he worked at Bendix Corporation.

Leatha passed on 3 December 1961 in La Porte after suffering a heart attack at home. Clarence died on 24 July 1990 in Bradenton, Florida. Clarence and Leatha are interred together at Pine Lake cemetery in La Porte.

Leatha Cecelia Haag – Birth Certificate

This is a copy of Leatha Cecelia Haag's birth certificate. Leatha was born on 1 February 1916 in Bicknell, Indiana.

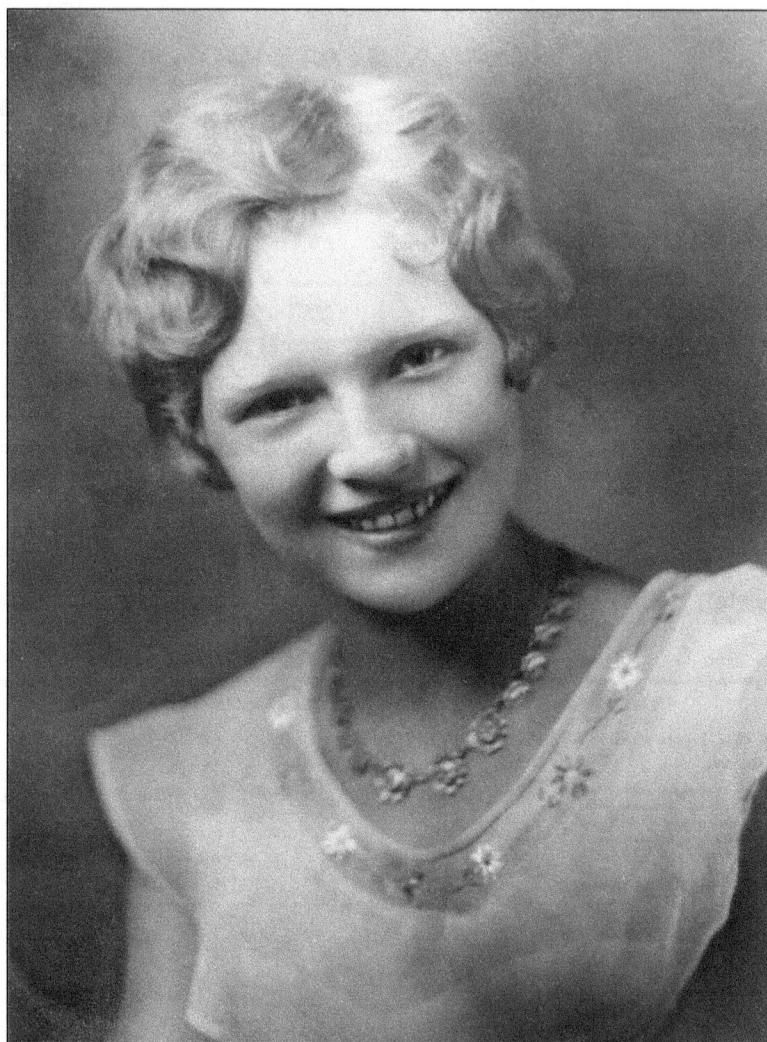

Leatha Cecelia Haag Portrait

This is an undated portrait of Leatha Cecelia Haag, but it was possibly taken near or after high school graduation, placing it in the early 1930s.

LEATHA HAAG

"A northern girl with a southern drawl."

C. C. H. S. 1
Girl Reserves 2, 3, 4
S. A. Club 1
Basketball 1
Prom Committee 3

Leatha Cecelia Haag – La Porte High School

This is a picture and caption from the 1933 La Porte High School yearbook, the *El-Pe*. This is Leatha's senior year in high school.

Leatha Cecelia Haag

This is an undated portrait of Leatha Haag may be from about the mid-1930s.

Leatha Cecelia Haag

The above two photos of Leatha Haag were taken on 11 March 1939 in front of the Harry Haag home at 311 McCollum Street in La Porte, Indiana. A description on the back of the photo on the left reads: *"Punch drunk" Leatha in front of Haag's on Helen's 21st Birthday.* The photo on the right has a description that reads: *Leatha in front of Oogt's car in La Porte, Indiana, U.S.A. March 11, 1939.* It is unsure if Oogt is an actual name or a nickname. Oogt is an old Dutch word that means appear or look.

Leatha Cecelia Haag

The photo on the left was taken 11 March 1939 in the front yard of the Harry Haag home on 311 McCollum Street in La Porte, Indiana. The photo on the right is undated, but it may be the early 1940s. Leatha would now be Leatha Hilgendorf as it is assumed this was taken after her marriage to Dutch Hilgendorf.

Leatha (Haag) Hilgendorf

These are undated photos, maybe from the early 1940s. The photo on the left is Dutch and Leatha. The photo of Leatha on the right is obviously taken in the same general location and same time-frame. These photos may be from their honeymoon.

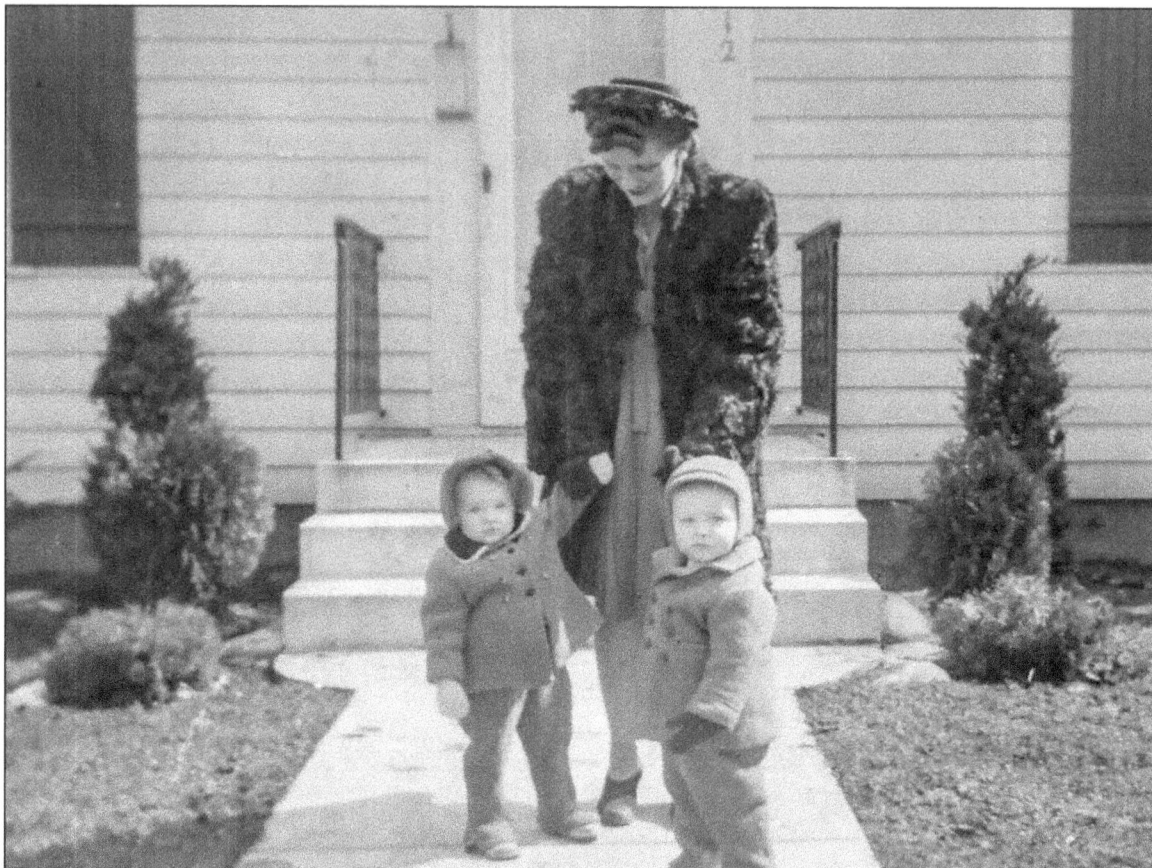

Leatha Hilgendorf, Sally Hilgendorf and Dave Parker

This photo in front of Dutch and Leatha's home at 1212 Weller Avenue in La Porte, Indiana, was taken about 1942. Leatha is with her daughter Sally (left) and her nephew Dave Parker (right).

Deaths

MRS. LEATHA HILGENDORF

Mrs. Leatha Hilgendorf, 45, of 1212 Weller avenue, died suddenly at 4 a. m. yesterday at the Holy Family hospital apparently as the result of a heart seizure.

She was born Feb. 1, 1916 in Bicknell, Ind., to Harry and Mable (Boze) Haag and had lived in La-Porte most of her life.

She was married Sept. 14, 1940 in LaPorte to Clarence (Dutch) Hilgendorf. Mrs. Hilgendorf was a member of St. Peter's Catholic church, St. Peter's Rosary society and the St. Peter's Home and School guild.

Surviving are her husband; three daughters; Mrs. Dennis Biege, LaPorte; Miss Mary Jane and Miss Martha Ann, both at home; two sons, Kenneth and Clarence, Jr., at home; her parents, and one sister, Mrs. John Parker, Jr., LaPorte.

Funeral services will be held at 9 a. m. Wednesday at St. Peter's Catholic church with the Rev. Lawrence T. Grothouse officiating. Burial will be in Pine Lake cemetery.

Friends may call at the Essling Funeral home from today and until time of services. The rosary will be recited tomorrow at 8 p. m. at the Essling chapel.

Leatha (Haag) Hilgendorf – Obituary

This is the obituary for Leatha (Haag) Hilgendorf from the *La Porte Herald-Argus* newspaper.

INDIANA STATE BOARD OF HEALTH
DIVISION OF VITAL RECORDS
MEDICAL CERTIFICATE OF DEATH

Local No. 61-332S

'61-041911
State No.

EMBALMER'S NAME Vincent Essling
LICENSE No. 1190
FUNERAL DIRECTOR'S LICENSE No. 2454

1. PLACE OF DEATH a. COUNTY LaPorte,	2. USUAL RESIDENCE (Where deceased lived. If institution: Residence before admission) a. STATE Indiana b. COUNTY LaPorte
b. CITY, TOWN, OR LOCATION LaPorte, c. Length of Stay in 1b 46 yrs	c. CITY, TOWN, OR LOCATION LaPorte.
d. NAME OF HOSPITAL OR INSTITUTION Holy Family Hospital	d. STREET ADDRESS 1212 Weller Ave.
e. IS PLACE OF DEATH INSIDE CITY LIMITS? YES ✗ NO ☐	e. IS RESIDENCE INSIDE CITY LIMITS? YES ✗ NO ☐ f. IS RESIDENCE ON A FARM? YES ☐ NO ✗

3. NAME OF DECEASED (Type or print) First Leatha Middle C. Last Hilgendorf
4. DATE OF DEATH Month 12 Day 3 Year 61

5. SEX Female 6. COLOR OR RACE White 7. MARRIED ✗ NEVER MARRIED ☐ WIDOWED ☐ DIVORCED ☐
8. DATE OF BIRTH 2-1-16 9. AGE (In years last birthday) 45 IF UNDER 1 YEAR Months Days IF UNDER 24 HRS. Hours Min.

10a. USUAL OCCUPATION (Give kind of work done during most of working life, even if retired). Housewife.
10b. KIND OF BUSINESS OR INDUSTRY
11. BIRTHPLACE (State or foreign country) Indiana
12. CITIZEN OF WHAT COUNTRY? U.S.A.

13. FATHER'S NAME HARRY HAAG
14. MOTHER'S MAIDEN NAME Mable Boze

15. WAS DECEASED EVER IN U. S. ARMED FORCES? (Yes, no, or unknown)(If yes, give war or dates of service) NO
17a. INFORMANT'S NAME Clarence Hilgendorf.

17b. INFORMANT'S ADDRESS 1212 Weller Ave. LaPorte Indiana
17c. RELATIONSHIP TO DECEASED Husband.

18. CAUSE OF DEATH [Enter only one cause per line for (a), (b), and (c).]
PART I. DEATH WAS CAUSED BY:
IMMEDIATE CAUSE (a) Coronary Thrombosis
INTERVAL BETWEEN ONSET AND DEATH Few Hours

Conditions, if any, which gave rise to above cause (a) stating the underlying cause last.
DUE TO (b)_____
DUE TO (c)_____

PART II. OTHER SIGNIFICANT CONDITIONS CONTRIBUTING TO DEATH BUT NOT RELATED TO THE TERMINAL DISEASE CONDITION GIVEN IN PART I (a).
19. WAS AUTOPSY PERFORMED? YES ☐ NO ✗

20a. ACCIDENT ☐ SUICIDE ☐ HOMICIDE ☐
20b. DESCRIBE HOW INJURY OCCURRED. (Enter nature of injury in Part I or Part II of item 18.)

20c. TIME OF INJURY Hour a. m. p. m. Month Day Year
20d. INJURY OCCURRED WHILE AT ☐ NOT WHILE ☐ WORK   AT WORK
20e. PLACE OF INJURY (e. g., in or about home, farm, factory, street, office bldg., etc.)
20f. CITY, TOWN, OR LOCATION COUNTY STATE

21. ATTENDING PHYSICIAN: I certify that I attended the deceased from 10/3/60
to 12/3/61 and last saw her him alive on 11/25/61 Death occurred at 4:00 A M (C.S.T.) on the date stated above; and to the best of my knowledge, from the causes stated.

22. HEALTH OFFICER: I certify that I investigated cause of death of deceased and find that death occurred at____ ____ M (C.S.T.) from causes stated and on above date.

23a. Signature of Attending Physician or Health Officer. Francis B. Schild M.D.
23b. ADDRESS 1201 Maple
23c. DATE SIGNED 12/4/61

24a. BURIAL, CREMATION, REMOVAL (Specify) Burial 24b. DATE 12-6-61 24c. NAME OF CEMETERY OR CREMATORY Pine Lake 24d. LOCATION LaPorte Ind.

DATE REC'D BY LOCAL HEALTH OFFICER 12-9-61 SIGNATURE OF HEALTH OFFICER R. McKinley M.D.
25. FUNERAL DIRECTOR Vincent Essling ADDRESS LaPorte Ind.

S.B.H.—6-24-3—Revised 1955 U. S. Department Health, Education and Welfare. Form Approved Budget Bureau No. 68-R375.

Leatha (Haag) Hilgendorf – Death Certificate

This is a copy of the death certificate for Leatha (Haag) Hilgendorf. She died on 3 December 1961 in La Porte, Indiana. The cause of death is listed as Coronary Thrombosis (a blood clot in the heart).

Helen Elizabeth Haag (1918 – 2002)

Helen was the second child of Harry and Mabel (Boze) Haag born in 1918 in Bicknell, Indiana. The family is living at 1200 N. Main Street in Bicknell in 1918. In 1920, there are two children, Leatha, 3; and Helen, 1. Another sister was born in June of 1920, after the census was taken, but she passed sometime before the next census in 1930. At the time of the 1920 census, the family is living at 409 7th Street in Vincennes, Indiana.

The family moved to La Porte around 1924. The 1930 census finds the family at 311 McCollum Street, and Helen is now 12 years old.

A 1938 La Porte city directory notes that Helen is a telephone operator at Indiana Associated Telephone. In 1940, 22-year-old Helen is working as a saleslady at a retail store in La Porte. Both she and her sister Leatha are still living at home with their parents at the time of the census. In September of that year Helen married John Parker Jr.

Helen and John had four children; David, Susan, Robert and Sherry. Helen died in La Porte on 8 July 2002. John passed on 3 March 2008. They are buried in Pine Lake Cemetery in La Porte.

The following is Helen's obituary:

Mrs. Helena E. Parker, 84, of 2414 Monroe St., La Porte, died Thursday, July 18, 2002, at 9:15 a.m. at La Porte Hospital.

She was born March 11, 1918, in Ragsdale, Ind., to Harry J. and Mabel (Boze) Haag, and had lived in the La Porte area for 78 years, coming from Vincennes, Ind.

Mrs. Parker retired from Whirlpool Corporation as a customer service representative after 15 years. She was a member of St. Peter Catholic Church, St. Peter Rosary Society and St. Joan of Arc Circle, was a former Lady Elks member, and was a La Porte Hospital volunteer.

On Sept. 26, 1940, in La Porte, she married John Parker Jr., who survives.

Also surviving are one daughter, Sherry A. Benner of Indianapolis; two sons, David L. of Fort Lauderdale, Fla., and Robert A. of La Porte; and three grandchildren.

She was preceded in death by one daughter, Susan, and one sister, Leatha Hilgendorf.

A funeral Mass will be celebrated Saturday at 9:30 a.m. at St. Peter Catholic Church with Rev. George Vrabely officiating. Friends may call today at Essling Funeral Home from 4 to 8 p.m., where the rosary will be recited at 7 p.m. Burial will be in Pine Lake Cemetery.

Memorial contributions may be made to the charity of the donor's choice or to St. Peter Catholic Church.

Helen Elizabeth Haag – Birth Certificate

This is a copy of Helen Elizabeth Haag's birth certificate. Helen was born on 11 March 1918 in Bicknell, Indiana.

Helen Elizabeth Haag – High School

This is a picture of Helen Elizabeth Haag from the La Porte High School yearbook for 1935. She was in the junior class in high school at the time.

Helen Elizabeth Haag

This is a photo of Helen Elizabeth Haag (right) and her sister Leatha (left) on 11 March 1939, the date of Helen's 21st birthday. The photo was taken in the front yard of their home at 311 McCollum Street in La Porte, Indiana.

Helen Elizabeth Haag

This is a photo of Helen Elizabeth Haag (right) and her sister Leatha (left) with their children about 1951-52. In the front are Jane Hilgendorf and Bob Parker. Standing between the mothers are Ken Hilgendorf, Dave Parker and Sally Hilgendorf.

Susan Jeanne Parker – Death Certificate

This is the death certificate of John and Helen (Haag) Parker's second child Susan Parker. She died on 18 August 1946 in La Porte, Indiana, at the age of two years. The cause of death is listed as Paralytic Ileus (paralysis of the intestine). Other causes noted include Primary Peritonitis (an infection that develops in the membrane that forms the lining of the abdominal cavity) and peritoneum cocci septicemia (sepsis is the body's extreme and life-threatening response to an infection).

* ATTENTION ESTATE: Disclosure of the SS# is voluntary and there will be no penalty for refusal *

Local No. 238-02

INDIANA STATE DEPARTMENT OF HEALTH
CERTIFICATE OF DEATH

State No. 025186

THE RECORDS IN THIS SERIES ARE CONFIDENTIAL PER I.C 16-1-18-3

TYPE/PRINT IN PERMANENT BLACK INK

1. DECEASED - NAME (First, Middle, Last): **Helena E. Parker**
2. SEX: **Female**
3a. TIME OF DEATH: **9:15 AM**
3b. DATE OF DEATH (Mo.Day.Yr): **July 18 2002**

5a. AGE - Last Birthday (Years): **84**
5b. UNDER 1 YEAR: Months / Days
5c. UNDER 1 DAY: Hours / Minutes
6. DATE OF BIRTH (Mo.Day.Yr): **March 11 1918**
7. BIRTHPLACE (City, St or Country): **LaPorte, IN**

DECEDENT

8a. WAS DECEDENT A US VETERAN? **NO**
8b. YEAR LAST SERVED IN US. ARMED FORCES? **N/A**
9a. PLACE OF DEATH (Check Only One. See Instructions): HOSPITAL ✔ Inpatient / ER/Outpatient / DOA / OTHER: Nursing Home / Residence / Other (Specify)

9b. FACILITY NAME (If not institution, give street and number): **LaPorte Hospital**
9c. CITY, TOWN OR LOCATION OF DEATH: **La Porte**
9d. COUNTY OF DEATH: **La Porte**

10. MARITAL STATUS (Specify): **Married**
11. SURVIVING SPOUSE (If wife, give maiden name): **John Parker**
12a. DECEDENT'S USUAL OCCUPATION (Give kind of work done during most of working life. Do not use Retired): **Customer Service**
12b. KIND OF BUSINESS/INDUSTRY: **Appliance Industry**

13a. RESIDENCE - STATE: **IN**
13b. COUNTY: **La Porte**
13c. CITY, TOWN OR LOCATION: **La Porte**
13d. STREET AND NUMBER: **2414 Monroe Street**

13e. ZIP CODE: **46350**
13f. INSIDE CITY LIMITS: No / Yes ✔
13g. ON A FARM: No ✔ / Yes
14. CITIZEN OF WHAT COUNTRY? **U.S.A.**
15. WAS DECEDENT OF HISPANIC ORIGIN? No ✔ / YES (If YES specify Cuban, Mexican, Puerto Rican, Etc.)
16. RACE (American Indian, Black, White, Etc SPECIFY): **White**
17. DECEDENT'S EDUCATION (Specify only highest grade completed): Elementary/Secondary (0-12): **12** / College (1-4, 5+)

PARENTS

18. FATHER'S NAME (First, Middle, Last): **Harry A. Haag**
19. MOTHER'S NAME (First, Middle, Maiden, Surname): **Mabel Boze**

INFORMANT

20a. INFORMANT'S NAME (Type/Print): **John Parker Jr.**
20b. MAILING ADDRESS (Street number or Rural Route Number, City/Town, State, ZIP): **2414 Monroe Street LaPorte, IN 46350**
20c. RELATIONSHIP: **Husband**

DISPOSITION

21a. METHOD OF DISPOSITION: Burial ✔ / Cremation / Entombment / Removal from State / Donation / Other (Specify)
21b. DATE AND PLACE OF DISPOSITION (Name of cemetery, crematory, or other place): **July 20 2002 Pine Lake Cemetery**
21c. CITY/TOWN, STATE: **LaPorte, IN 46350**

22a. EMBALMER'S NAME: **Mark Busse**
22b. EMBALMER'S LICENSE NUMBER: **FDO88800151**
23. WAS DEATH REPORTED TO CORONER? No ✔ / Yes

24a. SIGNATURE OF FUNERAL DIRECTOR: *Mark E Essl*
24b. LICENSEE NUMBER (Or Licensee): **FDO1001104**
25. NAME, ADDRESS AND LICENSE NUMBER OF FUNERAL HOME: **Essling Funeral Home 1117 Indiana Ave LaPorte, IN 46350 FDH9994049**

CAUSE OF DEATH

26. PART I. Enter the diseases, injuries or complications that caused the death. Do not enter nonspecific terms such as cardiac or respiratory arrest, shock or heart failure. List only one cause on each line.

		Approximate interval between Onset and Death
IMMEDIATE CAUSE (Final disease or condition resulting in death)	a. *Respiratory failure*	*3 days*
DUE TO (Or as a consequence of)	b. *Adult respiratory distress syndrome*	*3 days*
Conditions, if any, which gave rise to the immediate cause, stating the underlying cause last.	c. *Fracture right hip*	*4 days*
DUE TO (Or as a consequence of)	d. *Osteoporosis*	*years*

PART II. Other significant conditions - Conditions contributing to death, but not resulting in the underlying cause given in Part I.
1) Acute deep vein thrombosis right lower extremity 2) Cerebrovascular disease old stroke

27. WAS DECEDENT PREGNANT OR 90 DAYS POSTPARTUM? (Yes or No): **NO**
28a. WAS AN AUTOPSY PERFORMED? (Yes or No): **NO**
28b. WERE AUTOPSY FINDINGS AVAILABLE PRIOR TO COMPLETION OF CAUSE OF DEATH? (Yes or No): **NO**

CERTIFIER

29a. CERTIFIER (Check only one): ✔ CERTIFYING PHYSICIAN / HEALTH OFFICER / CORONER
To the best of my knowledge, death occurred at the time, date and place, and due to the cause(s) as stated.

29b. SIGNATURE AND TITLE OF CERTIFIER: *Carol M Schobert MD*
29c. MEDICAL LICENSE NUMBER: **01029403**
29d. DATE SIGNED (Mo.Day.Yr): *July 19, 2002*

30. NAME AND ADDRESS OF PERSON WHO COMPLETED COMPLETED CAUSE OF DEATH (ITEM 26) (Type/Print): **Schobert, Carol 900 "T" St, LaPorte, IN, 46350**

HEALTH OFFICER

31. HEALTH OFFICER SIGNATURE: *John Kopis*
32. DATE FILED (Mo.Day.Yr): **JUL 19 2002**

Helen E. (Haag) Parker – Death Certificate

This is the death certificate of Helen Elizabeth (Haag) Parker. She died on 18 July 2002 in La Porte, Indiana. Note that her first name is Helena on the death certificate and in her obituary. Her birth certificate, however, shows the name as the shorter form, Helen. Her death was due to Respiratory Failure as a result of Adult Respiratory Distress Syndrome, or ARDS (sudden and serious lung failure that can occur in people who are critically ill or have major injuries).

THELMA L. HAAG (1920 – BEFORE 1930)

Thelma was born to Harry and Mabel (Boze) Haag on 16 June 1920 in Vincennes, Indiana. The family was living at 409 7th Street at this time. Unfortunately, there are no other records of Thelma. She does not appear in the next federal census for 1930, so she likely died prior to 1930. With little knowledge of Thelma in the family history, it is quite possible that she died not long after her birth.

FAMILY DESCENDANT CHARTS

The Hilgendorf-Haag family history covers only the core of both families from their known origins through to the direct line of ancestors leading to the connection of the two families. It is simply an undaunting task to develop a history for every individual of every line of the families.

If you should happen to belong to a family line that follows a different path, then by all means use this as a beginning and provide more detail for your own family. To assist anyone interested in taking up such as task, or simply to see more of the families, included is a chart of all the relatives that were located up to the time of publication.

All of the charts were produced with Legacy Family Tree genealogy software. All charts appearing in this book are separately page numbered as they were produced by the Legacy software. This is important to note as each separate family chart in the book contains its own index of names and places. This index allows you to easily locate someone within the referenced chart.

Each generation begins on a new page in the charts. Each individual is given a number in the chart. In this manner children of a generation are numbered on their parents' chart, then that number is is carried over as that individual's number for their own generation. Following their individual identification number is a designation for male (M) or female (F).

I have included as much information regarding birth, marriage and death dates as I have been able to obtain. In some instances, I may have no more than a name. Should you have more information, or should you notice an error, I am more than happy to have you contact me, and I will update my database. I will also update the book for any future printings.

Finally, just a couple of miscellaneous notes. First, place names on the charts are noted with city, county, state and country (in that order) when available. Secondly, as you get deeper into the chart, you will notice names in italics following a specific individual's name. These names are the family line from whom that individual is descended in reverse order (*parent, grandparent, great-grandparent*, etc.). The chart number of each italicized name is also noted in superscript after the name for ease of reference. All of this will become clear if you spend a little time in the charts.

Hilgendorf

Descendant Chart

Beginning with

Johann C. Hilgendorf (1824-1897)

Table of Contents

Produced by: James Patrick Barber, 630 Nancy Street, Warsaw, Indiana 46580, 574-269-3124, 574-265-7939, jim@barberfamily.org

Descendants of Johann (John) C. Hilgendorf (1824-1897)

First Generation

1. Johann (John) C. Hilgendorf was born on 26 Apr 1824 in Mecklenburg, Germany, died on 4 Mar 1897 in La Porte, La Porte Co., Indiana, USA at age 72, and was buried in St. John's Cemetery, La Porte, La Porte Co., Indiana, USA.

Johann married **Maria (Mary)** before 1848 in Germany. Maria was born on 1 Mar 1823 in Germany, died on 1 Sep 1902 in La Porte, La Porte Co., Indiana, USA at age 79, and was buried in St. John's Cemetery, La Porte, La Porte Co., Indiana, USA. Other names for Maria were Marie and Maria.

Children from this marriage were:

+ 2 F   i. **Friederike (Rika, Rickie) Hilgendorf** was born on 21 Jun 1848 in Germany, died on 30 Jan 1920 in La Porte, La Porte Co., Indiana, USA at age 71, and was buried in St. John's Cemetery, La Porte, La Porte Co., Indiana, USA.

+ 3 F   ii. **Wilhelmina (Minnie) Hilgendorf** was born on 30 Mar 1852 in Germany, died on 31 Aug 1907 in La Porte, La Porte Co., Indiana, USA at age 55, and was buried in St. John's Cemetery, La Porte, La Porte Co., Indiana, USA.

+ 4 M   iii. **Ludwig (Louis) Hilgendorf** was born on 20 Dec 1859 in La Porte, La Porte Co., Indiana, USA, died on 12 Mar 1928 in La Porte, La Porte Co., Indiana, USA at age 68, and was buried in St. John's Cemetery, La Porte, La Porte Co., Indiana, USA.

+ 5 M   iv. **John Edward Hilgendorf** was born on 20 Oct 1862 in La Porte, La Porte Co., Indiana, USA, died on 30 Sep 1942 in La Porte, La Porte Co., Indiana, USA at age 79, and was buried in Pine Lake Cemetery, La Porte, La Porte Co., Indiana, USA.

Produced by: James Patrick Barber, 630 Nancy Street, Warsaw, Indiana 46580, 574-269-3124, 574-265-7939, jim@barberfamily.org

Page 1

Descendants of Johann (John) C. Hilgendorf (1824-1897)

Second Generation (Children)

2. Friederike (Rika, Rickie) Hilgendorf *(Johann (John) C. [1])* was born on 21 Jun 1848 in Germany, died on 30 Jan 1920 in La Porte, La Porte Co., Indiana, USA at age 71, and was buried in St. John's Cemetery, La Porte, La Porte Co., Indiana, USA.

Friederike married **William (Wilhelm) L. Blankschein** on 21 Sep 1867 in La Porte, La Porte Co., Indiana, USA. William was born on 21 Apr 1845 in Germany and died on 16 Nov 1893 in La Porte, La Porte Co., Indiana, USA at age 48.

Children from this marriage were:

+ 6   F   i.   **Emma Blankschein** died in 1883 and was buried in St. John's Cemetery, La Porte, La Porte Co., Indiana, USA.

+ 7   M   ii.   **Fred L. Blankschein** was born in 1869 in La Porte, La Porte Co., Indiana, USA and died on 1 Feb 1926 in La Porte, La Porte Co., Indiana, USA at age 57.

+ 8   M   iii.   **George Blankschein** was born on 7 Aug 1878 in La Porte, La Porte Co., Indiana, USA and died on 22 Jun 1955 in La Porte, La Porte Co., Indiana, USA at age 76.

+ 9   M   iv.   **Charles (Carl) Julius Blankschein** was born on 24 Oct 1880 in La Porte, La Porte Co., Indiana, USA and died on 1 Jan 1960 in La Porte, La Porte Co., Indiana, USA at age 79.

+ 10   M   v.   **Walter Blankschein** was born on 13 Nov 1882 in La Porte, La Porte Co., Indiana, USA and died on 7 Mar 1959 in Michigan City, La Porte Co., Indiana, USA at age 76.

3. Wilhelmina (Minnie) Hilgendorf *(Johann (John) C. [1])* was born on 30 Mar 1852 in Germany, died on 31 Aug 1907 in La Porte, La Porte Co., Indiana, USA at age 55, and was buried in St. John's Cemetery, La Porte, La Porte Co., Indiana, USA.

Wilhelmina married **Theodore Martin** on 15 Mar 1880 in La Porte, La Porte Co., Indiana, USA. Other names for Theodore are Theodore Marten and Theodore Martins.

Children from this marriage were:

+ 11   F   i.   **Louisa Martin** was born about Jan 1880 in Illinois, USA.

+ 12   M   ii.   **John Martin** was born in Mar 1882 in Illinois, USA.

+ 13   M   iii.   **Paul Martin** was born in Aug 1887 in Illinois, USA.

+ 14   M   iv.   **Louis Martin** was born in Jun 1893 in Illinois, USA.

4. Ludwig (Louis) Hilgendorf *(Johann (John) C. [1])* was born on 20 Dec 1859 in La Porte, La Porte Co., Indiana, USA, died on 12 Mar 1928 in La Porte, La Porte Co., Indiana, USA at age 68, and was buried in St. John's Cemetery, La Porte, La Porte Co., Indiana, USA. Another name for Ludwig was Ludwig.

Ludwig married **Wilhelmina (Minnie) Raddatz**, daughter of **Herman Raddatz** and **Wilhelmina Stephans**, on 3 Apr 1882 in La Porte, La Porte Co., Indiana, USA. Wilhelmina was born on 14 Dec 1863 in Germany, died on 29 Aug 1942 in La Porte, La Porte Co., Indiana, USA at age 78, and was buried in St. John's Cemetery, La Porte, La Porte Co., Indiana, USA. Another name for Wilhelmina was Wilhelmina Rothets.

Children from this marriage were:

+ 15   M   i.   **Paul Herman Hilgendorf** was born on 3 Jun 1884 in La Porte, La Porte Co., Indiana, USA, died on 16 Jan 1952 in La Porte, La Porte Co., Indiana, USA at age 67, and was buried in St. John's Cemetery, La Porte, La Porte Co., Indiana, USA.

+ 16   M   ii.   **Leo Hilgendorf** was born in Aug 1887 in La Porte, La Porte Co., Indiana, USA.

+ 17   F   iii.   **Elsie Caroline Hilgendorf** was born on 21 Feb 1889 in La Porte, La Porte Co., Indiana, USA and died in Mar 1986 in La Porte, La Porte Co., Indiana, USA at age 97.

+ 18   M   iv.   **Lawrence Hilgendorf** was born on 5 Nov 1891 in La Porte, La Porte Co., Indiana, USA and died on 1 Sep 1892 in La Porte, La Porte Co., Indiana, USA.

+ 19   F   v.   **Clara Hilgendorf** was born on 7 Dec 1892 in La Porte, La Porte Co., Indiana, USA, died on 14 Dec 1918 in La Porte, La Porte Co., Indiana, USA at age 26, and was buried in St. John's Cemetery, La Porte, La Porte Co., Indiana, USA.

+ 20   M   vi.   **Alfred Hilgendorf** was born on 7 Aug 1895 in La Porte, La Porte Co., Indiana, USA and was buried on 14 May 1896 in La Porte, La Porte Co., Indiana, USA.

Produced by: James Patrick Barber, 630 Nancy Street, Warsaw, Indiana 46580, 574-269-3124, 574-265-7939, jim@barberfamily.org

Page 2

+ 21 F vii. **Ruth Hilgendorf** was born on 26 Mar 1897 in La Porte, La Porte Co., Indiana, USA, died on 1 May 1989 in Chicago, Cook Co., Illinois, USA at age 92, and was buried in Montrose Cemetery, Chicago, Cook Co., Illinois.

+ 22 M viii. **Herbert Clarence Carl Hilgendorf** was born on 21 Mar 1899 in La Porte, La Porte Co., Indiana, USA, died on 7 Aug 1980 in La Porte, La Porte Co., Indiana, USA at age 81, and was buried in Pine Lake Cemetery, La Porte, La Porte Co., Indiana, USA.

+ 23 M ix. **Herman Hilgendorf** was born on 12 Nov 1901 in La Porte, La Porte Co., Indiana, USA, died on 28 May 1964 in Logansport, Cass Co., Indiana, USA at age 62, and was buried in Pine Lake Cemetery, La Porte, La Porte Co., Indiana, USA.

+ 24 F x. **Edna Hilgendorf** was born on 6 May 1904 in La Porte, La Porte Co., Indiana, USA and died on 11 Jan 1937 in La Porte, La Porte Co., Indiana, USA at age 32.

5. John Edward Hilgendorf *(Johann (John) C.* [1]*)* was born on 20 Oct 1862 in La Porte, La Porte Co., Indiana, USA, died on 30 Sep 1942 in La Porte, La Porte Co., Indiana, USA at age 79, and was buried in Pine Lake Cemetery, La Porte, La Porte Co., Indiana, USA.

John married **Fredericka (also Rickie, Ricka) Kuch** on 29 Mar 1885 in La Porte, La Porte Co., Indiana, USA. Fredericka was born on 3 Apr 1866 in Germany, died on 2 Mar 1935 in La Porte, La Porte Co., Indiana, USA at age 68, and was buried in Pine Lake Cemetery, La Porte, La Porte Co., Indiana, USA. Another name for Fredericka was Cook Fredericka (also Rickie, Ricka).

Children from this marriage were:

+ 25 M i. **Arthur John Hilgendorf** was born on 1 Jul 1885 in La Porte, La Porte Co., Indiana, USA, died on 18 Jan 1958 in La Porte, La Porte Co., Indiana, USA at age 72, and was buried in Pine Lake Cemetery, La Porte, La Porte Co., Indiana, USA.

+ 26 M ii. **Walter Frederick Hilgendorf** was born on 19 Mar 1887 in La Porte, La Porte Co., Indiana, USA, died on 21 Feb 1951 in La Porte, La Porte Co., Indiana, USA at age 63, and was buried in Pine Lake Cemetery, La Porte, La Porte Co., Indiana, USA.

+ 27 M iii. **Edwin William John Hilgendorf** was born on 4 Oct 1893 in Milwaukee, Milwaukee Co., Wisconsin, USA, died in 1956 in La Porte, La Porte Co., Indiana, USA at age 63, and was buried in Woodlawn Cemetery, Forest Park, Cook Co., Illinois, USA.

+ 28 F iv. **Mabel Louise Hilgendorf** was born on 13 May 1897 in La Porte, La Porte Co., Indiana, USA, died on 17 Apr 1985 in La Porte, La Porte Co., Indiana, USA at age 87, and was buried in Pine Lake Cemetery, La Porte, La Porte Co., Indiana, USA.

+ 29 F v. **Nora W. Hilgendorf** was born on 28 Jun 1899 in La Porte, La Porte Co., Indiana, USA, died on 23 Jan 1992 in La Porte, La Porte Co., Indiana, USA at age 92, and was buried in Pine Lake Cemetery, La Porte, La Porte Co., Indiana, USA.

+ 30 M vi. **William A. Hilgendorf** was born on 30 Dec 1901 in La Porte, La Porte Co., Indiana, USA, died on 21 Jan 1979 in La Porte, La Porte Co., Indiana, USA at age 77, and was buried in Patton Cemetery, La Porte, La Porte Co., Indiana, USA.

+ 31 M vii. **George F. Hilgendorf** was born on 21 Dec 1904 in La Porte, La Porte Co., Indiana, USA, died on 13 Dec 1966 in South Bend, St. Joseph Co., Indiana, USA at age 61, and was buried in Pine Lake Cemetery, La Porte, La Porte Co., Indiana, USA.

+ 32 M viii. **John Martin Leiter Hilgendorf** was born on 30 Sep 1909 in La Porte, La Porte Co., Indiana, USA, died on 15 Mar 1976 in La Porte, La Porte Co., Indiana, USA at age 66, and was buried in Pine Lake Cemetery, La Porte, La Porte Co., Indiana, USA.

Produced by: James Patrick Barber, 630 Nancy Street, Warsaw, Indiana 46580, 574-269-3124, 574-265-7939, jim@barberfamily.org

Page 3

Descendants of Johann (John) C. Hilgendorf (1824-1897)

Third Generation (Grandchildren)

6. Emma Blankschein *(Friederike (Rika, Rickie) Hilgendorf [2], Johann (John) C. [1])* died in 1883 and was buried in St. John's Cemetery, La Porte, La Porte Co., Indiana, USA.

7. Fred L. Blankschein *(Friederike (Rika, Rickie) Hilgendorf [2], Johann (John) C. [1])* was born in 1869 in La Porte, La Porte Co., Indiana, USA and died on 1 Feb 1926 in La Porte, La Porte Co., Indiana, USA at age 57.

8. George Blankschein *(Friederike (Rika, Rickie) Hilgendorf [2], Johann (John) C. [1])* was born on 7 Aug 1878 in La Porte, La Porte Co., Indiana, USA and died on 22 Jun 1955 in La Porte, La Porte Co., Indiana, USA at age 76.

9. Charles (Carl) Julius Blankschein *(Friederike (Rika, Rickie) Hilgendorf [2], Johann (John) C. [1])* was born on 24 Oct 1880 in La Porte, La Porte Co., Indiana, USA and died on 1 Jan 1960 in La Porte, La Porte Co., Indiana, USA at age 79.

10. Walter Blankschein *(Friederike (Rika, Rickie) Hilgendorf [2], Johann (John) C. [1])* was born on 13 Nov 1882 in La Porte, La Porte Co., Indiana, USA and died on 7 Mar 1959 in Michigan City, La Porte Co., Indiana, USA at age 76.

11. Louisa Martin *(Wilhelmina (Minnie) Hilgendorf [3], Johann (John) C. [1])* was born about Jan 1880 in Illinois, USA.

12. John Martin *(Wilhelmina (Minnie) Hilgendorf [3], Johann (John) C. [1])* was born in Mar 1882 in Illinois, USA.

13. Paul Martin *(Wilhelmina (Minnie) Hilgendorf [3], Johann (John) C. [1])* was born in Aug 1887 in Illinois, USA.

14. Louis Martin *(Wilhelmina (Minnie) Hilgendorf [3], Johann (John) C. [1])* was born in Jun 1893 in Illinois, USA.

15. Paul Herman Hilgendorf *(Ludwig (Louis) [4], Johann (John) C. [1])* was born on 3 Jun 1884 in La Porte, La Porte Co., Indiana, USA, died on 16 Jan 1952 in La Porte, La Porte Co., Indiana, USA at age 67, and was buried in St. John's Cemetery, La Porte, La Porte Co., Indiana, USA.

> Paul married **Louise M. Miller,** daughter of **Fred Miller** and **Louise Lurige,** on 24 Jun 1909 in La Porte, La Porte Co., Indiana, USA. Louise was born in 1881, died about 1962 in La Porte, La Porte Co., Indiana, USA about age 81, and was buried in St. John's Cemetery, La Porte, La Porte Co., Indiana, USA.

> The child from this marriage was:
> + 33 F   i. **Dorothy L. Hilgendorf** was born on 3 Sep 1911 in La Porte, La Porte Co., Indiana, USA and died on 15 May 1988 in La Porte, La Porte Co., Indiana, USA at age 76.

16. Leo Hilgendorf *(Ludwig (Louis) [4], Johann (John) C. [1])* was born in Aug 1887 in La Porte, La Porte Co., Indiana, USA.

17. Elsie Caroline Hilgendorf *(Ludwig (Louis) [4], Johann (John) C. [1])* was born on 21 Feb 1889 in La Porte, La Porte Co., Indiana, USA and died in Mar 1986 in La Porte, La Porte Co., Indiana, USA at age 97.

> Elsie married **Otto Alfred Droege,** son of **Frederick Herman Droege** and **Julia A. Backhaus,** on 18 Jun 1913 in La Porte, La Porte Co., Indiana, USA. Otto was born on 9 Jul 1887 in La Porte, La Porte Co., Indiana, USA and died on 3 Sep 1963 in La Porte, La Porte Co., Indiana, USA at age 76.

18. Lawrence Hilgendorf *(Ludwig (Louis) [4], Johann (John) C. [1])* was born on 5 Nov 1891 in La Porte, La Porte Co., Indiana, USA and died on 1 Sep 1892 in La Porte, La Porte Co., Indiana, USA.

Produced by: James Patrick Barber, 630 Nancy Street, Warsaw, Indiana 46580, 574-269-3124, 574-265-7939, jim@barberfamily.org

Page 4

Descendants of Johann (John) C. Hilgendorf (1824-1897)

19. Clara Hilgendorf *(Ludwig (Louis)⁴, Johann (John) C.¹)* was born on 7 Dec 1892 in La Porte, La Porte Co., Indiana, USA, died on 14 Dec 1918 in La Porte, La Porte Co., Indiana, USA at age 26, and was buried in St. John's Cemetery, La Porte, La Porte Co., Indiana, USA.

20. Alfred Hilgendorf *(Ludwig (Louis)⁴, Johann (John) C.¹)* was born on 7 Aug 1895 in La Porte, La Porte Co., Indiana, USA and was buried on 14 May 1896 in La Porte, La Porte Co., Indiana, USA.

21. Ruth Hilgendorf *(Ludwig (Louis)⁴, Johann (John) C.¹)* was born on 26 Mar 1897 in La Porte, La Porte Co., Indiana, USA, died on 1 May 1989 in Chicago, Cook Co., Illinois, USA at age 92, and was buried in Montrose Cemetery, Chicago, Cook Co., Illinois.

Ruth married **Walter J. Meister**. Walter was born about 1903 in Illinois, USA.

Children from this marriage were:
+ 34 M   i.   **Jacque Meister** was born about 1922 in Illinois, USA.
+ 35 M   ii.   **Richard Meister** was born about 1925 in Illinois, USA.

22. Herbert Clarence Carl Hilgendorf *(Ludwig (Louis)⁴, Johann (John) C.¹)* was born on 21 Mar 1899 in La Porte, La Porte Co., Indiana, USA, died on 7 Aug 1980 in La Porte, La Porte Co., Indiana, USA at age 81, and was buried in Pine Lake Cemetery, La Porte, La Porte Co., Indiana, USA.

Herbert married **Laura H. Schmidt,** daughter of **Edward Schmidt** and **Albertina,** on 14 Dec 1934 in La Porte, La Porte Co., Indiana, USA. Laura was born on 17 Sep 1898 in La Porte, La Porte Co., Indiana, USA, died on 27 Aug 1973 in La Porte, La Porte Co., Indiana, USA at age 74, and was buried in Pine Lake Cemetery, La Porte, La Porte Co., Indiana, USA. Another name for Laura was Schmidt.

23. Herman Hilgendorf *(Ludwig (Louis)⁴, Johann (John) C.¹)* was born on 12 Nov 1901 in La Porte, La Porte Co., Indiana, USA, died on 28 May 1964 in Logansport, Cass Co., Indiana, USA at age 62, and was buried in Pine Lake Cemetery, La Porte, La Porte Co., Indiana, USA.

Herman married **Veronica Schwartz** on 11 Mar 1926. Veronica was born on 23 Nov 1903 in Valparaiso, Porter Co., Indiana, USA, died on 7 Feb 1962 in La Porte, La Porte Co., Indiana, USA at age 58, and was buried in Pine Lake Cemetery, La Porte, La Porte Co., Indiana, USA.

The child from this marriage was:
+ 36 M   i.   **Richard L. Hilgendorf** was born on 20 Nov 1926 in La Porte, La Porte Co., Indiana, USA, died on 23 Oct 1982 in La Porte, La Porte Co., Indiana, USA at age 55, and was buried in Pine Lake Cemetery, La Porte, La Porte Co., Indiana, USA.

24. Edna Hilgendorf *(Ludwig (Louis)⁴, Johann (John) C.¹)* was born on 6 May 1904 in La Porte, La Porte Co., Indiana, USA and died on 11 Jan 1937 in La Porte, La Porte Co., Indiana, USA at age 32.

Edna married **Lafayette Figg** after 1930. Lafayette was born about 1896.

The child from this marriage was:
+ 37 M   i.   **Charles Warner Figg** was born on 11 Jan 1937 in La Porte, La Porte Co., Indiana, USA and died on 12 Jan 1937 in La Porte, La Porte Co., Indiana, USA.

25. Arthur John Hilgendorf *(John Edward⁵, Johann (John) C.¹)* was born on 1 Jul 1885 in La Porte, La Porte Co., Indiana, USA, died on 18 Jan 1958 in La Porte, La Porte Co., Indiana, USA at age 72, and was buried in Pine Lake Cemetery, La Porte, La Porte Co., Indiana, USA.

Arthur married **Mary Kramer**, daughter of **Mathias Kramer** and **Katherine Berg,** on 17 Dec 1907 in La Porte, La Porte Co., Indiana, USA. Mary was born on 21 Jan 1884 in La Porte, La Porte Co., Indiana, USA, died on 6 Dec 1960 in La Porte, La Porte Co., Indiana, USA at age 76, and was buried in Pine Lake Cemetery, La Porte, La Porte Co., Indiana, USA. Another name for Mary was Marie Kramer.

Children from this marriage were:
+ 38 M   i.   **Arthur Hilgendorf Jr.** was born on 27 May 1908 in La Porte, La Porte Co., Indiana, USA and died in 1908.

Produced by: James Patrick Barber, 630 Nancy Street, Warsaw, Indiana 46580, 574-269-3124, 574-265-7939, jim@barberfamily.org

Page 5

+ 39 M   ii.   **Lawrence Arthur Hilgendorf** was born on 25 Jul 1909 in La Porte, La Porte Co., Indiana, USA, died on 21 Apr 1999 in La Porte, La Porte Co., Indiana, USA at age 89, and was buried in Pine Lake Cemetery, La Porte, La Porte Co., Indiana, USA.

+ 40 M   iii.   **Clarence John Hilgendorf** was born on 30 Oct 1910 in La Porte, La Porte Co., Indiana, USA, died on 24 Jul 1990 in Bradenton, Manatee Co., Florida, USA at age 79, and was buried in La Porte, La Porte Co., Indiana, USA.

+ 41 M   iv.   **Roy Andrew Hilgendorf** was born on 7 Oct 1912 in La Porte, La Porte Co., Indiana, USA, died on 9 Apr 1970 in La Porte, La Porte Co., Indiana, USA at age 57, and was buried in Pine Lake Cemetery, La Porte, La Porte Co., Indiana, USA.

+ 42 M   v.   **Wilbur C. Hilgendorf** was born on 21 Oct 1914 in La Porte, La Porte Co., Indiana, USA, died on 1 May 1943 in Tunisia, Africa at age 28, and was buried in North Africa American Cemetery, Carthage, Tunisia, Africa.

+ 43 M   vi.   **Raymond J. Hilgendorf** was born on 5 Jul 1916 in La Porte, La Porte Co., Indiana, USA, died on 7 Jun 1981 in La Porte, La Porte Co., Indiana, USA at age 64, and was buried in Pine Lake Cemetery, La Porte, La Porte Co., Indiana, USA.

+ 44 M   vii.   **Arthur Hilgendorf Jr.** was born on 15 Mar 1919 in La Porte, La Porte Co., Indiana, USA, died on 10 Dec 1922 in La Porte, La Porte Co., Indiana, USA at age 3, and was buried in Pine Lake Cemetery, La Porte, La Porte Co., Indiana, USA.

+ 45 F   viii.   **Marie Elizabeth Hilgendorf** was born on 1 Apr 1922 in La Porte, La Porte Co., Indiana, USA, died on 1 Apr 2009 in La Porte, La Porte Co., Indiana, USA at age 87, and was buried in Kingsbury Cemetery, Kingsbury, La Porte Co., Indiana, USA.

+ 46 F   ix.   **Doris Hilgendorf** was born on 9 Jul 1924 in La Porte, La Porte Co., Indiana, USA and died on 22 Aug 2016 in Palatine, Cook Co., Illinois, USA at age 92.

26. Walter Frederick Hilgendorf *(John Edward⁵, Johann (John) C. ¹)* was born on 19 Mar 1887 in La Porte, La Porte Co., Indiana, USA, died on 21 Feb 1951 in La Porte, La Porte Co., Indiana, USA at age 63, and was buried in Pine Lake Cemetery, La Porte, La Porte Co., Indiana, USA.

Walter married **Minnie Pusch,** daughter of **Charles Pusch** and **Fredericka D. Jacob,** on 8 Jul 1909 in La Porte, La Porte Co., Indiana, USA. Minnie was born on 30 Oct 1888 in La Porte, La Porte Co., Indiana, USA and died on 19 Feb 1912 in La Porte, La Porte Co., Indiana, USA at age 23.

Walter next married **Emma Edith Mellenthin,** daughter of **Albert F. Mellenthin** and **Emma Boettcher,** on 28 Aug 1913 in La Porte, La Porte Co., Indiana, USA. Emma was born on 24 Jul 1894 in La Porte, La Porte Co., Indiana, USA, died on 5 Jan 1991 in La Porte, La Porte Co., Indiana, USA at age 96, and was buried in Pine Lake Cemetery, La Porte, La Porte Co., Indiana, USA. Another name for Emma was Mellenthein.

Children from this marriage were:

+ 47 M   i.   **Norman W. Hilgendorf** was born on 18 Mar 1914 in La Porte, La Porte Co., Indiana, USA, died on 15 Feb 1994 in La Porte, La Porte Co., Indiana, USA at age 79, and was buried in Pine Lake Cemetery, La Porte, La Porte Co., Indiana, USA.

+ 48 F   ii.   **Mildred Emma Hilgendorf** was born on 30 Sep 1915 in La Porte, La Porte Co., Indiana, USA, died on 12 Jul 2012 in La Porte, La Porte Co., Indiana, USA at age 96, and was buried in Pine Lake Cemetery, La Porte, La Porte Co., Indiana, USA.

+ 49 M   iii.   **Donald John Hilgendorf** was born on 19 Jul 1917 in La Porte, La Porte Co., Indiana, USA, died on 30 Oct 1999 in La Porte, La Porte Co., Indiana, USA at age 82, and was buried in Pine Lake Cemetery, La Porte, La Porte Co., Indiana, USA.

27. Edwin William John Hilgendorf *(John Edward⁵, Johann (John) C. ¹)* was born on 4 Oct 1893 in Milwaukee, Milwaukee Co., Wisconsin, USA, died in 1956 in La Porte, La Porte Co., Indiana, USA at age 63, and was buried in Woodlawn Cemetery, Forest Park, Cook Co., Illinois, USA.

Edwin married **Ella H. Krebs** about 1929. Ella was born on 13 May 1894 in Illinois, USA, died on 1 Jan 1973 in Cicero, Cook Co., Illinois, USA at age 78, and was buried in Woodlawn Cemetery, Forest Park, Cook Co., Illinois, USA.

28. Mabel Louise Hilgendorf *(John Edward⁵, Johann (John) C. ¹)* was born on 13 May 1897 in

Produced by: James Patrick Barber, 630 Nancy Street, Warsaw, Indiana 46580, 574-269-3124, 574-265-7939, jim@barberfamily.org

Page 6

La Porte, La Porte Co., Indiana, USA, died on 17 Apr 1985 in La Porte, La Porte Co., Indiana, USA at age 87, and was buried in Pine Lake Cemetery, La Porte, La Porte Co., Indiana, USA.

Noted events in her life were:
• Never Married.

29. Nora W. Hilgendorf *(John Edward [5], Johann (John) C. [1])* was born on 28 Jun 1899 in La Porte, La Porte Co., Indiana, USA, died on 23 Jan 1992 in La Porte, La Porte Co., Indiana, USA at age 92, and was buried in Pine Lake Cemetery, La Porte, La Porte Co., Indiana, USA.

Nora married **John Thomas Lingard** on 26 Nov 1927 in La Porte, La Porte Co., Indiana, USA. John was born on 28 Feb 1891 in Wills Township, La Porte Co., Indiana, USA, died on 22 Mar 1974 in La Porte, La Porte Co., Indiana, USA at age 83, and was buried in Pine Lake Cemetery, La Porte, La Porte Co., Indiana, USA.

30. William A. Hilgendorf *(John Edward [5], Johann (John) C. [1])* was born on 30 Dec 1901 in La Porte, La Porte Co., Indiana, USA, died on 21 Jan 1979 in La Porte, La Porte Co., Indiana, USA at age 77, and was buried in Patton Cemetery, La Porte, La Porte Co., Indiana, USA.

William married **Louise E. Pflugshaupt,** daughter of **Gottlieb Pflugshaupt** and **Theresa,** on 23 Feb 1924 in Knox, Starke County, Indiana, USA. Louise was born on 24 Feb 1901 in Michigan, USA, died on 30 Jun 1986 in La Porte, La Porte Co., Indiana, USA at age 85, and was buried in Patton Cemetery, La Porte, La Porte Co., Indiana, USA.

Children from this marriage were:
+ 50 F   i.   **Elaine Ruth Hilgendorf** was born on 28 Jan 1925 in La Porte, La Porte Co., Indiana, USA.
+ 51 F   ii.   **Viola June Hilgendorf** was born on 24 Nov 1928 in La Porte, La Porte Co., Indiana, USA and died on 25 Aug 2016 in La Porte, La Porte Co., Indiana, USA at age 87.
+ 52 M   iii.   **Ronald William Hilgendorf** was born on 25 Sep 1939 in La Porte, La Porte Co., Indiana, USA.

31. George F. Hilgendorf *(John Edward [5], Johann (John) C. [1])* was born on 21 Dec 1904 in La Porte, La Porte Co., Indiana, USA, died on 13 Dec 1966 in South Bend, St. Joseph Co., Indiana, USA at age 61, and was buried in Pine Lake Cemetery, La Porte, La Porte Co., Indiana, USA.

George married **Katherine Lucille Lindborg** about 1942-1945. Katherine was born on 17 Oct 1905 in La Porte, La Porte Co., Indiana, USA, died on 20 Jan 1993 in La Porte, La Porte Co., Indiana, USA at age 87, and was buried in Pine Lake Cemetery, La Porte, La Porte Co., Indiana, USA.

32. John Martin Leiter Hilgendorf *(John Edward [5], Johann (John) C. [1])* was born on 30 Sep 1909 in La Porte, La Porte Co., Indiana, USA, died on 15 Mar 1976 in La Porte, La Porte Co., Indiana, USA at age 66, and was buried in Pine Lake Cemetery, La Porte, La Porte Co., Indiana, USA.

John married **Ruth Ervin** on 23 Jun 1934. Ruth was born on 19 Jun 1908 in Fountain Green, Hancock Co., Illinois, USA, died on 18 Dec 2000 in La Porte, La Porte Co., Indiana, USA at age 92, and was buried in Pine Lake Cemetery, La Porte, La Porte Co., Indiana, USA.

Produced by: James Patrick Barber, 630 Nancy Street, Warsaw, Indiana 46580, 574-269-3124, 574-265-7939, jim@barberfamily.org

Page 7

Fourth Generation (Great-Grandchildren)

33. Dorothy L. Hilgendorf *(Paul Herman [15], Ludwig (Louis) [4], Johann (John) C. [1])* was born on 3 Sep 1911 in La Porte, La Porte Co., Indiana, USA and died on 15 May 1988 in La Porte, La Porte Co., Indiana, USA at age 76.

Dorothy married **Dorsha**.

34. Jacque Meister *(Ruth Hilgendorf [21], Ludwig (Louis) [4], Johann (John) C. [1])* was born about 1922 in Illinois, USA.

35. Richard Meister *(Ruth Hilgendorf [21], Ludwig (Louis) [4], Johann (John) C. [1])* was born about 1925 in Illinois, USA.

36. Richard L. Hilgendorf *(Herman [23], Ludwig (Louis) [4], Johann (John) C. [1])* was born on 20 Nov 1926 in La Porte, La Porte Co., Indiana, USA, died on 23 Oct 1982 in La Porte, La Porte Co., Indiana, USA at age 55, and was buried in Pine Lake Cemetery, La Porte, La Porte Co., Indiana, USA.

37. Charles Warner Figg *(Edna Hilgendorf [24], Ludwig (Louis) [4], Johann (John) C. [1])* was born on 11 Jan 1937 in La Porte, La Porte Co., Indiana, USA and died on 12 Jan 1937 in La Porte, La Porte Co., Indiana, USA.

38. Arthur Hilgendorf Jr. *(Arthur John [25], John Edward [5], Johann (John) C. [1])* was born on 27 May 1908 in La Porte, La Porte Co., Indiana, USA and died in 1908.

39. Lawrence Arthur Hilgendorf *(Arthur John [25], John Edward [5], Johann (John) C. [1])* was born on 25 Jul 1909 in La Porte, La Porte Co., Indiana, USA, died on 21 Apr 1999 in La Porte, La Porte Co., Indiana, USA at age 89, and was buried in Pine Lake Cemetery, La Porte, La Porte Co., Indiana, USA.

Lawrence married **Anna B. Dick,** daughter of **Frederick Dick** and **Rosa Mishler,** on 16 Dec 1933 in La Porte, La Porte Co., Indiana, USA. Anna was born on 19 May 1911 in Hanna, La Porte Co., Indiana, USA, died on 26 Feb 2006 in La Porte, La Porte Co., Indiana, USA at age 94, and was buried in Pine Lake Cemetery, La Porte, La Porte Co., Indiana, USA.

40. Clarence John Hilgendorf *(Arthur John [25], John Edward [5], Johann (John) C. [1])* was born on 30 Oct 1910 in La Porte, La Porte Co., Indiana, USA, died on 24 Jul 1990 in Bradenton, Manatee Co., Florida, USA at age 79, and was buried in La Porte, La Porte Co., Indiana, USA.

Clarence married **Leatha Cecelia Haag,** daughter of **Harry Joseph Haag** and **Mabel Iselem Boze,** on 14 Sep 1940 in La Porte, La Porte Co., Indiana, USA. Leatha was born on 1 Feb 1916 in Bicknell, Knox Co., Indiana, USA, died on 3 Dec 1961 in La Porte, La Porte Co., Indiana, USA at age 45, and was buried in La Porte, La Porte Co., Indiana, USA.

Children from this marriage were:

+ 53 F   i.   **Sally Joan Hilgendorf** was born on 23 Nov 1941 in La Porte, La Porte Co., Indiana, USA.
+ 54 M   ii.   **Kenneth Richard Hilgendorf** was born on 17 Jun 1943 in La Porte, La Porte Co., Indiana, USA.
+ 55 F   iii.   **Mary Jane Hilgendorf** was born on 3 Aug 1946 in La Porte, La Porte Co., Indiana, USA.
+ 56 F   iv.   **Martha Ann Hilgendorf** was born on 6 Apr 1951 in La Porte, La Porte Co., Indiana, USA.
+ 57 M   v.   **Clarence John Hilgendorf Jr.** was born on 14 Feb 1956 in La Porte, La Porte Co., Indiana, USA.

Clarence next married **Mary E. (Allen) Watson** about 1962. Mary was born on 30 Mar 1918 in Spencer, Owen Co., Indiana, USA and died on 12 Feb 2005 in Bradenton, Manatee Co., Florida, USA at age 86.

41. Roy Andrew Hilgendorf *(Arthur John [25], John Edward [5], Johann (John) C. [1])* was born on 7 Oct 1912 in La Porte, La Porte Co., Indiana, USA, died on 9 Apr 1970 in La Porte, La Porte Co., Indiana, USA at age 57, and was buried in Pine Lake Cemetery, La Porte, La Porte Co., Indiana, USA.

Produced by: James Patrick Barber, 630 Nancy Street, Warsaw, Indiana 46580, 574-269-3124, 574-265-7939, jim@barberfamily.org

Page 8

Roy married **Dorothy Marie Edwards,** daughter of **Ora C. Edwards** and **Carrie Buffum,** on 13 Nov 1936 in La Porte, La Porte Co., Indiana, USA. Dorothy was born on 21 Mar 1914 in Indiana, USA and died on 15 Jul 1992 in Santa Monica, Los Angeles Co., California, USA at age 78.

Children from this marriage were:
+ 58 M i. **James Hilgendorf** was born on 12 Jan 1940 in La Porte, La Porte Co., Indiana, USA.
+ 59 M ii. **John Thomas Hilgendorf** was born on 25 Jun 1951 in La Porte, La Porte Co., Indiana, USA and died on 29 Apr 2014 in Waitaki, New Zealand at age 62.

42. Wilbur C. Hilgendorf *(Arthur John ²⁵, John Edward ⁵, Johann (John) C. ¹)* was born on 21 Oct 1914 in La Porte, La Porte Co., Indiana, USA, died on 1 May 1943 in Tunisia, Africa at age 28, and was buried in North Africa American Cemetery, Carthage, Tunisia, Africa.

43. Raymond J. Hilgendorf *(Arthur John ²⁵, John Edward ⁵, Johann (John) C. ¹)* was born on 5 Jul 1916 in La Porte, La Porte Co., Indiana, USA, died on 7 Jun 1981 in La Porte, La Porte Co., Indiana, USA at age 64, and was buried in Pine Lake Cemetery, La Porte, La Porte Co., Indiana, USA.

Raymond married **Jean Cormick,** daughter of **Stephen Cormick** and **Hedvig Auney,** on 21 Dec 1936 in La Porte, La Porte Co., Indiana, USA. Jean was born on 11 Jul 1915 in Gary, Lake Co., Indiana, USA and died on 29 Apr 1997 in Michigan City, La Porte Co., Indiana, USA at age 81.

The child from this marriage was:
+ 60 F i. **Christine Hilgendorf.**

Raymond next married **Helen Louise Gray**, daughter of **Duane C. Gray** and **Eva Sage**. Helen was born on 23 Dec 1912 in Garber, Garfield Co., Oklahoma, USA, died on 29 Aug 1996 in La Porte, La Porte Co., Indiana, USA at age 83, and was buried in Pine Lake Cemetery, La Porte, La Porte Co., Indiana, USA.

44. Arthur Hilgendorf Jr. *(Arthur John ²⁵, John Edward ⁵, Johann (John) C. ¹)* was born on 15 Mar 1919 in La Porte, La Porte Co., Indiana, USA, died on 10 Dec 1922 in La Porte, La Porte Co., Indiana, USA at age 3, and was buried in Pine Lake Cemetery, La Porte, La Porte Co., Indiana, USA.

45. Marie Elizabeth Hilgendorf *(Arthur John ²⁵, John Edward ⁵, Johann (John) C. ¹)* was born on 1 Apr 1922 in La Porte, La Porte Co., Indiana, USA, died on 1 Apr 2009 in La Porte, La Porte Co., Indiana, USA at age 87, and was buried in Kingsbury Cemetery, Kingsbury, La Porte Co., Indiana, USA.

Marie married **George Raymond Wineholt,** son of **Daniel H. Wineholt** and **Lottie R. Clayton,** on 13 Sep 1947 in La Porte, La Porte Co., Indiana, USA. George was born on 16 Feb 1918 in La Porte Co., Indiana, USA, died on 16 Nov 1976 in La Porte, La Porte Co., Indiana, USA at age 58, and was buried in Kingsbury Cemetery, Kingsbury, La Porte Co., Indiana, USA.

Children from this marriage were:
+ 61 M i. **Dan Wineholt.**
+ 62 M ii. **Thomas Wineholt.**

46. Doris Hilgendorf *(Arthur John ²⁵, John Edward ⁵, Johann (John) C. ¹)* was born on 9 Jul 1924 in La Porte, La Porte Co., Indiana, USA and died on 22 Aug 2016 in Palatine, Cook Co., Illinois, USA at age 92.

Doris married **Richard K. Bowman,** son of **Orville S. Bowman** and **Mary C.,** on 19 Jun 1948 in La Porte, La Porte Co., Indiana, USA. Richard was born on 23 Jul 1924 in La Porte Co., Indiana, USA and died on 30 Jun 2012 in Palatine, Cook Co., Illinois, USA at age 87.

Children from this marriage were:
+ 63 M i. **Larry Bowman.**
+ 64 M ii. **Patrick Bowman.**

47. Norman W. Hilgendorf *(Walter Frederick ²⁶, John Edward ⁵, Johann (John) C. ¹)* was born on 18 Mar 1914 in La Porte, La Porte Co., Indiana, USA, died on 15 Feb 1994 in La Porte, La Porte Co., Indiana, USA at age 79, and was buried in Pine Lake Cemetery, La Porte, La Porte Co., Indiana, USA.

Produced by: James Patrick Barber, 630 Nancy Street, Warsaw, Indiana 46580, 574-269-3124, 574-265-7939, jim@barberfamily.org

Page 9

Norman married **Alberta**. Alberta was born about 1914 in Indiana, USA.

The child from this marriage was:
+ 65 F i. **Joan K. Hilgendorf** was born about 1939 in La Porte, La Porte Co., Indiana, USA.

Norman next married **Florence Marie**. Florence was born on 11 Sep 1916, died in Oct 1986 in La Porte, La Porte Co., Indiana, USA at age 70, and was buried in Pine Lake Cemetery, La Porte, La Porte Co., Indiana, USA.

48. Mildred Emma Hilgendorf *(Walter Frederick [26], John Edward [5], Johann (John) C. [1])* was born on 30 Sep 1915 in La Porte, La Porte Co., Indiana, USA, died on 12 Jul 2012 in La Porte, La Porte Co., Indiana, USA at age 96, and was buried in Pine Lake Cemetery, La Porte, La Porte Co., Indiana, USA.

Mildred married **Elmer H. Roempagel,** son of **Fred Roempagel** and **Louise Richter,** on 29 Aug 1936 in La Porte, La Porte Co., Indiana, USA. Elmer was born on 11 Jan 1908 and died on 10 Dec 1991 in La Porte, La Porte Co., Indiana, USA at age 83.

The child from this marriage was:
+ 66 F i. **Arlene Roempagel** was born about 1937 in La Porte, La Porte Co., Indiana, USA.

49. Donald John Hilgendorf *(Walter Frederick [26], John Edward [5], Johann (John) C. [1])* was born on 19 Jul 1917 in La Porte, La Porte Co., Indiana, USA, died on 30 Oct 1999 in La Porte, La Porte Co., Indiana, USA at age 82, and was buried in Pine Lake Cemetery, La Porte, La Porte Co., Indiana, USA.

Donald married **Anna Mae Carver**. Anna was born in 1917, died in 1980 in La Porte, La Porte Co., Indiana, USA at age 63, and was buried in Pine Lake Cemetery, La Porte, La Porte Co., Indiana, USA. Another name for Anna was Anna May.

The child from this marriage was:
+ 67 M i. **Thomas Donald Hilgendorf** was born on 1 Apr 1938 in La Porte, La Porte Co., Indiana, USA.

50. Elaine Ruth Hilgendorf *(William A. [30], John Edward [5], Johann (John) C. [1])* was born on 28 Jan 1925 in La Porte, La Porte Co., Indiana, USA.

Elaine married **Lawrence John Heidel,** son of **Ludwig Heidel** and **Lytha Mueller,** on 2 Jun 1946 in La Porte, La Porte Co., Indiana, USA. Lawrence was born on 2 Jun 1922 in Rolling Prairie, La Porte Co., Indiana, USA, died on 19 Feb 2006 in La Porte, La Porte Co., Indiana, USA at age 83, and was buried in Patton Cemetery, La Porte, La Porte Co., Indiana, USA.

Children from this marriage were:
+ 68 F i. **Sharon Heidel**.
+ 69 F ii. **Janice Heidel**.
+ 70 F iii. **Elyse Heidel**.
+ 71 M iv. **Rodney Heidel**.

51. Viola June Hilgendorf *(William A. [30], John Edward [5], Johann (John) C. [1])* was born on 24 Nov 1928 in La Porte, La Porte Co., Indiana, USA and died on 25 Aug 2016 in La Porte, La Porte Co., Indiana, USA at age 87.

Viola married **Carl E. Krentz** on 6 Apr 1951 in Rockville, Bates Co., Missouri, USA. Carl was born on 20 Jan 1928 in La Porte, La Porte Co., Indiana, USA and died on 4 Jan 2013 in La Porte, La Porte Co., Indiana, USA at age 84.

Children from this marriage were:
+ 72 M i. **Mark A. Krentz**.
+ 73 M ii. **Randall L. Krentz**.
+ 74 F iii. **Karla Krentz**.
+ 75 F iv. **Melinda Krentz**.
+ 76 F v. **Jennifer Krentz**.

Produced by: James Patrick Barber, 630 Nancy Street, Warsaw, Indiana 46580, 574-269-3124, 574-265-7939, jim@barberfamily.org

Page 10

52. Ronald William Hilgendorf *(William A. [30], John Edward [5], Johann (John) C. [1])* was born on 25 Sep 1939 in La Porte, La Porte Co., Indiana, USA.

Produced by: James Patrick Barber, 630 Nancy Street, Warsaw, Indiana 46580, 574-269-3124, 574-265-7939, jim@barberfamily.org

Page 11

Fifth Generation (Great Great-Grandchildren)

53. Sally Joan Hilgendorf *(Clarence John [40], Arthur John [25], John Edward [5], Johann (John) C. [1])* was born on 23 Nov 1941 in La Porte, La Porte Co., Indiana, USA.

Sally married **Dennis Lee Biege**, son of **James Kendall Biege** and **Angelina Sobko**, on 24 Jun 1961 in La Porte, La Porte Co., Indiana, USA. Dennis was born on 13 May 1941 in La Porte, La Porte Co., Indiana, USA.

Children from this marriage were:

    77 F   i.   **Tina Marie Biege** was born on 21 May 1962 in La Porte, La Porte Co., Indiana, USA.
        Tina married **Garry T. Bowers** on 17 Aug 1985 in La Porte, La Porte Co., Indiana, USA. Garry was born on 21 Aug 1960 in La Porte, La Porte Co., Indiana, USA.

    78 F   ii.   **Julie Ann Biege** was born on 5 Aug 1965 in La Porte, La Porte Co., Indiana, USA. Julie married **Tom Muller** on 3 Oct 1987 in La Porte, La Porte Co., Indiana, USA. Tom was born on 3 May 1964 in La Porte, La Porte Co., Indiana, USA and died on 18 Sep 2013 in La Porte, La Porte Co., Indiana, USA at age 49.

54. Kenneth Richard Hilgendorf *(Clarence John [40], Arthur John [25], John Edward [5], Johann (John) C. [1])* was born on 17 Jun 1943 in La Porte, La Porte Co., Indiana, USA.

Kenneth married **Sue Sternal**. Sue was born on 5 May 1954.

Children from this marriage were:

    79 F   i.   **Michelle Sue Hilgendorf** was born on 31 Mar 1966.
        Michelle married **Kurk William Steenhoek**. Kurk was born on 16 Apr 1965.

    80 M   ii.   **Kevin Thomas Hilgendorf** was born on 3 Apr 1968.
        Kevin married **Sharon Mary Steif**. Sharon was born on 5 May 1965.

55. Mary Jane Hilgendorf *(Clarence John [40], Arthur John [25], John Edward [5], Johann (John) C. [1])* was born on 3 Aug 1946 in La Porte, La Porte Co., Indiana, USA.

Mary married **Ronald Wayne Loeffler**, son of **Walter Charles Loeffler** and **Virginia Sobko**, on 28 May 1966 in La Porte, La Porte Co., Indiana, USA. Ronald was born on 2 Sep 1943 in La Porte, La Porte Co., Indiana, USA.

Children from this marriage were:

    81 M   i.   **Jeff Loeffler** was born on 21 Oct 1968 in La Porte, La Porte Co., Indiana, USA. Jeff married **Angie** on 21 Mar 2010.

    82 M   ii.   **Ryan Loeffler** was born on 1 Nov 1971 in La Porte, La Porte Co., Indiana, USA. Ryan married **Becky Womack**, daughter of **Robert Walter Womack** and **Karen Kay Kessler**, on 11 May 1996. Becky was born on 29 Oct 1974 in La Porte, La Porte Co., Indiana, USA.

    83 M   iii.   **Corey Loeffler** was born on 2 Jun 1978 in La Porte, La Porte Co., Indiana, USA. Corey married **Paula** on 23 Nov 2014.

56. Martha Ann Hilgendorf *(Clarence John [40], Arthur John [25], John Edward [5], Johann (John) C. [1])* was born on 6 Apr 1951 in La Porte, La Porte Co., Indiana, USA.

Martha married **James Patrick Barber**, son of **Ira Barber Jr.** and **Shirley Esther Wendt**, on 27 Nov 1970 in La Porte, La Porte Co., Indiana, USA. James was born on 9 Nov 1948 in La Porte, La Porte Co., Indiana, USA.

Children from this marriage were:

    84 M   i.   **Matthew James Barber** was born on 11 Dec 1971 in Warsaw, Kosciusko Co., Indiana, USA.
        Matthew married **Estera Corlan** on 6 Oct 2002 in Brentwood, Williamson Co., Tennessee, USA. Estera was born on 18 Oct 1975 in Drobeta Turnu Severin, , , Romania.

    85 M   ii.   **Joshua Ira Barber** was born on 1 Sep 1976 in Naples, Collier Co., Florida, USA.

Produced by: James Patrick Barber, 630 Nancy Street, Warsaw, Indiana 46580, 574-269-3124, 574-265-7939, jim@barberfamily.org

Page 12

Joshua married **Vanessa Lynn Cudney** on 12 Apr 1996 in Bourbon, Marshall Co., Indiana, USA. Vanessa was born on 4 Sep 1976.

86 F   iii. **Sarah Elizabeth Barber** was born on 1 Sep 1979 in Warsaw, Kosciusko Co., Indiana, USA.

Sarah married **Michael Dale Petersen**, son of **Marvin Petersen** and **Mary Oberlin**, on 4 Aug 2000 in Warsaw, Kosciusko Co., Indiana, USA. Michael was born on 28 Jul 1975 in Indiana, USA.

57. Clarence John Hilgendorf Jr. *(Clarence John [40], Arthur John [25], John Edward [5], Johann (John) C. [1])* was born on 14 Feb 1956 in La Porte, La Porte Co., Indiana, USA.

Clarence married **Dana Marie Alderman**. Dana was born on 10 May 1958.

The child from this marriage was:
87 M   i. **Christopher John Hilgendorf** was born on 18 Feb 1979.

58. James Hilgendorf *(Roy Andrew [41], Arthur John [25], John Edward [5], Johann (John) C. [1])* was born on 12 Jan 1940 in La Porte, La Porte Co., Indiana, USA.

59. John Thomas Hilgendorf *(Roy Andrew [41], Arthur John [25], John Edward [5], Johann (John) C. [1])* was born on 25 Jun 1951 in La Porte, La Porte Co., Indiana, USA and died on 29 Apr 2014 in Waitaki, New Zealand at age 62.

John married **Ernestina Annie Ozuna**.

John next married **Rebecca I. Cooper**.

60. Christine Hilgendorf *(Raymond J. [43], Arthur John [25], John Edward [5], Johann (John) C. [1]).*

61. Dan Wineholt *(Marie Elizabeth Hilgendorf [45], Arthur John [25], John Edward [5], Johann (John) C. [1]).*

62. Thomas Wineholt *(Marie Elizabeth Hilgendorf [45], Arthur John [25], John Edward [5], Johann (John) C. [1]).*

63. Larry Bowman *(Doris Hilgendorf [46], Arthur John [25], John Edward [5], Johann (John) C. [1]).*

64. Patrick Bowman *(Doris Hilgendorf [46], Arthur John [25], John Edward [5], Johann (John) C. [1]).*

65. Joan K. Hilgendorf *(Norman W. [47], Walter Frederick [26], John Edward [5], Johann (John) C. [1])* was born about 1939 in La Porte, La Porte Co., Indiana, USA.

66. Arlene Roempagel *(Mildred Emma Hilgendorf [48], Walter Frederick [26], John Edward [5], Johann (John) C. [1])* was born about 1937 in La Porte, La Porte Co., Indiana, USA.

Arlene married **Jimmie Hacker**.

Children from this marriage were:
88 F   i. **Janet Hacker**.
             Janet married **William Lockridge**.
89 M   ii. **David Hacker**.
             David married someone.

67. Thomas Donald Hilgendorf *(Donald John [49], Walter Frederick [26], John Edward [5], Johann (John) C. [1])* was born on 1 Apr 1938 in La Porte, La Porte Co., Indiana, USA.

68. Sharon Heidel *(Elaine Ruth Hilgendorf [50], William A. [30], John Edward [5], Johann (John) C. [1]).*

69. Janice Heidel *(Elaine Ruth Hilgendorf [50], William A. [30], John Edward [5], Johann (John) C. [1]).*

Produced by: James Patrick Barber, 630 Nancy Street, Warsaw, Indiana 46580, 574-269-3124, 574-265-7939, jim@barberfamily.org

Page 13

Descendants of Johann (John) C. Hilgendorf (1824-1897)

70. **Elyse Heidel** *(Elaine Ruth Hilgendorf [50], William A. [30], John Edward [5], Johann (John) C. [1]).*

71. **Rodney Heidel** *(Elaine Ruth Hilgendorf [50], William A. [30], John Edward [5], Johann (John) C. [1]).*

72. **Mark A. Krentz** *(Viola June Hilgendorf [51], William A. [30], John Edward [5], Johann (John) C. [1]).*

73. **Randall L. Krentz** *(Viola June Hilgendorf [51], William A. [30], John Edward [5], Johann (John) C. [1]).*

74. **Karla Krentz** *(Viola June Hilgendorf [51], William A. [30], John Edward [5], Johann (John) C. [1]).*

75. **Melinda Krentz** *(Viola June Hilgendorf [51], William A. [30], John Edward [5], Johann (John) C. [1]).*

76. **Jennifer Krentz** *(Viola June Hilgendorf [51], William A. [30], John Edward [5], Johann (John) C. [1]).*

Produced by: James Patrick Barber, 630 Nancy Street, Warsaw, Indiana 46580, 574-269-3124, 574-265-7939, jim@barberfamily.org

Page 14

Name Index

Produced by: James Patrick Barber, 630 Nancy Street, Warsaw, Indiana 46580, 574-269-3124, 574-265-7939, jim@barberfamily.org

Page 15

Name Index

Produced by: James Patrick Barber, 630 Nancy Street, Warsaw, Indiana 46580, 574-269-3124, 574-265-7939, jim@barberfamily.org

Name Index

Produced by: James Patrick Barber, 630 Nancy Street, Warsaw, Indiana 46580, 574-269-3124, 574-265-7939, jim@barberfamily.org

Location Index

Produced by: James Patrick Barber, 630 Nancy Street, Warsaw, Indiana 46580, 574-269-3124, 574-265-7939, jim@barberfamily.org

Haag

Descendant Chart

Beginning with

Hans Martin Haag (1647-1690)

Table of Contents

Produced by: James Patrick Barber, 630 Nancy Street, Warsaw, Indiana 46580, 574-269-3124, 574-265-7939, jim@barberfamily.org

First Generation

1. Hans Martin Hag was born in 1647 in Durlach, Stadt Karlsruhe, Baden-Wuerttemberg, Germany and died in 1690 in Durlach, Stadt Karlsruhe, Baden-Wuerttemberg, Germany at age 43. Another name for Hans was Hans Martin Haag.

Hans married **Catherina Sauerman** in 1671. Catherina was born on 8 Aug 1651 in Durlach, Stadt Karlsruhe, Baden-Wuerttemberg, Germany and died on 28 Jul 1731 in Durlach, Stadt Karlsruhe, Baden-Wuerttemberg, Germany at age 79.

Children from this marriage were:

+ 2 F   i.   **Johanna Elisabetha Hag** was born in May 1675 in Durlach, Stadt Karlsruhe, Baden-Wuerttemberg, Germany.

+ 3 F   ii.   **Anna Maria Hag** was born in Nov 1679 in Durlach, Stadt Karlsruhe, Baden-Wuerttemberg, Germany.

+ 4 M   iii.   **Hans Martin Hag** was born in Apr 1687 in Durlach, Stadt Karlsruhe, Baden-Wuerttemberg, Germany and died in Jul 1761 in Nottingen, Enzkreis, Baden-Wuerttemberg, Germany at age 74.

+ 5 M   iv.   **Jacob Haag** was born in Feb 1689 in Auerbach, Durlach, Baden, Germany and died on 7 Feb 1762 in Auerbach, Durlach, Baden, Germany at age 73.

Produced by: James Patrick Barber, 630 Nancy Street, Warsaw, Indiana 46580, 574-269-3124, 574-265-7939, jim@barberfamily.org

Page 1

Second Generation (Children)

2. Johanna Elisabetha Hag *(Hans Martin [1])* was born in May 1675 in Durlach, Stadt Karlsruhe, Baden-Wuerttemberg, Germany.

3. Anna Maria Hag *(Hans Martin [1])* was born in Nov 1679 in Durlach, Stadt Karlsruhe, Baden-Wuerttemberg, Germany.

4. Hans Martin Hag *(Hans Martin [1])* was born in Apr 1687 in Durlach, Stadt Karlsruhe, Baden-Wuerttemberg, Germany and died in Jul 1761 in Nottingen, Enzkreis, Baden-Wuerttemberg, Germany at age 74.

5. Jacob Haag *(Hans Martin [1])* was born in Feb 1689 in Auerbach, Durlach, Baden, Germany and died on 7 Feb 1762 in Auerbach, Durlach, Baden, Germany at age 73.

Jacob married **Anna Maria Leonhardt**. Anna was born on 11 Jun 1700 in Heiningen, Germany and died on 7 Aug 1767 in Auerbach, Durlach, Baden, Germany at age 67.

Children from this marriage were:

+ 6 F   i.   **Maria Christina Haag** was born on 27 May 1718 in Auerbach, Karlsruhe, Baden-Wuerttemberg, Germany and died on 7 Aug 1761 in Auerbach, Karlsruhe, Baden-Wuerttemberg, Germany at age 43.

+ 7 F   ii. **Anna Barbara Haag** was born in Aug 1720 in Auerbach, Karlsruhe, Baden-Wuerttemberg, Germany and died on 16 Jun 1754 in Obermutchelbach, Baden-Wuerttemberg, Germany at age 33.

+ 8 F   iii. **Anna Catharina Haag** was born on 5 Mar 1722 in Auerbach, Karlsruhe, Baden-Wuerttemberg, Germany and died in 1778 at age 56.

+ 9 M   iv. **Phillip Haag** was born on 31 Mar 1726 in Untermutschelbach, Karlsruhe, Baden-Wuerttemberg, Germany and died on 17 Aug 1763 in Auerbach, Karlsruhe, Baden-Wuerttemberg, Germany at age 37.

+ 10 M v. **Hans Jacob Haag** was born on 16 Jun 1729 in Auerbach, Karlsruhe, Baden-Wuerttemberg, Germany and died in 1732 at age 3.

+ 11 M vi. **Matthias Haag** was born in Mar 1730 in Auerbach, Karlsruhe, Baden-Wuerttemberg, Germany.

+ 12 M vii. **Johannes Jacob Haag** was born on 14 Sep 1732 in Durlach, Stadt Karlsruhe, Baden-Wuerttemberg, Germany and died on 2 Jun 1797 in Durlach, Stadt Karlsruhe, Baden-Wuerttemberg, Germany at age 64.

Produced by: James Patrick Barber, 630 Nancy Street, Warsaw, Indiana 46580, 574-269-3124, 574-265-7939, jim@barberfamily.org

Page 2

Third Generation (Grandchildren)

6. Maria Christina Haag *(Jacob [5], Hans Martin [1])* was born on 27 May 1718 in Auerbach, Karlsruhe, Baden-Wuerttemberg, Germany and died on 7 Aug 1761 in Auerbach, Karlsruhe, Baden-Wuerttemberg, Germany at age 43.

7. Anna Barbara Haag *(Jacob [5], Hans Martin [1])* was born in Aug 1720 in Auerbach, Karlsruhe, Baden-Wuerttemberg, Germany and died on 16 Jun 1754 in Obermutchelbach, Baden-Wuerttemberg, Germany at age 33.

8. Anna Catharina Haag *(Jacob [5], Hans Martin [1])* was born on 5 Mar 1722 in Auerbach, Karlsruhe, Baden-Wuerttemberg, Germany and died in 1778 at age 56.

9. Phillip Haag *(Jacob [5], Hans Martin [1])* was born on 31 Mar 1726 in Untermutschelbach, Karlsruhe, Baden-Wuerttemberg, Germany and died on 17 Aug 1763 in Auerbach, Karlsruhe, Baden-Wuerttemberg, Germany at age 37.

10. Hans Jacob Haag *(Jacob [5], Hans Martin [1])* was born on 16 Jun 1729 in Auerbach, Karlsruhe, Baden-Wuerttemberg, Germany and died in 1732 at age 3.

11. Matthias Haag *(Jacob [5], Hans Martin [1])* was born in Mar 1730 in Auerbach, Karlsruhe, Baden-Wuerttemberg, Germany.

12. Johannes Jacob Haag *(Jacob [5], Hans Martin [1])* was born on 14 Sep 1732 in Durlach, Stadt Karlsruhe, Baden-Wuerttemberg, Germany and died on 2 Jun 1797 in Durlach, Stadt Karlsruhe, Baden-Wuerttemberg, Germany at age 64.

Johannes married someone.

His children were:

+ 13 F   i. **Catharina Haag** was born on 14 Aug 1757 in Auerbach, Karlsruhe, Baden-Wuerttemberg, Germany.

+ 14 M   ii. **Friederich Haag** was born on 14 Sep 1760 in Auerbach, Karlsruhe, Baden-Wuerttemberg, Germany and died on 29 Oct 1760 in Auerbach, Karlsruhe, Baden-Wuerttemberg, Germany.

+ 15 F   iii. **Christina Haag** was born on 2 Mar 1762 in Auerbach, Karlsruhe, Baden-Wuerttemberg, Germany and died on 13 May 1828 at age 66.

+ 16 M   iv. **Johann Jacob Haag** was born on 8 Mar 1765 in Auerbach, Karlsruhe, Baden-Wuerttemberg, Germany and died on 23 Jun 1765 in Auerbach, Karlsruhe, Baden-Wuerttemberg, Germany.

+ 17 M   v. **Johann Jacob Frederick Haag** was born on 20 Nov 1766 in Auerbach, Karlsruhe, Baden-Wuerttemberg, Germany and died on 6 Jul 1839 in Walsheim, Saarpfalz-Kreis, Saarland, Germany at age 72.

+ 18 M   vi. **Phillip Haag** was born on 13 Oct 1769 in Auerbach, Karlsruhe, Baden-Wuerttemberg, Germany and died in 1770 at age 1.

+ 19 M   vii. **Johann Martin Haag** was born on 2 Nov 1771 in Auerbach, Karlsruhe, Baden-Wuerttemberg, Germany and died on 20 Feb 1772 in Auerbach, Karlsruhe, Baden-Wuerttemberg, Germany.

+ 20 M   viii. **Michael Haag** was born on 27 Jan 1774 in Unter Auerbach, Baden, Germany and died in 1839 in Unter Auerbach, Baden, Germany at age 65.

+ 21 M   ix. **Phillip Haag** was born on 22 Mar 1780 in Auerbach, Karlsruhe, Baden-Wuerttemberg, Germany and died on 15 May 1846 in Auerbach, Karlsruhe, Baden-Wuerttemberg, Germany at age 66.

Produced by: James Patrick Barber, 630 Nancy Street, Warsaw, Indiana 46580, 574-269-3124, 574-265-7939, jim@barberfamily.org

Page 3

Fourth Generation (Great-Grandchildren)

13. Catharina Haag *(Johannes Jacob [12], Jacob [5], Hans Martin [1])* was born on 14 Aug 1757 in Auerbach, Karlsruhe, Baden-Wuerttemberg, Germany.

14. Friederich Haag *(Johannes Jacob [12], Jacob [5], Hans Martin [1])* was born on 14 Sep 1760 in Auerbach, Karlsruhe, Baden-Wuerttemberg, Germany and died on 29 Oct 1760 in Auerbach, Karlsruhe, Baden-Wuerttemberg, Germany.

15. Christina Haag *(Johannes Jacob [12], Jacob [5], Hans Martin [1])* was born on 2 Mar 1762 in Auerbach, Karlsruhe, Baden-Wuerttemberg, Germany and died on 13 May 1828 at age 66.

16. Johann Jacob Haag *(Johannes Jacob [12], Jacob [5], Hans Martin [1])* was born on 8 Mar 1765 in Auerbach, Karlsruhe, Baden-Wuerttemberg, Germany and died on 23 Jun 1765 in Auerbach, Karlsruhe, Baden-Wuerttemberg, Germany.

17. Johann Jacob Frederick Haag *(Johannes Jacob [12], Jacob [5], Hans Martin [1])* was born on 20 Nov 1766 in Auerbach, Karlsruhe, Baden-Wuerttemberg, Germany and died on 6 Jul 1839 in Walsheim, Saarpfalz-Kreis, Saarland, Germany at age 72.

> Johann married **Elizabeth Kramer** on 17 Oct 1797 in Walsheim, Saarpfalz-Kreis, Saarland, Germany. Elizabeth was born on 13 Nov 1780 in Walsheim, Saar-Pfatz Kreis, Saarland, Germany and died on 9 Dec 1837 in Walsheim, Saar-Pfatz Kreis, Saarland, Germany at age 57.
>
> Children from this marriage were:
>
> + 22 M   i.   **Nikolaus Haag** was born in Walsheim, Saarpfalz-Kreis, Saarland, Germany.
> + 23 M   ii.   **Johann Peter Haag** was born in Walsheim, Saarpfalz-Kreis, Saarland, Germany and died on 20 Nov 1834 in Walsheim, Saarpfalz-Kreis, Saarland, Germany.
> + 24 M   iii.   **Johannes Daniel Haag** was born on 10 Dec 1806 in Reinheim, Saar-Pfatz Kreis, Saarland, Germany and died in 1851 in Wittersheim, Saarpfalz-Kreis, Saarland, Germany at age 45.
> + 25 M   iv.   **Michael Haag** was born on 6 Mar 1813 in Walsheim, Saarland, Germany, died on 8 May 1890 in Terre Haute, Vigo Co., Indiana, USA at age 77, and was buried in St. Joseph Cemetery, Terre Haute, Vigo Co., Indiana, USA.
> + 26 F   v.   **Maria Anna Haag** was born on 9 Jun 1815 in Zweibrucken, Germany, died on 8 Oct 1876 in New Orleans, Orleans Parish, Louisiana, USA at age 61, and was buried in Lafayette Cemetery No. 1, New Orleans, Orleans Parish, Louisiana, USA.

18. Phillip Haag *(Johannes Jacob [12], Jacob [5], Hans Martin [1])* was born on 13 Oct 1769 in Auerbach, Karlsruhe, Baden-Wuerttemberg, Germany and died in 1770 at age 1.

19. Johann Martin Haag *(Johannes Jacob [12], Jacob [5], Hans Martin [1])* was born on 2 Nov 1771 in Auerbach, Karlsruhe, Baden-Wuerttemberg, Germany and died on 20 Feb 1772 in Auerbach, Karlsruhe, Baden-Wuerttemberg, Germany.

20. Michael Haag *(Johannes Jacob [12], Jacob [5], Hans Martin [1])* was born on 27 Jan 1774 in Unter Auerbach, Baden, Germany and died in 1839 in Unter Auerbach, Baden, Germany at age 65.

21. Phillip Haag *(Johannes Jacob [12], Jacob [5], Hans Martin [1])* was born on 22 Mar 1780 in Auerbach, Karlsruhe, Baden-Wuerttemberg, Germany and died on 15 May 1846 in Auerbach, Karlsruhe, Baden-Wuerttemberg, Germany at age 66.

Produced by: James Patrick Barber, 630 Nancy Street, Warsaw, Indiana 46580, 574-269-3124, 574-265-7939, jim@barberfamily.org

Page 4

Fifth Generation (Great Great-Grandchildren)

22. Nikolaus Haag *(Johann Jacob Frederick [17], Johannes Jacob [12], Jacob [5], Hans Martin [1])* was born in Walsheim, Saarpfalz-Kreis, Saarland, Germany.

23. Johann Peter Haag *(Johann Jacob Frederick [17], Johannes Jacob [12], Jacob [5], Hans Martin [1])* was born in Walsheim, Saarpfalz-Kreis, Saarland, Germany and died on 20 Nov 1834 in Walsheim, Saarpfalz-Kreis, Saarland, Germany.

24. Johannes Daniel Haag *(Johann Jacob Frederick [17], Johannes Jacob [12], Jacob [5], Hans Martin [1])* was born on 10 Dec 1806 in Reinheim, Saar-Pfatz Kreis, Saarland, Germany and died in 1851 in Wittersheim, Saarpfalz-Kreis, Saarland, Germany at age 45.

25. Michael Haag *(Johann Jacob Frederick [17], Johannes Jacob [12], Jacob [5], Hans Martin [1])* was born on 6 Mar 1813 in Walsheim, Saarland, Germany, died on 8 May 1890 in Terre Haute, Vigo Co., Indiana, USA at age 77, and was buried in St. Joseph Cemetery, Terre Haute, Vigo Co., Indiana, USA.

Michael married **Juliana Guthneck** on 12 May 1841 in Jasper Co., Illinois, USA. Juliana was born in 1816 in Alsace, France, died on 18 Apr 1868 in Terre Haute, Vigo Co., Indiana, USA at age 52, and was buried in St. Joseph Cemetery, Terre Haute, Vigo Co., Indiana, USA. Another name for Juliana was Juliana Guthnick.

Children from this marriage were:

+ 27 M   i.   **Louis August Haag** was born on 29 Aug 1842 in Madison, Jefferson Co., Indiana, USA, died on 27 Jan 1922 in Cannelburg, Daviess Co., Indiana, USA at age 79, and was buried in St. Peter's Cemetery, Montgomery, Daviess Co., Indiana, USA.

+ 28 M   ii.   **John Haag** was born on 16 Oct 1845 in Hinds Co., Mississippi, USA, died on 23 Jul 1893 in Paducah, McCracken Co., Kentucky, USA at age 47, and was buried in Mount Carmel Cemetery, Paducah, McCracken Co., Kentucky, USA.

+ 29 M   iii.   **George Haag** was born in 1847 in Hinds Co., Mississippi, USA and died before 1860.

+ 30 F   iv.   **Catherine Haag** was born in 1849 in Hinds Co., Mississippi, USA, died on 30 May 1874 in Sugar Creek Township, Vigo Co., Indiana, USA at age 25, and was buried in St. Joseph Cemetery, Terre Haute, Vigo Co., Indiana, USA.

+ 31 M   v.   **Hubert Charles Haag** was born on 16 Jul 1851 in West Terre Haute, Vigo Co., Indiana, USA, died on 28 May 1919 in Oak Grove Mine, Daviess Co., Indiana, USA at age 67, and was buried in St. Peter's Cemetery, Montgomery, Daviess Co., Indiana, USA.

Michael next married **Mary Magdalene Balzar** on 20 Oct 1868 in Vigo Co., Indiana, USA. Mary was born in May 1821 in Alsace, France, died on 10 Dec 1903 in Indianapolis, Marion Co., Indiana, USA at age 82, and was buried in St. Joseph Cemetery, Terre Haute, Vigo Co., Indiana, USA. Another name for Mary was Mary Magdalene Smith (from first marriage).

26. Maria Anna Haag *(Johann Jacob Frederick [17], Johannes Jacob [12], Jacob [5], Hans Martin [1])* was born on 9 Jun 1815 in Zweibrucken, Germany, died on 8 Oct 1876 in New Orleans, Orleans Parish, Louisiana, USA at age 61, and was buried in Lafayette Cemetery No. 1, New Orleans, Orleans Parish, Louisiana, USA.

Maria married **Charles Lauer**. Charles was born on 24 Jun 1817 in Hasslach, Ortenaukreis, Baden-Wuerttemberg, Germany, died on 13 Dec 1874 in New Orleans, Orleans Parish, Louisiana, USA at age 57, and was buried in Lafayette Cemetery No. 1, New Orleans, Orleans Parish, Louisiana, USA.

Children from this marriage were:

+ 32 F   i.   **Louisa Lauer** was born in 1844 and died in 1930 at age 86.

+ 33 M   ii.   **Charles Lauer Jr.** was born on 28 Dec 1845 in Louisiana, USA and died on 17 Sep 1874 at age 28.

+ 34 M   iii.   **Gustav Lauer** was born about 1851 in Louisiana, USA.

+ 35 F   iv.   **Therese Lauer** was born on 3 Oct 1852 in Louisiana, USA and died on 15 Jan 1887 at age 34.

Produced by: James Patrick Barber, 630 Nancy Street, Warsaw, Indiana 46580, 574-269-3124, 574-265-7939, jim@barberfamily.org

Page 5

+ 36 F v. **Henrietta Lauer** was born about 1856 in Louisiana, USA.

Produced by: James Patrick Barber, 630 Nancy Street, Warsaw, Indiana 46580, 574-269-3124, 574-265-7939, jim@barberfamily.org

Page 6

Sixth Generation (3rd Great-Grandchildren)

27. Louis August Haag *(Michael [25], Johann Jacob Frederick [17], Johannes Jacob [12], Jacob [5], Hans Martin [1])* was born on 29 Aug 1842 in Madison, Jefferson Co., Indiana, USA, died on 27 Jan 1922 in Cannelburg, Daviess Co., Indiana, USA at age 79, and was buried in St. Peter's Cemetery, Montgomery, Daviess Co., Indiana, USA. Another name for Louis was Lewis Haag.

Louis married **Elizabeth Shirley**. Elizabeth was born in 1847 in Sumner, Lawrence Co., Illinois, USA, died in 1924 in Cannelburg, Daviess Co., Indiana, USA at age 77, and was buried in St. Peter's Cemetery, Montgomery, Daviess Co., Indiana, USA.

Children from this marriage were:

+ 37 M   i.   **Joseph Haag** was born about 1869 in Indiana, USA.
+ 38 M   ii.   **John Haag** was born about 1872 in Indiana, USA, died on 22 Jun 1936 in Terre Haute, Vigo Co., Indiana, USA about age 64, and was buried in Montgomery, Daviess Co., Indiana, USA.
+ 39 F   iii.   **Mary E. Haag** was born about 1876 in Indiana, USA.
+ 40 M   iv.   **William H. Haag** was born about 1879 in Indiana, USA.
+ 41 F   v.   **Ola V. Haag** was born in 1881 in Indiana, USA.
+ 42 F   vi.   **Anna Haag** was born in 1882 in Indiana, USA.

28. John Haag *(Michael [25], Johann Jacob Frederick [17], Johannes Jacob [12], Jacob [5], Hans Martin [1])* was born on 16 Oct 1845 in Hinds Co., Mississippi, USA, died on 23 Jul 1893 in Paducah, McCracken Co., Kentucky, USA at age 47, and was buried in Mount Carmel Cemetery, Paducah, McCracken Co., Kentucky, USA.

John married **Elizabeth Forbeck** on 12 Sep 1866 in Marshall, Clark Co., Illinois, USA. Elizabeth was born on 17 Feb 1847 in Kuttawa, Lyon Co., Kentucky, USA, died on 18 Jun 1923 in Paducah, McCracken Co., Kentucky, USA at age 76, and was buried in Mount Carmel Cemetery, Paducah, McCracken Co., Kentucky, USA.

Children from this marriage were:

+ 43 F   i.   **Mary Haag** was born in Sep 1870 in Illinois, USA.
+ 44 F   ii.   **Josephine Haag** was born in Nov 1873 in Illinois, USA.
+ 45 F   iii.   **Emma Haag** was born on 30 Apr 1876 in Illinois, USA and died on 2 Feb 1950 in Mount Carmel Cemetery, Paducah, McCracken Co., Kentucky, USA at age 73.
+ 46 F   iv.   **Catherine Haag** was born in Jan 1880 in Kentucky, USA and died on 5 Nov 1964 in Fort Worth, Tarrant Co., Texas, USA at age 84.
+ 47 M   v.   **Leo Vincent Haag** was born on 1 Feb 1886 in Paducah, McCracken Co., Kentucky, USA and died on 12 Sep 1941 in Paducah, McCracken Co., Kentucky, USA at age 55.

29. George Haag *(Michael [25], Johann Jacob Frederick [17], Johannes Jacob [12], Jacob [5], Hans Martin [1])* was born in 1847 in Hinds Co., Mississippi, USA and died before 1860.

Noted events in his life were:

• Death: George appears in both the federal census and the Mississippi states census at age 3 in 1850. He does not, however, appear in the next federal census in 1860 when he would have been age 13 and likely still at home. He does not appear in any subsequent records with the family, and no other records were located for him.

30. Catherine Haag *(Michael [25], Johann Jacob Frederick [17], Johannes Jacob [12], Jacob [5], Hans Martin [1])* was born in 1849 in Hinds Co., Mississippi, USA, died on 30 May 1874 in Sugar Creek Township, Vigo Co., Indiana, USA at age 25, and was buried in St. Joseph Cemetery, Terre Haute, Vigo Co., Indiana, USA. Another name for Catherine was Elizabeth Catherine Haag.

Catherine married someone.

Produced by: James Patrick Barber, 630 Nancy Street, Warsaw, Indiana 46580, 574-269-3124, 574-265-7939, jim@barberfamily.org

Page 7

Her child was:

+ 48 U   i.   --?-- was born on 11 May 1874 in Sugar Creek Township, Vigo Co., Indiana, USA, died on 11 May 1874 in Sugar Creek Township, Vigo Co., Indiana, USA, and was buried in Woodlawn Cemetery, Terre Haute, Vigo Co., Indiana, USA.

31. Hubert Charles Haag *(Michael [25], Johann Jacob Frederick [17], Johannes Jacob [12], Jacob [5], Hans Martin [1])* was born on 16 Jul 1851 in West Terre Haute, Vigo Co., Indiana, USA, died on 28 May 1919 in Oak Grove Mine, Daviess Co., Indiana, USA at age 67, and was buried in St. Peter's Cemetery, Montgomery, Daviess Co., Indiana, USA.

Hubert married **Mariah J. Satterfield** on 26 Aug 1870 in Daviess Co., Indiana, USA. Mariah was born on 2 Jan 1851 in Indiana, USA, died on 15 Aug 1880 in Cannelburg, Daviess Co., Indiana, USA at age 29, and was buried in St. Peter's Cemetery, Montgomery, Daviess Co., Indiana, USA.

Children from this marriage were:

+ 49 F   i.   **Julia A. Haag** was born about 1870 in Indiana, USA.

+ 50 M   ii.   **John Edward Haag** was born in 1872-1874 in Indiana, USA, died on 15 Sep 1956 in Montgomery, Daviess Co., Indiana, USA at age 84, and was buried in St. Peter's Cemetery, Montgomery, Daviess Co., Indiana, USA.

+ 51 M   iii.   **George Francis Haag** was born on 2 Feb 1875 in Vigo Co., Indiana, USA, died on 22 Jun 1943 in Linton, Greene Co., Indiana, USA at age 68, and was buried in Fairview Cemetery, Linton, Greene Co., Indiana, USA.

+ 52 F   iv.   **Nancy E. Haag** was born on 1 Mar 1878 in Indiana, USA and died on 18 Mar 1879 in Cannelburg, Daviess Co., Indiana, USA at age 1.

+ 53 M   v.   **Charles Hubert Haag** was born on 14 Apr 1880 in Daviess Co., Indiana, USA, died in Aug 1963 at age 83, and was buried in St. John's Cemetery, Washington, Daviess Co., Indiana, USA.

Hubert next married **Mary H. Shirley** on 12 Jan 1881 in Daviess Co., Indiana, USA. Mary was born on 3 Sep 1861 in Jasper Co., Illinois, USA and died on 14 Mar 1930 in Washington, Daviess Co., Indiana, USA at age 68.

Children from this marriage were:

+ 54 M   i.   **James Albert Haag** was born in 1881 and died in 1898 at age 17.

+ 55 M   ii.   **Oscar Eugene Haag** was born in 1883 and died in 1947 at age 64.

+ 56 F   iii.   **Alodia F. Haag** was born in Dec 1886 and died in 1929 at age 43.

+ 57 M   iv.   **Terrence Vincent Haag** was born in Jan 1889 and died in 1967 at age 78.

+ 58 M   v.   **Herman L. Haag** was born in Apr 1891 and died in 1956 at age 65.

+ 59 M   vi.   **Kevin Michael Haag** was born in Aug 1894 and died in 1917 at age 23.

+ 60 M   vii.   **Ralph J. Haag** was born in Mar 1897 and died in 1935 at age 38.

+ 61 F   viii.   **Mary Rosa Haag** was born in 1899 and died in 1903 at age 4.

+ 62 F   ix.   **Dolah Marie Haag** was born on 5 Dec 1903 and died in 1986 at age 83.

32. Louisa Lauer *(Maria Anna Haag [26], Johann Jacob Frederick [17], Johannes Jacob [12], Jacob [5], Hans Martin [1])* was born in 1844 and died in 1930 at age 86.

33. Charles Lauer Jr. *(Maria Anna Haag [26], Johann Jacob Frederick [17], Johannes Jacob [12], Jacob [5], Hans Martin [1])* was born on 28 Dec 1845 in Louisiana, USA and died on 17 Sep 1874 at age 28.

34. Gustav Lauer *(Maria Anna Haag [26], Johann Jacob Frederick [17], Johannes Jacob [12], Jacob [5], Hans Martin [1])* was born about 1851 in Louisiana, USA.

35. Therese Lauer *(Maria Anna Haag [26], Johann Jacob Frederick [17], Johannes Jacob [12], Jacob [5], Hans Martin [1])* was born on 3 Oct 1852 in Louisiana, USA and died on 15 Jan 1887 at age 34.

36. Henrietta Lauer *(Maria Anna Haag [26], Johann Jacob Frederick [17], Johannes Jacob [12], Jacob [5], Hans Martin [1])* was born about 1856 in Louisiana, USA.

Produced by: James Patrick Barber, 630 Nancy Street, Warsaw, Indiana 46580, 574-269-3124, 574-265-7939, jim@barberfamily.org

Page 8

Seventh Generation (4th Great-Grandchildren)

37. Joseph Haag *(Louis August²⁷, Michael²⁵, Johann Jacob Frederick¹⁷, Johannes Jacob¹², Jacob⁵, Hans Martin¹)* was born about 1869 in Indiana, USA.

38. John Haag *(Louis August²⁷, Michael²⁵, Johann Jacob Frederick¹⁷, Johannes Jacob¹², Jacob⁵, Hans Martin¹)* was born about 1872 in Indiana, USA, died on 22 Jun 1936 in Terre Haute, Vigo Co., Indiana, USA about age 64, and was buried in Montgomery, Daviess Co., Indiana, USA.

39. Mary E. Haag *(Louis August²⁷, Michael²⁵, Johann Jacob Frederick¹⁷, Johannes Jacob¹², Jacob⁵, Hans Martin¹)* was born about 1876 in Indiana, USA.

40. William H. Haag *(Louis August²⁷, Michael²⁵, Johann Jacob Frederick¹⁷, Johannes Jacob¹², Jacob⁵, Hans Martin¹)* was born about 1879 in Indiana, USA.

41. Ola V. Haag *(Louis August²⁷, Michael²⁵, Johann Jacob Frederick¹⁷, Johannes Jacob¹², Jacob⁵, Hans Martin¹)* was born in 1881 in Indiana, USA.

42. Anna Haag *(Louis August²⁷, Michael²⁵, Johann Jacob Frederick¹⁷, Johannes Jacob¹², Jacob⁵, Hans Martin¹)* was born in 1882 in Indiana, USA.

43. Mary Haag *(John²⁸, Michael²⁵, Johann Jacob Frederick¹⁷, Johannes Jacob¹², Jacob⁵, Hans Martin¹)* was born in Sep 1870 in Illinois, USA.

44. Josephine Haag *(John²⁸, Michael²⁵, Johann Jacob Frederick¹⁷, Johannes Jacob¹², Jacob⁵, Hans Martin¹)* was born in Nov 1873 in Illinois, USA.

45. Emma Haag *(John²⁸, Michael²⁵, Johann Jacob Frederick¹⁷, Johannes Jacob¹², Jacob⁵, Hans Martin¹)* was born on 30 Apr 1876 in Illinois, USA and died on 2 Feb 1950 in Mount Carmel Cemetery, Paducah, McCracken Co., Kentucky, USA at age 73.

Emma married **Bailey**.

46. Catherine Haag *(John²⁸, Michael²⁵, Johann Jacob Frederick¹⁷, Johannes Jacob¹², Jacob⁵, Hans Martin¹)* was born in Jan 1880 in Kentucky, USA and died on 5 Nov 1964 in Fort Worth, Tarrant Co., Texas, USA at age 84.

Catherine married **Charles Arthur Mills**.

47. Leo Vincent Haag *(John²⁸, Michael²⁵, Johann Jacob Frederick¹⁷, Johannes Jacob¹², Jacob⁵, Hans Martin¹)* was born on 1 Feb 1886 in Paducah, McCracken Co., Kentucky, USA and died on 12 Sep 1941 in Paducah, McCracken Co., Kentucky, USA at age 55.

48. --?-- *(Catherine Haag³⁰, Michael²⁵, Johann Jacob Frederick¹⁷, Johannes Jacob¹², Jacob⁵, Hans Martin¹)* was born on 11 May 1874 in Sugar Creek Township, Vigo Co., Indiana, USA, died on 11 May 1874 in Sugar Creek Township, Vigo Co., Indiana, USA, and was buried in Woodlawn Cemetery, Terre Haute, Vigo Co., Indiana, USA.

49. Julia A. Haag *(Hubert Charles³¹, Michael²⁵, Johann Jacob Frederick¹⁷, Johannes Jacob¹², Jacob⁵, Hans Martin¹)* was born about 1870 in Indiana, USA.

Julia married **Lawrence McGee** on 1 Jun 1886 in Daviess Co., Indiana, USA.

50. John Edward Haag *(Hubert Charles³¹, Michael²⁵, Johann Jacob Frederick¹⁷, Johannes Jacob¹², Jacob⁵, Hans Martin¹)* was born in 1872-1874 in Indiana, USA, died on 15 Sep 1956 in Montgomery, Daviess Co., Indiana, USA at age 84, and was buried in St. Peter's Cemetery, Montgomery,

Produced by: James Patrick Barber, 630 Nancy Street, Warsaw, Indiana 46580, 574-269-3124, 574-265-7939, jim@barberfamily.org

Page 9

Daviess Co., Indiana, USA.

Noted events in his life were:
• He has conflicting birth information of Jan 1872.

John married **Gertrude S. Carrico,** daughter of **Joseph Bede Carrico** and **Appolonia McAtee,** on 27 Jan 1891 in Daviess Co., Indiana, USA. Gertrude was born on 17 Feb 1872 in Indiana, USA, died on 19 Jul 1908 in Montgomery, Daviess Co., Indiana, USA at age 36, and was buried in St. Peter's Cemetery, Montgomery, Daviess Co., Indiana, USA.

Noted events in her life were:
• She has conflicting birth information of 17 Feb 1873.

Children from this marriage were:

+ 63 F i. **Cleophas F. Haag** was born in Mar 1894 in Indiana, USA and died before 1935.
+ 64 M ii. **Harry Joseph Haag** was born on 4 Sep 1895 in LaSalle, LaSalle Co. Illinois, USA, died on 1 Aug 1963 in La Porte, La Porte Co., Indiana, USA at age 67, and was buried in Pine Lake Cemetery, La Porte, La Porte Co., Indiana, USA.
+ 65 M iii. **John LeRoy Haag** was born in Mar 1900 in LaSalle, LaSalle Co. Illinois, USA, died on 29 Jul 1916 in Bicknell, Knox Co., Indiana, USA at age 16, and was buried in Mount Calvary Cemetery, Vincennes, Knox Co., Indiana, USA.
+ 66 M iv. **Michael Bernard Haag** was born on 19 Oct 1902 in Illinois, USA, died on 29 Jul 1980 in La Porte, La Porte Co., Indiana, USA at age 77, and was buried in Pine Lake Cemetery, La Porte, La Porte Co., Indiana, USA.
+ 67 M v. **Vincent Bartholomew Haag** was born on 14 Jan 1906 in La Salle, La Salle, Illinois, USA and died on 8 Mar 1970 in Sebring, Highlands Co., Florida, USA at age 64.
+ 68 F vi. **Mary Agnes Haag** was born on 27 Jun 1908 in Bicknell, Knox Co., Indiana, USA and died on 2 Aug 1908 in Bicknell, Knox Co., Indiana, USA.

John next married **Francis A. McAtee** about 1909. Francis was born on 3 Oct 1861 in Indiana, USA and died on 13 Oct 1926 in Vincennes, Knox Co., Indiana, USA at age 65. Another name for Francis was Francis A. McAtee (maiden).

Children from this marriage were:

+ 69 F i. **Mary A. Haag** was born about 1909 in Kentucky, USA.
+ 70 M ii. **Charles Haag** was born about 1922. (Relationship to Father: Adopted)
+ 71 F iii. **Margaret Haag** was born on 3 Apr 1922 in Indiana, USA and died on 1 Dec 1992 at age 70.

John next married **Jean McArthur** on 5 Aug 1927 in La Porte, La Porte Co., Indiana, USA. Jean was born on 2 Jun 1901 in Scotland, died on 27 May 1964 in Vincennes, Knox Co., Indiana, USA at age 62, and was buried in St. Peter's Cemetery, Montgomery, Daviess Co., Indiana, USA.

Children from this marriage were:

+ 72 M i. **John Robert Haag** was born on 29 Nov 1927 in La Porte, La Porte Co., Indiana, USA and died on 8 Mar 1991 at age 63.
+ 73 F ii. **Francis G. Haag** was born on 24 Sep 1929 in Indiana, USA and died on 18 Apr 1995 in Vincennes, Knox Co., Indiana, USA at age 65.
+ 74 F iii. **Mary Jean Haag** was born on 20 Nov 1930 in Ragsdale, Knox Co., Indiana, USA and died on 29 Aug 2008 in Jasper, Dubois Co., Indiana, USA at age 77.
+ 75 M iv. **James William Haag** was born on 3 Nov 1932 in Bicknell, Knox Co., Indiana, USA and died on 6 Aug 2008 in Lebanon, Warren Co., Ohio, USA at age 75.
+ 76 F v. **Martha Rose Haag** was born on 23 Sep 1934 in Bicknell, Knox Co., Indiana, USA and died on 2 Feb 1935 in Bicknell, Knox Co., Indiana, USA.
+ 77 M vi. **Thomas Adrian Haag** was born on 14 Sep 1935 in Bicknell, Knox Co., Indiana, USA and died on 7 Jun 1936 in Bicknell, Knox Co., Indiana, USA.

51. George Francis Haag *(Hubert Charles [31], Michael [25], Johann Jacob Frederick [17], Johannes Jacob [12],*

Produced by: James Patrick Barber, 630 Nancy Street, Warsaw, Indiana 46580, 574-269-3124, 574-265-7939, jim@barberfamily.org

Page 10

Jacob⁵, Hans Martin¹) was born on 2 Feb 1875 in Vigo Co., Indiana, USA, died on 22 Jun 1943 in Linton, Greene Co., Indiana, USA at age 68, and was buried in Fairview Cemetery, Linton, Greene Co., Indiana, USA.

George married **Addie L. Graves**. Addie was born on 12 Jul 1873 in Kentucky, USA, died on 27 Jun 1960 at age 86, and was buried in Fairview Cemetery, Linton, Greene Co., Indiana, USA.

Children from this marriage were:
+ 78 M i. **Leo Haag** was born in 1897 and died in 1956 at age 59.
+ 79 M ii. **Raymond Haag** was born in 1901 and died in 1956 at age 55.
+ 80 M iii. **Earl A. Haag** was born about 1906.

52. Nancy E. Haag *(Hubert Charles³¹, Michael²⁵, Johann Jacob Frederick¹⁷, Johannes Jacob¹², Jacob⁵, Hans Martin¹)* was born on 1 Mar 1878 in Indiana, USA and died on 18 Mar 1879 in Cannelburg, Daviess Co., Indiana, USA at age 1.

53. Charles Hubert Haag *(Hubert Charles³¹, Michael²⁵, Johann Jacob Frederick¹⁷, Johannes Jacob¹², Jacob⁵, Hans Martin¹)* was born on 14 Apr 1880 in Daviess Co., Indiana, USA, died in Aug 1963 at age 83, and was buried in St. John's Cemetery, Washington, Daviess Co., Indiana, USA.

Charles married **Lillie Victoria Wilson** about 1898. Lillie was born in 1882 and died in Jul 1968 at age 86.

Children from this marriage were:
+ 81 F i. **Frances Haag** was born on 28 Aug 1899 in Daviess Co., Indiana, USA and died on 8 Jan 1919 in Bicknell, Knox Co., Indiana, USA at age 19.
+ 82 F ii. **May Haag** was born in 1902.
+ 83 F iii. **Gertrude Calesta Haag** was born on 3 Mar 1905 in Linton, Greene Co., Indiana, USA and died on 11 Feb 1998 in Carmel, Hamilton Co., Indiana, USA at age 92.
+ 84 F iv. **Lucile Haag** was born on 28 Sep 1909 in Bicknell, Knox Co., Indiana, USA.
+ 85 M v. **James Alvin Haag** was born on 6 Apr 1911 in Bicknell, Knox Co., Indiana, USA, died on 16 Mar 1944 in Indianapolis, Marion Co., Indiana, USA at age 32, and was buried in St. John's Cemetery, Washington, Daviess Co., Indiana, USA.
+ 86 F vi. **Mary Haag** was born on 26 Jun 1913 in Knox Co., Indiana, USA and died on 13 Oct 1921 in Bicknell, Knox Co., Indiana, USA at age 8.
+ 87 F vii. **Loretta V. Haag** was born on 21 Jan 1915 in Bicknell, Knox Co., Indiana, USA and died on 19 Oct 1916 in Bicknell, Knox Co., Indiana, USA at age 1.
+ 88 M viii. **Joseph R. Haag** was born on 27 Oct 1920 in Knox Co., Indiana, USA, died on 17 Feb 2004 at age 83, and was buried in Calvary Cemetery, Indianapolis, Marion Co., Indiana, USA.

54. James Albert Haag *(Hubert Charles³¹, Michael²⁵, Johann Jacob Frederick¹⁷, Johannes Jacob¹², Jacob⁵, Hans Martin¹)* was born in 1881 and died in 1898 at age 17.

55. Oscar Eugene Haag *(Hubert Charles³¹, Michael²⁵, Johann Jacob Frederick¹⁷, Johannes Jacob¹², Jacob⁵, Hans Martin¹)* was born in 1883 and died in 1947 at age 64.

56. Alodia F. Haag *(Hubert Charles³¹, Michael²⁵, Johann Jacob Frederick¹⁷, Johannes Jacob¹², Jacob⁵, Hans Martin¹)* was born in Dec 1886 and died in 1929 at age 43. Another name for Alodia was Francis Alodia.

57. Terrence Vincent Haag *(Hubert Charles³¹, Michael²⁵, Johann Jacob Frederick¹⁷, Johannes Jacob¹², Jacob⁵, Hans Martin¹)* was born in Jan 1889 and died in 1967 at age 78.

58. Herman L. Haag *(Hubert Charles³¹, Michael²⁵, Johann Jacob Frederick¹⁷, Johannes Jacob¹², Jacob⁵, Hans Martin¹)* was born in Apr 1891 and died in 1956 at age 65.

59. Kevin Michael Haag *(Hubert Charles³¹, Michael²⁵, Johann Jacob Frederick¹⁷, Johannes Jacob¹², Jacob⁵, Hans Martin¹)* was born in Aug 1894 and died in 1917 at age 23.

Produced by: James Patrick Barber, 630 Nancy Street, Warsaw, Indiana 46580, 574-269-3124, 574-265-7939, jim@barberfamily.org

Page 11

60. Ralph J. Haag *(Hubert Charles [31], Michael [25], Johann Jacob Frederick [17], Johannes Jacob [12], Jacob [5], Hans Martin [1])* was born in Mar 1897 and died in 1935 at age 38.

61. Mary Rosa Haag *(Hubert Charles [31], Michael [25], Johann Jacob Frederick [17], Johannes Jacob [12], Jacob [5], Hans Martin [1])* was born in 1899 and died in 1903 at age 4.

62. Dolah Marie Haag *(Hubert Charles [31], Michael [25], Johann Jacob Frederick [17], Johannes Jacob [12], Jacob [5], Hans Martin [1])* was born on 5 Dec 1903 and died in 1986 at age 83.

Dolah married **Samuel Perry Lannan** on 24 Oct 1922 in Washington, Daviess Co., Indiana, USA.

Produced by: James Patrick Barber, 630 Nancy Street, Warsaw, Indiana 46580, 574-269-3124, 574-265-7939, jim@barberfamily.org

Page 12

Eighth Generation (5th Great-Grandchildren)

63. Cleophas F. Haag *(John Edward [50], Hubert Charles [31], Michael [25], Johann Jacob Frederick [17], Johannes Jacob [12], Jacob [5], Hans Martin [1])* was born in Mar 1894 in Indiana, USA and died before 1935.

Cleophas married **Walter Friedley Clinton**. Walter was born on 2 Oct 1889 and died on 25 Mar 1963 at age 73.

Children from this marriage were:
+ 89 F   i.   **Grace Leora Clinton** was born in 1917 and died in 2002 at age 85.
+ 90 M   ii.   **John Steven Clinton** was born in 1919 and died in 1923 at age 4.

64. Harry Joseph Haag *(John Edward [50], Hubert Charles [31], Michael [25], Johann Jacob Frederick [17], Johannes Jacob [12], Jacob [5], Hans Martin [1])* was born on 4 Sep 1895 in LaSalle, LaSalle Co. Illinois, USA, died on 1 Aug 1963 in La Porte, La Porte Co., Indiana, USA at age 67, and was buried in Pine Lake Cemetery, La Porte, La Porte Co., Indiana, USA. Another name for Harry was Joseph Harry.

Harry married **Mabel Iselem Boze**, daughter of **Charles E. Boze** and **Martha "Mattie" McCollum**, on 26 Nov 1913 in Vincennes, Knox Co., Indiana, USA. Mabel was born in May 1895 in Illinois, USA, died on 10 Jul 1969 in La Porte, La Porte Co., Indiana, USA at age 74, and was buried in St. John's Cemetery, La Porte, La Porte Co., Indiana, USA.

Children from this marriage were:
+ 91 F   i.   **Leatha Cecelia Haag** was born on 1 Feb 1916 in Bicknell, Knox Co., Indiana, USA, died on 3 Dec 1961 in La Porte, La Porte Co., Indiana, USA at age 45, and was buried in La Porte, La Porte Co., Indiana, USA.
+ 92 F   ii.   **Helen Elizabeth Haag** was born on 11 Mar 1918 in Bicknell, Knox Co., Indiana, USA, died on 18 Jul 2002 in La Porte, La Porte Co., Indiana, USA at age 84, and was buried in Pine Lake Cemetery, La Porte, La Porte Co., Indiana, USA.
+ 93 F   iii.   **Thelma L. Haag** was born on 16 Jun 1920 in Vincennes, Knox Co., Indiana, USA and died before 1930.

65. John LeRoy Haag *(John Edward [50], Hubert Charles [31], Michael [25], Johann Jacob Frederick [17], Johannes Jacob [12], Jacob [5], Hans Martin [1])* was born in Mar 1900 in LaSalle, LaSalle Co. Illinois, USA, died on 29 Jul 1916 in Bicknell, Knox Co., Indiana, USA at age 16, and was buried in Mount Calvary Cemetery, Vincennes, Knox Co., Indiana, USA.

Noted events in his life were:
• He has conflicting birth information of 15 Mar 1898. In the June 1900 Census, his age is listed as 3 months, and his birth is noted as March 1900. His death certificate, however, lists his date of birth as 15 Mar 1898.

66. Michael Bernard Haag *(John Edward [50], Hubert Charles [31], Michael [25], Johann Jacob Frederick [17], Johannes Jacob [12], Jacob [5], Hans Martin [1])* was born on 19 Oct 1902 in Illinois, USA, died on 29 Jul 1980 in La Porte, La Porte Co., Indiana, USA at age 77, and was buried in Pine Lake Cemetery, La Porte, La Porte Co., Indiana, USA. Another name for Michael was Bernard M.

Michael married **Frances G. Dueppe**, daughter of **Fredrick G. Dueppe** and **Elizabeth A.,** about 1922. Frances was born on 4 Jan 1899 in Washington, Daviess Co., Indiana, USA, died on 23 Feb 1934 in La Porte, La Porte Co., Indiana, USA at age 35, and was buried in St. Joseph's Cemetery, La Porte, La Porte Co., Indiana, USA.

Children from this marriage were:
+ 94 M   i.   **Joseph Haag** was born about 1923 in Indiana, USA.
+ 95 M   ii.   **Charles Edward Haag** was born on 3 Dec 1933 in La Porte, La Porte Co., Indiana, USA and died on 2 May 2000 in Winter Park, Orange Co., Florida, USA at age 66.

Produced by: James Patrick Barber, 630 Nancy Street, Warsaw, Indiana 46580, 574-269-3124, 574-265-7939, jim@barberfamily.org

Page 13

Michael next married **Mary Lee Goodson** on 21 Oct 1934 in La Porte, La Porte Co., Indiana, USA. Mary was born on 12 Mar 1912 in Wellsboro, La Porte Co., Indiana, USA and died on 23 Sep 1995 in La Porte, La Porte Co., Indiana, USA at age 83. Another name for Mary was Mary L. Gallo.

Children from this marriage were:
+ 96 M   i.   **Bernard M. Haag Jr.** was born on 23 Sep 1935 in La Porte, La Porte Co., Indiana, USA.
+ 97 F   ii.   **Judith A. Haag** was born about 1939 in La Porte, La Porte Co., Indiana, USA.

67. Vincent Bartholomew Haag *(John Edward [50], Hubert Charles [31], Michael [25], Johann Jacob Frederick [17], Johannes Jacob [12], Jacob [5], Hans Martin [1])* was born on 14 Jan 1906 in La Salle, La Salle, Illinois, USA and died on 8 Mar 1970 in Sebring, Highlands Co., Florida, USA at age 64.

Vincent married **Mary Louise Ueding** about 1924. Mary was born on 5 Jul 1905 in Vincennes, Knox Co., Indiana, USA and died in Jan 1987 in La Porte, La Porte Co., Indiana, USA at age 81.

Children from this marriage were:
+ 98 M   i.   **John Vincent Haag** was born on 15 Nov 1925 in La Porte, La Porte Co., Indiana, USA.
+ 99 F   ii.   **Patricia Ann Haag** was born on 6 Oct 1927 in La Porte, La Porte Co., Indiana, USA and died on 1 Feb 2004 at age 76.
+ 100 F   iii.   **Margaret Helen Haag** was born on 12 Apr 1930 in La Porte, La Porte Co., Indiana, USA.
+ 101 M   iv.   **Vincent L. Haag** was born 11 Feb 1935 in La Porte, La Porte Co., Indiana, USA, died on 3 Aug 2005 in Hebron, Porter Co., Indiana, USA at age 69, and was buried in Saint Mary's Cemetery, Crown Point, Lake Co., Indiana, USA.

68. Mary Agnes Haag *(John Edward [50], Hubert Charles [31], Michael [25], Johann Jacob Frederick [17], Johannes Jacob [12], Jacob [5], Hans Martin [1])* was born on 27 Jun 1908 in Bicknell, Knox Co., Indiana, USA and died on 2 Aug 1908 in Bicknell, Knox Co., Indiana, USA.

69. Mary A. Haag *(John Edward [50], Hubert Charles [31], Michael [25], Johann Jacob Frederick [17], Johannes Jacob [12], Jacob [5], Hans Martin [1])* was born about 1909 in Kentucky, USA.

70. Charles Haag *(John Edward [50], Hubert Charles [31], Michael [25], Johann Jacob Frederick [17], Johannes Jacob [12], Jacob [5], Hans Martin [1])* was born about 1922.

71. Margaret Haag *(John Edward [50], Hubert Charles [31], Michael [25], Johann Jacob Frederick [17], Johannes Jacob [12], Jacob [5], Hans Martin [1])* was born on 3 Apr 1922 in Indiana, USA and died on 1 Dec 1992 at age 70.

72. John Robert Haag *(John Edward [50], Hubert Charles [31], Michael [25], Johann Jacob Frederick [17], Johannes Jacob [12], Jacob [5], Hans Martin [1])* was born on 29 Nov 1927 in La Porte, La Porte Co., Indiana, USA and died on 8 Mar 1991 at age 63.

73. Francis G. Haag *(John Edward [50], Hubert Charles [31], Michael [25], Johann Jacob Frederick [17], Johannes Jacob [12], Jacob [5], Hans Martin [1])* was born on 24 Sep 1929 in Indiana, USA and died on 18 Apr 1995 in Vincennes, Knox Co., Indiana, USA at age 65.

74. Mary Jean Haag *(John Edward [50], Hubert Charles [31], Michael [25], Johann Jacob Frederick [17], Johannes Jacob [12], Jacob [5], Hans Martin [1])* was born on 20 Nov 1930 in Ragsdale, Knox Co., Indiana, USA and died on 29 Aug 2008 in Jasper, Dubois Co., Indiana, USA at age 77.

Mary married **Hand**.

75. James William Haag *(John Edward [50], Hubert Charles [31], Michael [25], Johann Jacob Frederick [17], Johannes Jacob [12], Jacob [5], Hans Martin [1])* was born on 3 Nov 1932 in Bicknell, Knox Co., Indiana, USA and died on 6 Aug 2008 in Lebanon, Warren Co., Ohio, USA at age 75.

76. Martha Rose Haag *(John Edward [50], Hubert Charles [31], Michael [25], Johann Jacob Frederick [17], Johannes Jacob [12], Jacob [5], Hans Martin [1])* was born on 23 Sep 1934 in Bicknell, Knox Co., Indiana, USA and died on 2 Feb

Produced by: James Patrick Barber, 630 Nancy Street, Warsaw, Indiana 46580, 574-269-3124, 574-265-7939, jim@barberfamily.org

Page 14

1935 in Bicknell, Knox Co., Indiana, USA.

77. Thomas Adrian Haag *(John Edward* [50]*, Hubert Charles* [31]*, Michael* [25]*, Johann Jacob Frederick* [17]*, Johannes Jacob* [12]*, Jacob* [5]*, Hans Martin* [1]*)* was born on 14 Sep 1935 in Bicknell, Knox Co., Indiana, USA and died on 7 Jun 1936 in Bicknell, Knox Co., Indiana, USA.

78. Leo Haag *(George Francis* [51]*, Hubert Charles* [31]*, Michael* [25]*, Johann Jacob Frederick* [17]*, Johannes Jacob* [12]*, Jacob* [5]*, Hans Martin* [1]*)* was born in 1897 and died in 1956 at age 59.

79. Raymond Haag *(George Francis* [51]*, Hubert Charles* [31]*, Michael* [25]*, Johann Jacob Frederick* [17]*, Johannes Jacob* [12]*, Jacob* [5]*, Hans Martin* [1]*)* was born in 1901 and died in 1956 at age 55.

80. Earl A. Haag *(George Francis* [51]*, Hubert Charles* [31]*, Michael* [25]*, Johann Jacob Frederick* [17]*, Johannes Jacob* [12]*, Jacob* [5]*, Hans Martin* [1]*)* was born about 1906.

81. Frances Haag *(Charles Hubert* [53]*, Hubert Charles* [31]*, Michael* [25]*, Johann Jacob Frederick* [17]*, Johannes Jacob* [12]*, Jacob* [5]*, Hans Martin* [1]*)* was born on 28 Aug 1899 in Daviess Co., Indiana, USA and died on 8 Jan 1919 in Bicknell, Knox Co., Indiana, USA at age 19.

Frances married **Albert Haper**. Albert was born in 1892 and died in 1965 at age 73.

82. May Haag *(Charles Hubert* [53]*, Hubert Charles* [31]*, Michael* [25]*, Johann Jacob Frederick* [17]*, Johannes Jacob* [12]*, Jacob* [5]*, Hans Martin* [1]*)* was born in 1902.

83. Gertrude Calesta Haag *(Charles Hubert* [53]*, Hubert Charles* [31]*, Michael* [25]*, Johann Jacob Frederick* [17]*, Johannes Jacob* [12]*, Jacob* [5]*, Hans Martin* [1]*)* was born on 3 Mar 1905 in Linton, Greene Co., Indiana, USA and died on 11 Feb 1998 in Carmel, Hamilton Co., Indiana, USA at age 92.

Gertrude married **Stark**.

84. Lucile Haag *(Charles Hubert* [53]*, Hubert Charles* [31]*, Michael* [25]*, Johann Jacob Frederick* [17]*, Johannes Jacob* [12]*, Jacob* [5]*, Hans Martin* [1]*)* was born on 28 Sep 1909 in Bicknell, Knox Co., Indiana, USA. Another name for Lucile was Hazel Lucile Haag.

Lucile married **Ira E. Fields**. Ira was born about 1903.

The child from this marriage was:
+ 102 M   i. **Charles R. Fields**.

85. James Alvin Haag *(Charles Hubert* [53]*, Hubert Charles* [31]*, Michael* [25]*, Johann Jacob Frederick* [17]*, Johannes Jacob* [12]*, Jacob* [5]*, Hans Martin* [1]*)* was born on 6 Apr 1911 in Bicknell, Knox Co., Indiana, USA, died on 16 Mar 1944 in Indianapolis, Marion Co., Indiana, USA at age 32, and was buried in St. John's Cemetery, Washington, Daviess Co., Indiana, USA.

James married **Mary**. Mary was born about 1912.

86. Mary Haag *(Charles Hubert* [53]*, Hubert Charles* [31]*, Michael* [25]*, Johann Jacob Frederick* [17]*, Johannes Jacob* [12]*, Jacob* [5]*, Hans Martin* [1]*)* was born on 26 Jun 1913 in Knox Co., Indiana, USA and died on 13 Oct 1921 in Bicknell, Knox Co., Indiana, USA at age 8.

87. Loretta V. Haag *(Charles Hubert* [53]*, Hubert Charles* [31]*, Michael* [25]*, Johann Jacob Frederick* [17]*, Johannes Jacob* [12]*, Jacob* [5]*, Hans Martin* [1]*)* was born on 21 Jan 1915 in Bicknell, Knox Co., Indiana, USA and died on 19 Oct 1916 in Bicknell, Knox Co., Indiana, USA at age 1.

88. Joseph R. Haag *(Charles Hubert* [53]*, Hubert Charles* [31]*, Michael* [25]*, Johann Jacob Frederick* [17]*, Johannes Jacob* [12]*, Jacob* [5]*, Hans Martin* [1]*)* was born on 27 Oct 1920 in Knox Co., Indiana, USA, died on 17 Feb 2004 at age 83, and was buried in Calvary Cemetery, Indianapolis, Marion Co., Indiana, USA.

Produced by: James Patrick Barber, 630 Nancy Street, Warsaw, Indiana 46580, 574-269-3124, 574-265-7939, jim@barberfamily.org

Page 15

Joseph married **Helen Jeanne Koch** on 6 Sep 1941 in Boone Co., Indiana, USA.

Produced by: James Patrick Barber, 630 Nancy Street, Warsaw, Indiana 46580, 574-269-3124, 574-265-7939, jim@barberfamily.org

Page 16

Ninth Generation (6th Great-Grandchildren)

89. Grace Leora Clinton *(Cleophas F. Haag [63], John Edward [50], Hubert Charles [31], Michael [25], Johann Jacob Frederick [17], Johannes Jacob [12], Jacob [5], Hans Martin [1])* was born in 1917 and died in 2002 at age 85.

90. John Steven Clinton *(Cleophas F. Haag [63], John Edward [50], Hubert Charles [31], Michael [25], Johann Jacob Frederick [17], Johannes Jacob [12], Jacob [5], Hans Martin [1])* was born in 1919 and died in 1923 at age 4.

91. Leatha Cecelia Haag *(Harry Joseph [64], John Edward [50], Hubert Charles [31], Michael [25], Johann Jacob Frederick [17], Johannes Jacob [12], Jacob [5], Hans Martin [1])* was born on 1 Feb 1916 in Bicknell, Knox Co., Indiana, USA, died on 3 Dec 1961 in La Porte, La Porte Co., Indiana, USA at age 45, and was buried in La Porte, La Porte Co., Indiana, USA.

Leatha married **Clarence John Hilgendorf,** son of **Arthur John Hilgendorf** and **Mary Kramer,** on 14 Sep 1940 in La Porte, La Porte Co., Indiana, USA. Clarence was born on 30 Oct 1910 in La Porte, La Porte Co., Indiana, USA, died on 24 Jul 1990 in Bradenton, Manatee Co., Florida, USA at age 79, and was buried in La Porte, La Porte Co., Indiana, USA.

Children from this marriage were:

+ 103 F   i.   **Sally Joan Hilgendorf** was born on 23 Nov 1941 in La Porte, La Porte Co., Indiana, USA.
+ 104 M   ii.   **Kenneth Richard Hilgendorf** was born on 17 Jun 1943 in La Porte, La Porte Co., Indiana, USA.
+ 105 F   iii.   **Mary Jane Hilgendorf** was born on 3 Aug 1946 in La Porte, La Porte Co., Indiana, USA.
+ 106 F   iv.   **Martha Ann Hilgendorf** was born on 6 Apr 1951 in La Porte, La Porte Co., Indiana, USA.
+ 107 M   v.   **Clarence John Hilgendorf Jr.** was born on 14 Feb 1956 in La Porte, La Porte Co., Indiana, USA.

92. Helen Elizabeth Haag *(Harry Joseph [64], John Edward [50], Hubert Charles [31], Michael [25], Johann Jacob Frederick [17], Johannes Jacob [12], Jacob [5], Hans Martin [1])* was born on 11 Mar 1918 in Bicknell, Knox Co., Indiana, USA, died on 18 Jul 2002 in La Porte, La Porte Co., Indiana, USA at age 84, and was buried in Pine Lake Cemetery, La Porte, La Porte Co., Indiana, USA.

Helen married **John Parker Jr.,** son of **John A. Parker** and **Fannie Gooden,** on 26 Sep 1940 in La Porte, La Porte Co., Indiana, USA. John was born on 9 Sep 1917 in La Porte, La Porte Co., Indiana, USA, died on 3 Mar 2008 in La Porte, La Porte Co., Indiana, USA at age 90, and was buried in Pine Lake Cemetery, La Porte, La Porte Co., Indiana, USA.

Children from this marriage were:

+ 108 M   i.   **David Lee Parker** was born on 19 Sep 1941 in La Porte, La Porte Co., Indiana, USA.
+ 109 F   ii.   **Susan Jeanne Parker** was born on 3 Jan 1944 in La Porte, La Porte Co., Indiana, USA and died on 18 Aug 1946 in La Porte, La Porte Co., Indiana, USA at age 2.
+ 110 M   iii.   **Robert Alan Parker** was born on 27 Oct 1948 in La Porte, La Porte Co., Indiana, USA.
+ 111 M   iv.   **Sherry Ann Parker** was born on 6 Nov 1951 in La Porte, La Porte Co., Indiana, USA.

93. Thelma L. Haag *(Harry Joseph [64], John Edward [50], Hubert Charles [31], Michael [25], Johann Jacob Frederick [17], Johannes Jacob [12], Jacob [5], Hans Martin [1])* was born on 16 Jun 1920 in Vincennes, Knox Co., Indiana, USA and died before 1930.

94. Joseph Haag *(Michael Bernard [66], John Edward [50], Hubert Charles [31], Michael [25], Johann Jacob Frederick [17], Johannes Jacob [12], Jacob [5], Hans Martin [1])* was born about 1923 in Indiana, USA.

95. Charles Edward Haag *(Michael Bernard [66], John Edward [50], Hubert Charles [31], Michael [25], Johann Jacob Frederick [17], Johannes Jacob [12], Jacob [5], Hans Martin [1])* was born on 3 Dec 1933 in La Porte, La Porte Co., Indiana, USA and died on 2 May 2000 in Winter Park, Orange Co., Florida, USA at age 66.

Charles married **Betty Pate** on 24 Apr 1957 in La Porte, La Porte Co., Indiana, USA.

Produced by: James Patrick Barber, 630 Nancy Street, Warsaw, Indiana 46580, 574-269-3124, 574-265-7939, jim@barberfamily.org

Page 17

Children from this marriage were:

+ 112 F   i. **Kippy Haag**.
+ 113 M   ii. **Kevin Haag**.

96. Bernard M. Haag Jr. *(Michael Bernard [66], John Edward [50], Hubert Charles [31], Michael [25], Johann Jacob Frederick [17], Johannes Jacob [12], Jacob [5], Hans Martin [1])* was born on 23 Sep 1935 in La Porte, La Porte Co., Indiana, USA.

Bernard married **Karel Craft** on 24 Aug 1957 in La Porte, La Porte Co., Indiana, USA. Karel was born on 26 Jul 1936 in La Porte, La Porte Co., Indiana, USA.

Children from this marriage were:

+ 114 F   i. **Beth Ann Haag**.
+ 115 F   ii. **Jennifer Haag**.

97. Judith A. Haag *(Michael Bernard [66], John Edward [50], Hubert Charles [31], Michael [25], Johann Jacob Frederick [17], Johannes Jacob [12], Jacob [5], Hans Martin [1])* was born about 1939 in La Porte, La Porte Co., Indiana, USA.

Judith married **Phillip Carichoff** on 18 Jul 1959 in La Porte, La Porte Co., Indiana, USA.

98. John Vincent Haag *(Vincent Bartholomew [67], John Edward [50], Hubert Charles [31], Michael [25], Johann Jacob Frederick [17], Johannes Jacob [12], Jacob [5], Hans Martin [1])* was born on 15 Nov 1925 in La Porte, La Porte Co., Indiana, USA.

99. Patricia Ann Haag *(Vincent Bartholomew [67], John Edward [50], Hubert Charles [31], Michael [25], Johann Jacob Frederick [17], Johannes Jacob [12], Jacob [5], Hans Martin [1])* was born on 6 Oct 1927 in La Porte, La Porte Co., Indiana, USA and died on 1 Feb 2004 at age 76.

Patricia married **Robert J. Minich**. Robert was born about 1925 and died about 1985 about age 60.

100. Margaret Helen Haag *(Vincent Bartholomew [67], John Edward [50], Hubert Charles [31], Michael [25], Johann Jacob Frederick [17], Johannes Jacob [12], Jacob [5], Hans Martin [1])* was born on 12 Apr 1930 in La Porte, La Porte Co., Indiana, USA.

Margaret married **Royce Cattron**.

101. Vincent L. Haag *(Vincent Bartholomew [67], John Edward [50], Hubert Charles [31], Michael [25], Johann Jacob Frederick [17], Johannes Jacob [12], Jacob [5], Hans Martin [1])* was born 11 Feb1935 in La Porte, La Porte Co., Indiana, USA, died on 3 Aug 2005 in Hebron, Porter Co., Indiana, USA at age 69, and was buried in Saint Mary's Cemetery, Crown Point, Lake Co., Indiana, USA.

Vincent married **Kay Maureen Blood** about 1957. Kay was born on 27 Nov 1936 in Porter Co., Indiana, USA, died on 1 May 2006 in Hebron, Porter Co., Indiana, USA at age 69, and was buried in Saint Mary's Cemetery, Crown Point, Lake Co., Indiana, USA.

102. Charles R. Fields *(Lucile Haag [84], Charles Hubert [53], Hubert Charles [31], Michael [25], Johann Jacob Frederick [17], Johannes Jacob [12], Jacob [5], Hans Martin [1])*.

Produced by: James Patrick Barber, 630 Nancy Street, Warsaw, Indiana 46580, 574-269-3124, 574-265-7939, jim@barberfamily.org

Page 18

Tenth Generation (7th Great-Grandchildren)

103. Sally Joan Hilgendorf *(Leatha Cecelia Haag [91], Harry Joseph [64], John Edward [50], Hubert Charles [31], Michael [25], Johann Jacob Frederick [17], Johannes Jacob [12], Jacob [5], Hans Martin [1])* was born on 23 Nov 1941 in La Porte, La Porte Co., Indiana, USA.

Sally married **Dennis Lee Biege,** son of **James Kendall Biege** and **Angelina Sobko,** on 24 Jun 1961 in La Porte, La Porte Co., Indiana, USA. Dennis was born on 13 May 1941 in La Porte, La Porte Co., Indiana, USA.

Children from this marriage were:

116	F	i.	**Tina Marie Biege** was born on 21 May 1962 in La Porte, La Porte Co., Indiana, USA. Tina married **Garry T. Bowers** on 17 Aug 1985 in La Porte, La Porte Co., Indiana, USA. Garry was born on 21 Aug 1960 in La Porte, La Porte Co., Indiana, USA.
117	F	ii.	**Julie Ann Biege** was born on 5 Aug 1965 in La Porte, La Porte Co., Indiana, USA. Julie married **Tom Muller** on 3 Oct 1987 in La Porte, La Porte Co., Indiana, USA. Tom was born on 3 May 1964 in La Porte, La Porte Co., Indiana, USA and died on 18 Sep 2013 in La Porte, La Porte Co., Indiana, USA at age 49.

104. Kenneth Richard Hilgendorf *(Leatha Cecelia Haag [91], Harry Joseph [64], John Edward [50], Hubert Charles [31], Michael [25], Johann Jacob Frederick [17], Johannes Jacob [12], Jacob [5], Hans Martin [1])* was born on 17 Jun 1943 in La Porte, La Porte Co., Indiana, USA.

Kenneth married **Sue Sternal.** Sue was born on 5 May 1954.

Children from this marriage were:

118	F	i.	**Michelle Sue Hilgendorf** was born on 31 Mar 1966. Michelle married **Kurk William Steenhoek.** Kurk was born on 16 Apr 1965.
119	M	ii.	**Kevin Thomas Hilgendorf** was born on 3 Apr 1968. Kevin married **Sharon Mary Steif.** Sharon was born on 5 May 1965.

105. Mary Jane Hilgendorf *(Leatha Cecelia Haag [91], Harry Joseph [64], John Edward [50], Hubert Charles [31], Michael [25], Johann Jacob Frederick [17], Johannes Jacob [12], Jacob [5], Hans Martin [1])* was born on 3 Aug 1946 in La Porte, La Porte Co., Indiana, USA.

Mary married **Ronald Wayne Loeffler,** son of **Walter Charles Loeffler** and **Virginia Sobko,** on 28 May 1966 in La Porte, La Porte Co., Indiana, USA. Ronald was born on 2 Sep 1943 in La Porte, La Porte Co., Indiana, USA.

Children from this marriage were:

120	M	i.	**Jeff Loeffler** was born on 21 Oct 1968 in La Porte, La Porte Co., Indiana, USA. Jeff married **Angie** on 21 Mar 2010.
121	M	ii.	**Ryan Loeffler** was born on 1 Nov 1971 in La Porte, La Porte Co., Indiana, USA. Ryan married **Becky Womack,** daughter of **Robert Walter Womack** and **Karen Kay Kessler,** on 11 May 1996. Becky was born on 29 Oct 1974 in La Porte, La Porte Co., Indiana, USA.
122	M	iii.	**Corey Loeffler** was born on 2 Jun 1978 in La Porte, La Porte Co., Indiana, USA. Corey married **Paula** on 23 Nov 2014.

106. Martha Ann Hilgendorf *(Leatha Cecelia Haag [91], Harry Joseph [64], John Edward [50], Hubert Charles [31], Michael [25], Johann Jacob Frederick [17], Johannes Jacob [12], Jacob [5], Hans Martin [1])* was born on 6 Apr 1951 in La Porte, La Porte Co., Indiana, USA.

Martha married **James Patrick Barber,** son of **Ira Barber Jr.** and **Shirley Esther Wendt,** on 27 Nov 1970 in La Porte, La Porte Co., Indiana, USA. James was born on 9 Nov 1948 in La Porte, La Porte Co., Indiana, USA.

Children from this marriage were:

123	M	i.	**Matthew James Barber** was born on 11 Dec 1971 in Warsaw, Kosciusko Co., Indiana, USA.

Produced by: James Patrick Barber, 630 Nancy Street, Warsaw, Indiana 46580, 574-269-3124, 574-265-7939, jim@barberfamily.org

Page 19

Matthew married **Estera Corlan** on 6 Oct 2002 in Brentwood, Williamson Co., Tennessee, USA. Estera was born on 18 Oct 1975 in Drobeta Turnu Severin, , , Romania.

124 M ii. **Joshua Ira Barber** was born on 1 Sep 1976 in Naples, Collier Co., Florida, USA.
Joshua married **Vanessa Lynn Cudney** on 12 Apr 1996 in Bourbon, Marshall Co., Indiana, USA. Vanessa was born on 4 Sep 1976.

125 F iii. **Sarah Elizabeth Barber** was born on 1 Sep 1979 in Warsaw, Kosciusko Co., Indiana, USA.
Sarah married **Michael Dale Petersen**, son of **Marvin Petersen** and **Mary Oberlin**, on 4 Aug 2000 in Warsaw, Kosciusko Co., Indiana, USA. Michael was born on 28 Jul 1975 in Indiana, USA.

107. Clarence John Hilgendorf Jr. *(Leatha Cecelia Haag [91], Harry Joseph [64], John Edward [50], Hubert Charles [31], Michael [25], Johann Jacob Frederick [17], Johannes Jacob [12], Jacob [5], Hans Martin [1])* was born on 14 Feb 1956 in La Porte, La Porte Co., Indiana, USA.

Clarence married **Dana Marie Alderman**. Dana was born on 10 May 1958.

The child from this marriage was:

126 M i. **Christopher John Hilgendorf** was born on 18 Feb 1979.

108. David Lee Parker *(Helen Elizabeth Haag [92], Harry Joseph [64], John Edward [50], Hubert Charles [31], Michael [25], Johann Jacob Frederick [17], Johannes Jacob [12], Jacob [5], Hans Martin [1])* was born on 19 Sep 1941 in La Porte, La Porte Co., Indiana, USA.

109. Susan Jeanne Parker *(Helen Elizabeth Haag [92], Harry Joseph [64], John Edward [50], Hubert Charles [31], Michael [25], Johann Jacob Frederick [17], Johannes Jacob [12], Jacob [5], Hans Martin [1])* was born on 3 Jan 1944 in La Porte, La Porte Co., Indiana, USA and died on 18 Aug 1946 in La Porte, La Porte Co., Indiana, USA at age 2.

110. Robert Alan Parker *(Helen Elizabeth Haag [92], Harry Joseph [64], John Edward [50], Hubert Charles [31], Michael [25], Johann Jacob Frederick [17], Johannes Jacob [12], Jacob [5], Hans Martin [1])* was born on 27 Oct 1948 in La Porte, La Porte Co., Indiana, USA.

111. Sherry Ann Parker *(Helen Elizabeth Haag [92], Harry Joseph [64], John Edward [50], Hubert Charles [31], Michael [25], Johann Jacob Frederick [17], Johannes Jacob [12], Jacob [5], Hans Martin [1])* was born on 6 Nov 1951 in La Porte, La Porte Co., Indiana, USA.

112. Kippy Haag *(Charles Edward [95], Michael Bernard [66], John Edward [50], Hubert Charles [31], Michael [25], Johann Jacob Frederick [17], Johannes Jacob [12], Jacob [5], Hans Martin [1]).*

113. Kevin Haag *(Charles Edward [95], Michael Bernard [66], John Edward [50], Hubert Charles [31], Michael [25], Johann Jacob Frederick [17], Johannes Jacob [12], Jacob [5], Hans Martin [1]).*

114. Beth Ann Haag *(Bernard M. Jr. [96], Michael Bernard [66], John Edward [50], Hubert Charles [31], Michael [25], Johann Jacob Frederick [17], Johannes Jacob [12], Jacob [5], Hans Martin [1]).*

115. Jennifer Haag *(Bernard M. Jr. [96], Michael Bernard [66], John Edward [50], Hubert Charles [31], Michael [25], Johann Jacob Frederick [17], Johannes Jacob [12], Jacob [5], Hans Martin [1]).*

Produced by: James Patrick Barber, 630 Nancy Street, Warsaw, Indiana 46580, 574-269-3124, 574-265-7939, jim@barberfamily.org

Page 20

Name Index

Produced by: James Patrick Barber, 630 Nancy Street, Warsaw, Indiana 46580, 574-269-3124, 574-265-7939, jim@barberfamily.org

Name Index

Produced by: James Patrick Barber, 630 Nancy Street, Warsaw, Indiana 46580, 574-269-3124, 574-265-7939, jim@barberfamily.org

Page 22

Name Index

Produced by: James Patrick Barber, 630 Nancy Street, Warsaw, Indiana 46580, 574-269-3124, 574-265-7939, jim@barberfamily.org

Page 23

Location Index

Location Index

Produced by: James Patrick Barber, 630 Nancy Street, Warsaw, Indiana 46580, 574-269-3124, 574-265-7939, jim@barberfamily.org

Page 25

Kramer

Descendant Chart

Beginning with

Thomas Kramer (1817-1900)

In following the Hilgendorf family, we find that Arthur Hilgendorf (1885-1958), the father of Clarence "Dutch" Hilgendorf, was married to Mary Kramer (1884-1960) in La Porte, Indiana. The family descendant chart on the following pages looks at Mary Kramer's ancestry beginning with Thomas Kramer, born in 1817 in Germany.

Table of Contents

Produced by: James Patrick Barber, 630 Nancy Street, Warsaw, Indiana 46580, 574-269-3124, 574-265-7939, jim@barberfamily.org

First Generation

1. Thomas Kramer was born on 19 Aug 1817 in Germany, died on 28 Jun 1900 in La Porte, La Porte Co., Indiana, USA at age 82, and was buried in St. Joseph's Cemetery, La Porte, La Porte Co., Indiana, USA.

Thomas married **Catherine Johnson**. Catherine was born in Germany, died in Germany, and was buried in Germany. Another name for Catherine was Katherine.

Children from this marriage were:

+ 2 M   i.   **Nicholas Kramer** was born on 19 Jun 1837, died on 19 May 1909 in La Porte, La Porte Co., Indiana, USA at age 71, and was buried in Rossburg Cemetery, , La Porte Co., Indiana, USA.

+ 3 M   ii.   **Peter Kramer**.

+ 4 F   iii.   **Kramer**.

+ 5 F   iv.   **Kramer**.

+ 6 M   v.   **Mathias Kramer** was born on 1 Jun 1842 in Germany, died on 20 Dec 1920 in La Porte, La Porte Co., Indiana, USA at age 78, and was buried in St. Joseph's Cemetery, La Porte, La Porte Co., Indiana, USA.

Produced by: James Patrick Barber, 630 Nancy Street, Warsaw, Indiana 46580, 574-269-3124, 574-265-7939, jim@barberfamily.org

Page 1

Second Generation (Children)

2. Nicholas Kramer *(Thomas [1])* was born on 19 Jun 1837, died on 19 May 1909 in La Porte, La Porte Co., Indiana, USA at age 71, and was buried in Rossburg Cemetery, , La Porte Co., Indiana, USA.

Nicholas married **Caroline Nebbleseck**. Caroline died in La Porte, La Porte Co., Indiana, USA and was buried in Rossburg Cemetery, , La Porte Co., Indiana, USA.

Children from this marriage were:
- \+ 7   M   i.   **Thomas M. Kramer**.
- \+ 8   F   ii.   **Minnie Kramer**.
- \+ 9   F   iii.   **Carries Kramer**.
- \+ 10   F   iv.   **Mary Kramer**.

3. Peter Kramer *(Thomas [1])*.

4. Kramer *(Thomas [1])*.

5. Kramer *(Thomas [1])*.

6. Mathias Kramer *(Thomas [1])* was born on 1 Jun 1842 in Germany, died on 20 Dec 1920 in La Porte, La Porte Co., Indiana, USA at age 78, and was buried in St. Joseph's Cemetery, La Porte, La Porte Co., Indiana, USA. Another name for Mathias was Mat.

Mathias married **Katherine Berg**, daughter of **John Berg** and **Hanna Dora Winmueller**, about 1874. Katherine was born on 4 Jun 1856 in Chicago, Cook Co., Illinois, USA, died on 5 Jan 1917 in La Porte, La Porte Co., Indiana, USA at age 60, and was buried in St. Joseph's Cemetery, La Porte, La Porte Co., Indiana, USA. Other names for Katherine were Bergland and Catherine Burg.

Children from this marriage were:
- \+ 11   M   i.   **Thomas J. Kramer** was born on 6 Nov 1874 in Indiana, USA, died on 29 Jun 1942 in Michigan City, La Porte Co., Indiana, USA at age 67, and was buried in Greenwood Cemetery, Michigan City, La Porte Co., Indiana, USA.
- \+ 12   F   ii.   **Louisa Kramer** was born on 6 May 1875 in La Porte, La Porte Co., Indiana, USA, died on 21 Mar 1935 in Michigan City, La Porte Co., Indiana, USA at age 59, and was buried in Greenwood Cemetery, Michigan City, La Porte Co., Indiana, USA.
- \+ 13   F   iii.   **Anna Kramer** was born on 2 Oct 1876, died on 8 Mar 1958 at age 81, and was buried in Dodge Grove Cemetery, Mattoon, Coles County, Illinois, USA.
- \+ 14   F   iv.   **Dora G. Kramer** was born on 27 Aug 1878 in La Porte, La Porte Co., Indiana, USA, died on 6 May 1968 in La Porte, La Porte Co., Indiana, USA at age 89, and was buried in St. Joseph's Cemetery, La Porte, La Porte Co., Indiana, USA.
- \+ 15   F   v.   **Katherine Kramer** was born on 15 May 1881 in La Porte, La Porte Co., Indiana, USA, died on 20 Jun 1909 in La Porte, La Porte Co., Indiana, USA at age 28, and was buried in St. Joseph's Cemetery, La Porte, La Porte Co., Indiana, USA.
- \+ 16   F   vi.   **Mary Kramer** was born on 21 Jan 1884 in La Porte, La Porte Co., Indiana, USA, died on 6 Dec 1960 in La Porte, La Porte Co., Indiana, USA at age 76, and was buried in Pine Lake Cemetery, La Porte, La Porte Co., Indiana, USA.
- \+ 17   M   vii.   **John Kramer** was born on 6 Jun 1885 in La Porte, La Porte Co., Indiana, USA, died on 14 Aug 1973 in La Porte, La Porte Co., Indiana, USA at age 88, and was buried in St. Joseph's Cemetery, La Porte, La Porte Co., Indiana, USA.
- \+ 18   U   viii.   **Kramer**.
- \+ 19   U   ix.   **Kramer**.

Produced by: James Patrick Barber, 630 Nancy Street, Warsaw, Indiana 46580, 574-269-3124, 574-265-7939, jim@barberfamily.org

Page 2

Third Generation (Grandchildren)

7. Thomas M. Kramer *(Nicholas [2], Thomas [1])*.

8. Minnie Kramer *(Nicholas [2], Thomas [1])*.

9. Carries Kramer *(Nicholas [2], Thomas [1])*.

10. Mary Kramer *(Nicholas [2], Thomas [1])*.

11. Thomas J. Kramer *(Mathias [6], Thomas [1])* was born on 6 Nov 1874 in Indiana, USA, died on 29 Jun 1942 in Michigan City, La Porte Co., Indiana, USA at age 67, and was buried in Greenwood Cemetery, Michigan City, La Porte Co., Indiana, USA.

Thomas married **Elizabeth Fisch**.

Children from this marriage were:
+ 20 F   i.   **Matilda K. Kramer** was born about 1902 in Indiana, USA.
+ 21 F   ii. **Florence G. Kramer** was born about 1904 in Indiana, USA.
+ 22 F   iii. **Irene M. Kramer** was born about 1908 in Indiana, USA.
+ 23 F   iv. **Hazel K. Kramer** was born about 1909 in Indiana, USA.
+ 24 F   v.   **Helen Kramer** was born about 1912 in Indiana, USA.
+ 25 M   vi. **Elmer Kramer** was born about 1914 in Indiana, USA.

12. Louisa Kramer *(Mathias [6], Thomas [1])* was born on 6 May 1875 in La Porte, La Porte Co., Indiana, USA, died on 21 Mar 1935 in Michigan City, La Porte Co., Indiana, USA at age 59, and was buried in Greenwood Cemetery, Michigan City, La Porte Co., Indiana, USA.

Louisa married **Mathias Phillips**.

Children from this marriage were:
+ 26 M   i.   **Lawrence Phillips**.
+ 27 M   ii.   **Leo Phillips**.
+ 28 M   iii. **Katherine Phillips**.
+ 29 F   iv.   **Margaret Phillips**.
+ 30 F   v.   **Leona Phillips**.
+ 31 F   vi.   **Ruth Phillips**.
+ 32 M   vii. **William Phillips**.
+ 33 F   viii. **Mathilda Phillips**.

13. Anna Kramer *(Mathias [6], Thomas [1])* was born on 2 Oct 1876, died on 8 Mar 1958 at age 81, and was buried in Dodge Grove Cemetery, Mattoon, Coles County, Illinois, USA.

Anna married **John William Albert**. John was born about 1870 and died about 1950 about age 80.

Children from this marriage were:
+ 34 M   i.   **Agnes Albert** was born in Aug 1897.
+ 35 M   ii. **Paul M. Albert** was born about 1903 and died about 1983 about age 80.

14. Dora G. Kramer *(Mathias [6], Thomas [1])* was born on 27 Aug 1878 in La Porte, La Porte Co., Indiana, USA, died on 6 May 1968 in La Porte, La Porte Co., Indiana, USA at age 89, and was buried in St. Joseph's Cemetery, La Porte, La Porte Co., Indiana, USA.

Dora married **Clement Siegmund**. Clement was born in Oct 1875 and died in May 1945 at age 69.

The child from this marriage was:
+ 36 F   i.   **Ruth Siegmund** was born about 1905 and died about 1983 about age 78.

15. Katherine Kramer *(Mathias [6], Thomas [1])* was born on 15 May 1881 in La Porte, La Porte Co.,

Produced by: James Patrick Barber, 630 Nancy Street, Warsaw, Indiana 46580, 574-269-3124, 574-265-7939, jim@barberfamily.org

Page 3

Indiana, USA, died on 20 Jun 1909 in La Porte, La Porte Co., Indiana, USA at age 28, and was buried in St. Joseph's Cemetery, La Porte, La Porte Co., Indiana, USA.

16. Mary Kramer *(Mathias [6], Thomas [1])* was born on 21 Jan 1884 in La Porte, La Porte Co., Indiana, USA, died on 6 Dec 1960 in La Porte, La Porte Co., Indiana, USA at age 76, and was buried in Pine Lake Cemetery, La Porte, La Porte Co., Indiana, USA. Another name for Mary was Marie Kramer.

> Mary married **Arthur John Hilgendorf, son of John Edward Hilgendorf** and **Fredericka (also Rickie, Ricka) Kuch,** on 17 Dec 1907 in La Porte, La Porte Co., Indiana, USA. Arthur was born on 1 Jul 1885 in La Porte, La Porte Co., Indiana, USA, died on 18 Jan 1958 in La Porte, La Porte Co., Indiana, USA at age 72, and was buried in Pine Lake Cemetery, La Porte, La Porte Co., Indiana, USA.

> Children from this marriage were:

> + 37 M   i.   **Arthur Hilgendorf Jr.** was born on 27 May 1908 in La Porte, La Porte Co., Indiana, USA and died in 1908.

> + 38 M   ii.   **Lawrence Arthur Hilgendorf** was born on 25 Jul 1909 in La Porte, La Porte Co., Indiana, USA, died on 21 Apr 1999 in La Porte, La Porte Co., Indiana, USA at age 89, and was buried in Pine Lake Cemetery, La Porte, La Porte Co., Indiana, USA.

> + 39 M   iii.   **Clarence John Hilgendorf** was born on 30 Oct 1910 in La Porte, La Porte Co., Indiana, USA, died on 24 Jul 1990 in Bradenton, Manatee Co., Florida, USA at age 79, and was buried in La Porte, La Porte Co., Indiana, USA.

> + 40 M   iv.   **Roy Andrew Hilgendorf** was born on 7 Oct 1912 in La Porte, La Porte Co., Indiana, USA, died on 9 Apr 1970 in La Porte, La Porte Co., Indiana, USA at age 57, and was buried in Pine Lake Cemetery, La Porte, La Porte Co., Indiana, USA.

> + 41 M   v.   **Wilbur C. Hilgendorf** was born on 21 Oct 1914 in La Porte, La Porte Co., Indiana, USA, died on 1 May 1943 in Tunisia, Africa at age 28, and was buried in North Africa American Cemetery, Carthage, Tunisia, Africa.

> + 42 M   vi.   **Raymond J. Hilgendorf** was born on 5 Jul 1916 in La Porte, La Porte Co., Indiana, USA, died on 7 Jun 1981 in La Porte, La Porte Co., Indiana, USA at age 64, and was buried in Pine Lake Cemetery, La Porte, La Porte Co., Indiana, USA.

> + 43 M   vii.   **Arthur Hilgendorf Jr.** was born on 15 Mar 1919 in La Porte, La Porte Co., Indiana, USA, died on 10 Dec 1922 in La Porte, La Porte Co., Indiana, USA at age 3, and was buried in Pine Lake Cemetery, La Porte, La Porte Co., Indiana, USA.

> + 44 F   viii.   **Marie Elizabeth Hilgendorf** was born on 1 Apr 1922 in La Porte, La Porte Co., Indiana, USA, died on 1 Apr 2009 in La Porte, La Porte Co., Indiana, USA at age 87, and was buried in Kingsbury Cemetery, Kingsbury, La Porte Co., Indiana, USA.

> + 45 F   ix.   **Doris Hilgendorf** was born on 9 Jul 1924 in La Porte, La Porte Co., Indiana, USA and died on 22 Aug 2016 in Palatine, Cook Co., Illinois, USA at age 92.

17. John Kramer *(Mathias [6], Thomas [1])* was born on 6 Jun 1885 in La Porte, La Porte Co., Indiana, USA, died on 14 Aug 1973 in La Porte, La Porte Co., Indiana, USA at age 88, and was buried in St. Joseph's Cemetery, La Porte, La Porte Co., Indiana, USA.

> John married **Susan H. Rose**. Susan was born in 1888 and died in 1988 at age 100.

> Children from this marriage were:

> + 46 M   i.   **Leo J. Kramer** was born on 7 Aug 1910 in La Porte, La Porte Co., Indiana, USA, died on 14 Nov 1984 in Bluffton, Wells Co., Indiana, USA at age 74, and was buried in St. John's Cemetery, La Porte, La Porte Co., Indiana, USA.

> + 47 F   ii.   **Evelyn M. Kramer** was born on 23 Feb 1915 in La Porte, La Porte Co., Indiana, USA, died on 18 Feb 1941 in La Porte, La Porte Co., Indiana, USA at age 25, and was buried in St. Joseph's Cemetery, La Porte, La Porte Co., Indiana, USA.

18. Kramer *(Mathias [6], Thomas [1])*.

19. Kramer *(Mathias [6], Thomas [1])*.

Produced by: James Patrick Barber, 630 Nancy Street, Warsaw, Indiana 46580, 574-269-3124, 574-265-7939, jim@barberfamily.org

Page 4

Fourth Generation (Great-Grandchildren)

20. Matilda K. Kramer *(Thomas J. [11], Mathias [6], Thomas [1])* was born about 1902 in Indiana, USA.

21. Florence G. Kramer *(Thomas J. [11], Mathias [6], Thomas [1])* was born about 1904 in Indiana, USA.

22. Irene M. Kramer *(Thomas J. [11], Mathias [6], Thomas [1])* was born about 1908 in Indiana, USA.

23. Hazel K. Kramer *(Thomas J. [11], Mathias [6], Thomas [1])* was born about 1909 in Indiana, USA.

24. Helen Kramer *(Thomas J. [11], Mathias [6], Thomas [1])* was born about 1912 in Indiana, USA.

25. Elmer Kramer *(Thomas J. [11], Mathias [6], Thomas [1])* was born about 1914 in Indiana, USA.

26. Lawrence Phillips *(Louisa Kramer [12], Mathias [6], Thomas [1])*.

27. Leo Phillips *(Louisa Kramer [12], Mathias [6], Thomas [1])*.

28. Katherine Phillips *(Louisa Kramer [12], Mathias [6], Thomas [1])*.

29. Margaret Phillips *(Louisa Kramer [12], Mathias [6], Thomas [1])*.

30. Leona Phillips *(Louisa Kramer [12], Mathias [6], Thomas [1])*.

31. Ruth Phillips *(Louisa Kramer [12], Mathias [6], Thomas [1])*.

32. William Phillips *(Louisa Kramer [12], Mathias [6], Thomas [1])*.

33. Mathilda Phillips *(Louisa Kramer [12], Mathias [6], Thomas [1])*.

34. Agnes Albert *(Anna Kramer [13], Mathias [6], Thomas [1])* was born in Aug 1897.

35. Paul M. Albert *(Anna Kramer [13], Mathias [6], Thomas [1])* was born about 1903 and died about 1983 about age 80.

36. Ruth Siegmund *(Dora G. Kramer [14], Mathias [6], Thomas [1])* was born about 1905 and died about 1983 about age 78.

37. Arthur Hilgendorf Jr. *(Mary Kramer [16], Mathias [6], Thomas [1])* was born on 27 May 1908 in La Porte, La Porte Co., Indiana, USA and died in 1908.

38. Lawrence Arthur Hilgendorf *(Mary Kramer [16], Mathias [6], Thomas [1])* was born on 25 Jul 1909 in La Porte, La Porte Co., Indiana, USA, died on 21 Apr 1999 in La Porte, La Porte Co., Indiana, USA at age 89, and was buried in Pine Lake Cemetery, La Porte, La Porte Co., Indiana, USA.

> Lawrence married **Anna B. Dick,** daughter of **Frederick Dick** and **Rosa Mishler,** on 16 Dec 1933 in La Porte, La Porte Co., Indiana, USA. Anna was born on 19 May 1911 in Hanna, La Porte Co., Indiana, USA, died on 26 Feb 2006 in La Porte, La Porte Co., Indiana, USA at age 94, and was buried in Pine Lake Cemetery, La Porte, La Porte Co., Indiana, USA.

39. Clarence John Hilgendorf *(Mary Kramer [16], Mathias [6], Thomas [1])* was born on 30 Oct 1910 in La Porte, La Porte Co., Indiana, USA, died on 24 Jul 1990 in Bradenton, Manatee Co., Florida, USA at age 79, and was buried in La Porte, La Porte Co., Indiana, USA.

Produced by: James Patrick Barber, 630 Nancy Street, Warsaw, Indiana 46580, 574-269-3124, 574-265-7939, jim@barberfamily.org

Page 5

Clarence married **Leatha Cecelia Haag,** daughter of **Harry Joseph Haag** and **Mabel Iselem Boze,** on 14 Sep 1940 in La Porte, La Porte Co., Indiana, USA. Leatha was born on 1 Feb 1916 in Bicknell, Knox Co., Indiana, USA, died on 3 Dec 1961 in La Porte, La Porte Co., Indiana, USA at age 45, and was buried in La Porte, La Porte Co., Indiana, USA.

Children from this marriage were:
- 48 F i. **Sally Joan Hilgendorf** was born on 23 Nov 1941 in La Porte, La Porte Co., Indiana, USA. Sally married **Dennis Lee Biege,** son of **James Kendall Biege** and **Angelina Sobko,** on 24 Jun 1961 in La Porte, La Porte Co., Indiana, USA. Dennis was born on 13 May 1941 in La Porte, La Porte Co., Indiana, USA.
- 49 M ii. **Kenneth Richard Hilgendorf** was born on 17 Jun 1943 in La Porte, La Porte Co., Indiana, USA.
  Kenneth married **Sue Sternal.** Sue was born on 5 May 1954.
- 50 F iii. **Mary Jane Hilgendorf** was born on 3 Aug 1946 in La Porte, La Porte Co., Indiana, USA. Mary married **Ronald Wayne Loeffler,** son of **Walter Charles Loeffler** and **Virginia Sobko,** on 28 May 1966 in La Porte, La Porte Co., Indiana, USA. Ronald was born on 2 Sep 1943 in La Porte, La Porte Co., Indiana, USA.
- 51 F iv. **Martha Ann Hilgendorf** was born on 6 Apr 1951 in La Porte, La Porte Co., Indiana, USA. Martha married **James Patrick Barber,** son of **Ira Barber Jr.** and **Shirley Esther Wendt,** on 27 Nov 1970 in La Porte, La Porte Co., Indiana, USA. James was born on 9 Nov 1948 in La Porte, La Porte Co., Indiana, USA.
- 52 M v. **Clarence John Hilgendorf Jr.** was born on 14 Feb 1956 in La Porte, La Porte Co., Indiana, USA.
  Clarence married **Dana Marie Alderman.** Dana was born on 10 May 1958.

Clarence next married **Mary E. (Allen) Watson** about 1962. Mary was born on 30 Mar 1918 in Spencer, Owen Co., Indiana, USA and died on 12 Feb 2005 in Bradenton, Manatee Co., Florida, USA at age 86.

40. Roy Andrew Hilgendorf *(Mary Kramer [16], Mathias [6], Thomas [1])* was born on 7 Oct 1912 in La Porte, La Porte Co., Indiana, USA, died on 9 Apr 1970 in La Porte, La Porte Co., Indiana, USA at age 57, and was buried in Pine Lake Cemetery, La Porte, La Porte Co., Indiana, USA.

Roy married **Dorothy Marie Edwards,** daughter of **Ora C. Edwards** and **Carrie Buffum,** on 13 Nov 1936 in La Porte, La Porte Co., Indiana, USA. Dorothy was born on 21 Mar 1914 in Indiana, USA and died on 15 Jul 1992 in Santa Monica, Los Angeles Co., California, USA at age 78.

Children from this marriage were:
- 53 M i. **James Hilgendorf** was born on 12 Jan 1940 in La Porte, La Porte Co., Indiana, USA.
- 54 M ii. **John Thomas Hilgendorf** was born on 25 Jun 1951 in La Porte, La Porte Co., Indiana, USA and died on 29 Apr 2014 in Waitaki, New Zealand at age 62.
  John married **Ernestina Annie Ozuna.**
  John next married **Rebecca I. Cooper.**

41. Wilbur C. Hilgendorf *(Mary Kramer [16], Mathias [6], Thomas [1])* was born on 21 Oct 1914 in La Porte, La Porte Co., Indiana, USA, died on 1 May 1943 in Tunisia, Africa at age 28, and was buried in North Africa American Cemetery, Carthage, Tunisia, Africa.

42. Raymond J. Hilgendorf *(Mary Kramer [16], Mathias [6], Thomas [1])* was born on 5 Jul 1916 in La Porte, La Porte Co., Indiana, USA, died on 7 Jun 1981 in La Porte, La Porte Co., Indiana, USA at age 64, and was buried in Pine Lake Cemetery, La Porte, La Porte Co., Indiana, USA.

Raymond married **Jean Cormick,** daughter of **Stephen Cormick** and **Hedvig Auney,** on 21 Dec 1936 in La Porte, La Porte Co., Indiana, USA. Jean was born on 11 Jul 1915 in Gary, Lake Co., Indiana, USA and died on 29 Apr 1997 in Michigan City, La Porte Co., Indiana, USA at age 81.

The child from this marriage was:
- 55 F i. **Christine Hilgendorf.**

Produced by: James Patrick Barber, 630 Nancy Street, Warsaw, Indiana 46580, 574-269-3124, 574-265-7939, jim@barberfamily.org

Page 6

Raymond next married **Helen Louise Gray**, daughter of **Duane C. Gray** and **Eva Sage**. Helen was born on 23 Dec 1912 in Garber, Garfield Co., Oklahoma, USA, died on 29 Aug 1996 in La Porte, La Porte Co., Indiana, USA at age 83, and was buried in Pine Lake Cemetery, La Porte, La Porte Co., Indiana, USA.

43. Arthur Hilgendorf Jr. *(Mary Kramer [16], Mathias [6], Thomas [1])* was born on 15 Mar 1919 in La Porte, La Porte Co., Indiana, USA, died on 10 Dec 1922 in La Porte, La Porte Co., Indiana, USA at age 3, and was buried in Pine Lake Cemetery, La Porte, La Porte Co., Indiana, USA.

44. Marie Elizabeth Hilgendorf *(Mary Kramer [16], Mathias [6], Thomas [1])* was born on 1 Apr 1922 in La Porte, La Porte Co., Indiana, USA, died on 1 Apr 2009 in La Porte, La Porte Co., Indiana, USA at age 87, and was buried in Kingsbury Cemetery, Kingsbury, La Porte Co., Indiana, USA.

Marie married **George Raymond Wineholt,** son of **Daniel H. Wineholt** and **Lottie R. Clayton,** on 13 Sep 1947 in La Porte, La Porte Co., Indiana, USA. George was born on 16 Feb 1918 in La Porte Co., Indiana, USA, died on 16 Nov 1976 in La Porte, La Porte Co., Indiana, USA at age 58, and was buried in Kingsbury Cemetery, Kingsbury, La Porte Co., Indiana, USA.

Children from this marriage were:
   56   M   i.   **Dan Wineholt**.
   57   M   ii.   **Thomas Wineholt**.

45. Doris Hilgendorf *(Mary Kramer [16], Mathias [6], Thomas [1])* was born on 9 Jul 1924 in La Porte, La Porte Co., Indiana, USA and died on 22 Aug 2016 in Palatine, Cook Co., Illinois, USA at age 92.

Doris married **Richard K. Bowman,** son of **Orville S. Bowman** and **Mary C.,** on 19 Jun 1948 in La Porte, La Porte Co., Indiana, USA. Richard was born on 23 Jul 1924 in La Porte Co., Indiana, USA and died on 30 Jun 2012 in Palatine, Cook Co., Illinois, USA at age 87.

Children from this marriage were:
   58   M   i.   **Larry Bowman**.
   59   M   ii.   **Patrick Bowman**.

46. Leo J. Kramer *(John [17], Mathias [6], Thomas [1])* was born on 7 Aug 1910 in La Porte, La Porte Co., Indiana, USA, died on 14 Nov 1984 in Bluffton, Wells Co., Indiana, USA at age 74, and was buried in St. John's Cemetery, La Porte, La Porte Co., Indiana, USA.

Leo married **Isabella Eckstein**.

Children from this marriage were:
   60   M   i.   **Kenneth Kramer**.
   61   M   ii.   **Allen Kramer**.
   62   F   iii.   **Loretta Kramer**.
   63   F   iv.   **Marie Kramer**.
   64   F   v.   **Karen Kramer**.

47. Evelyn M. Kramer *(John [17], Mathias [6], Thomas [1])* was born on 23 Feb 1915 in La Porte, La Porte Co., Indiana, USA, died on 18 Feb 1941 in La Porte, La Porte Co., Indiana, USA at age 25, and was buried in St. Joseph's Cemetery, La Porte, La Porte Co., Indiana, USA.

Evelyn married **Roman J. Levendoski**. Roman was born in 1912 and died in 1996 at age 84.

The child from this marriage was:
   65   M   i.   **Ronald Levendoski**.

Produced by: James Patrick Barber, 630 Nancy Street, Warsaw, Indiana 46580, 574-269-3124, 574-265-7939, jim@barberfamily.org

Page 7

Name Index

Produced by: James Patrick Barber, 630 Nancy Street, Warsaw, Indiana 46580, 574-269-3124, 574-265-7939, jim@barberfamily.org

Name Index

Produced by: James Patrick Barber, 630 Nancy Street, Warsaw, Indiana 46580, 574-269-3124, 574-265-7939, jim@barberfamily.org

Page 9

Location Index

Produced by: James Patrick Barber, 630 Nancy Street, Warsaw, Indiana 46580, 574-269-3124, 574-265-7939, jim@barberfamily.org

Boze

Descendant Chart

Beginning with

William Boze (1800-1871)

In following the Haag family, we find that Harry Joseph Haag (1895-1963), the father of Leatha Haag, was married Mabel Boze (1895-1969) in La Porte, Indiana. The family descendant chart on the following pages looks at Mable Boze's ancestry beginning with William Boze, born in 1800 in Lynchburg, Virginia.

Table of Contents

Produced by: James Patrick Barber, 630 Nancy Street, Warsaw, Indiana 46580, 574-269-3124, 574-265-7939, jim@barberfamily.org

Descendants of William Boze (1800-1871)

First Generation

1. William Boze was born on 23 Mar 1800 in Lynchburg, , Virginia, USA and died on 23 May 1871 in Barnhill, Wayne Co., Illinois, USA at age 71. Other names for William were Boas and Boaz.

William married **Harriet Simpson** on 4 May 1822 in Lebanon, Wilson Co., Tennessee, USA. Harriet was born about 1808 in Tennessee, USA and died about 1886 about age 78.

Children from this marriage were:

+ 2   M   i.   **William S. Boze**.

+ 3   M   ii.   **Presley Corbin Boze** was born in 1834 in Illinois, USA and died in 1886 in Illinois, USA at age 52.

Produced by: James Patrick Barber, 630 Nancy Street, Warsaw, Indiana 46580, 574-269-3124, 574-265-7939, jim@barberfamily.org

Second Generation (Children)

2. William S. Boze *(William* [1]*)*.

3. Presley Corbin Boze *(William* [1]*)* was born in 1834 in Illinois, USA and died in 1886 in Illinois, USA at age 52.

Presley married **Sarah**. Sarah was born about 1844 in Illinois, USA.

Children from this marriage were:
+ 4 F   i. **Mary Boze** was born about 1866.
+ 5 M   ii. **Charles E. Boze** was born in Apr 1871 in Fairfield, Wayne Co., Illinois, USA and died on 8 Jun 1900 in Vincennes, Knox Co., Indiana, USA at age 29.
+ 6 M iii. **William O. Boze** was born about 1872.
+ 7 M iv. **James J. Boze** was born about 1876.

Produced by: James Patrick Barber, 630 Nancy Street, Warsaw, Indiana 46580, 574-269-3124, 574-265-7939, jim@barberfamily.org

Page 2

Third Generation (Grandchildren)

4. Mary Boze *(Presley Corbin³, William¹)* was born about 1866.

5. Charles E. Boze *(Presley Corbin³, William¹)* was born in Apr 1871 in Fairfield, Wayne Co., Illinois, USA and died on 8 Jun 1900 in Vincennes, Knox Co., Indiana, USA at age 29.

Charles married **Martha "Mattie" McCollum** about 1891 in Illinois, USA. Martha was born 13 Dec 1868 or 1869 in Illinois, USA and died on 21 Apr 1922 in Indiana, USA at age 53. Another name for Martha was McCallum.

Children from this marriage were:

+ 8 M   i. **Harry Alvin Boze** was born in Aug 1893 in Illinois, USA and died on 7 Aug 1909 in Vincennes, Knox Co., Indiana, USA at age 16.

+ 9 F   ii. **Mabel Iselem Boze** was born in May 1895 in Illinois, USA, died on 10 Jul 1969 in La Porte, La Porte Co., Indiana, USA at age 74, and was buried in St. John's Cemetery, La Porte, La Porte Co., Indiana, USA.

+ 10 F   iii. **Blanche Marie Boze** was born on 25 Jul 1897 in Indiana, USA and died on 21 Oct 1979 in Los Angeles, Los Angeles Co., California, USA at age 82.

+ 11 F   iv. **Ethel Louise Boze** was born on 19 Nov 1899 in Indiana, USA and died on 7 Dec 1937 at age 38.

6. William O. Boze *(Presley Corbin³, William¹)* was born about 1872.

7. James J. Boze *(Presley Corbin³, William¹)* was born about 1876.

Produced by: James Patrick Barber, 630 Nancy Street, Warsaw, Indiana 46580, 574-269-3124, 574-265-7939, jim@barberfamily.org

Page 3

Fourth Generation (Great-Grandchildren)

8. Harry Alvin Boze *(Charles E.*[5]*, Presley Corbin*[3]*, William*[1]*)* was born in Aug 1893 in Illinois, USA and died on 7 Aug 1909 in Vincennes, Knox Co., Indiana, USA at age 16.

9. Mabel Iselem Boze *(Charles E.*[5]*, Presley Corbin*[3]*, William*[1]*)* was born in May 1895 in Illinois, USA, died on 10 Jul 1969 in La Porte, La Porte Co., Indiana, USA at age 74, and was buried in St. John's Cemetery, La Porte, La Porte Co., Indiana, USA.

Mabel married **Harry Joseph Haag,** son of **John Edward Haag** and **Gertrude S. Carrico,** on 26 Nov 1913 in Vincennes, Knox Co., Indiana, USA. Harry was born on 4 Sep 1895 in LaSalle, LaSalle Co. Illinois, USA, died on 1 Aug 1963 in La Porte, La Porte Co., Indiana, USA at age 67, and was buried in Pine Lake Cemetery, La Porte, La Porte Co., Indiana, USA. Another name for Harry was Joseph Harry.

Children from this marriage were:

+ 12 F   i.   **Leatha Cecelia Haag** was born on 1 Feb 1916 in Bicknell, Knox Co., Indiana, USA, died on 3 Dec 1961 in La Porte, La Porte Co., Indiana, USA at age 45, and was buried in La Porte, La Porte Co., Indiana, USA.

+ 13 F   ii. **Helen Elizabeth Haag** was born on 11 Mar 1918 in Bicknell, Knox Co., Indiana, USA, died on 18 Jul 2002 in La Porte, La Porte Co., Indiana, USA at age 84, and was buried in Pine Lake Cemetery, La Porte, La Porte Co., Indiana, USA.

+ 14 F   iii. **Thelma L. Haag** was born on 16 Jun 1920 in Vincennes, Knox Co., Indiana, USA and died before 1930.

Mabel next married **Wilbur Smith**.

10. Blanche Marie Boze *(Charles E.*[5]*, Presley Corbin*[3]*, William*[1]*)* was born on 25 Jul 1897 in Indiana, USA and died on 21 Oct 1979 in Los Angeles, Los Angeles Co., California, USA at age 82.

Blanche married **Paul Reel** about 1918. Paul was born about 1896.

Children from this marriage were:

+ 15 M   i.   **Robert Reel**.
+ 16 M   ii. **Paul Reel**.
+ 17 M   iii. **Howard Reel**.
+ 18 F   iv. **Mary Reel** was born on 17 Jan 1923 in Mansfield, Richard Co., Ohio, USA and died on 2 Jan 2011 at age 87.

11. Ethel Louise Boze *(Charles E.*[5]*, Presley Corbin*[3]*, William*[1]*)* was born on 19 Nov 1899 in Indiana, USA and died on 7 Dec 1937 at age 38.

Produced by: James Patrick Barber, 630 Nancy Street, Warsaw, Indiana 46580, 574-269-3124, 574-265-7939, jim@barberfamily.org

Page 4

Fifth Generation (Great Great-Grandchildren)

12. Leatha Cecelia Haag *(Mabel Iselem Boze [9], Charles E. [5], Presley Corbin [3], William [1])*
was born on 1 Feb 1916 in Bicknell, Knox Co., Indiana, USA, died on 3 Dec 1961 in La Porte, La Porte Co., Indiana, USA at age 45, and was buried in La Porte, La Porte Co., Indiana, USA.

Leatha married **Clarence John Hilgendorf,** son of **Arthur John Hilgendorf** and **Mary Kramer,** on 14 Sep 1940 in La Porte, La Porte Co., Indiana, USA. Clarence was born on 30 Oct 1910 in La Porte, La Porte Co., Indiana, USA, died 24 Jul 1990 in Bradenton, Manatee Co., Florida, USA at age 79, and was buried in La Porte, La Porte Co., Indiana, USA.

Children from this marriage were:
- 19 F i. **Sally Joan Hilgendorf** was born on 23 Nov 1941 in La Porte, La Porte Co., Indiana, USA. Sally married **Dennis Lee Biege,** son of **James Kendall Biege** and **Angelina Sobko,** on 24 Jun 1961 in La Porte, La Porte Co., Indiana, USA. Dennis was born on 13 May 1941 in La Porte, La Porte Co., Indiana, USA.
- 20 M ii. **Kenneth Richard Hilgendorf** was born on 17 Jun 1943 in La Porte, La Porte Co., Indiana, USA. Kenneth married **Sue Sternal.** Sue was born on 5 May 1954.
- 21 F iii. **Mary Jane Hilgendorf** was born on 3 Aug 1946 in La Porte, La Porte Co., Indiana, USA. Mary married **Ronald Wayne Loeffler,** son of **Walter Charles Loeffler** and **Virginia Sobko,** on 28 May 1966 in La Porte, La Porte Co., Indiana, USA. Ronald was born on 2 Sep 1943 in La Porte, La Porte Co., Indiana, USA.
- 22 F iv. **Martha Ann Hilgendorf** was born on 6 Apr 1951 in La Porte, La Porte Co., Indiana, USA. Martha married **James Patrick Barber,** son of **Ira Barber Jr.** and **Shirley Esther Wendt,** on 27 Nov 1970 in La Porte, La Porte Co., Indiana, USA. James was born on 9 Nov 1948 in La Porte, La Porte Co., Indiana, USA.
- 23 M v. **Clarence John Hilgendorf Jr.** was born on 14 Feb 1956 in La Porte, La Porte Co., Indiana, USA. Clarence married **Dana Marie Alderman.** Dana was born on 10 May 1958.

13. Helen Elizabeth Haag *(Mabel Iselem Boze [9], Charles E. [5], Presley Corbin [3], William [1])*
was born on 11 Mar 1918 in Bicknell, Knox Co., Indiana, USA, died on 18 Jul 2002 in La Porte, La Porte Co., Indiana, USA at age 84, and was buried in Pine Lake Cemetery, La Porte, La Porte Co., Indiana, USA.

Helen married **John Parker Jr.,** son of **John A. Parker** and **Fannie Gooden,** on 26 Sep 1940 in La Porte, La Porte Co., Indiana, USA. John was born on 9 Sep 1917 in La Porte, La Porte Co., Indiana, USA, died on 3 Mar 2008 in La Porte, La Porte Co., Indiana, USA at age 90, and was buried in Pine Lake Cemetery, La Porte, La Porte Co., Indiana, USA.

Children from this marriage were:
- 24 M i. **David Lee Parker** was born on 19 Sep 1941 in La Porte, La Porte Co., Indiana, USA.
- 25 F ii. **Susan Jeanne Parker** was born on 3 Jan 1944 in La Porte, La Porte Co., Indiana, USA and died on 18 Aug 1946 in La Porte, La Porte Co., Indiana, USA at age 2.
- 26 M iii. **Robert Alan Parker** was born on 27 Oct 1948 in La Porte, La Porte Co., Indiana, USA.
- 27 M iv. **Sherry Ann Parker** was born on 6 Nov 1951 in La Porte, La Porte Co., Indiana, USA.

14. Thelma L. Haag *(Mabel Iselem Boze [9], Charles E. [5], Presley Corbin [3], William [1])* was born on 16 Jun 1920 in Vincennes, Knox Co., Indiana, USA and died before 1930.

15. Robert Reel *(Blanche Marie Boze [10], Charles E. [5], Presley Corbin [3], William [1]).*

16. Paul Reel *(Blanche Marie Boze [10], Charles E. [5], Presley Corbin [3], William [1]).*

17. Howard Reel *(Blanche Marie Boze [10], Charles E. [5], Presley Corbin [3], William [1]).*

18. Mary Reel *(Blanche Marie Boze [10], Charles E. [5], Presley Corbin [3], William [1])* was born on 17 Jan 1923 in

Produced by: James Patrick Barber, 630 Nancy Street, Warsaw, Indiana 46580, 574-269-3124, 574-265-7939, jim@barberfamily.org

Page 5

Mansfield, Richard Co., Ohio, USA and died on 2 Jan 2011 at age 87.

Mary married **Kenneth F. Sass** on 15 Feb 1942. Kenneth died on 22 Jul 1993.

Children from this marriage were:

28	F	i.	**Carol Sass**.
29	F	ii.	**Martha Sass**.
30	F	iii.	**Paula Sass**.
31	F	iv.	**Mary Sass**.
32	M	v.	**Robert Sass**.

Produced by: James Patrick Barber, 630 Nancy Street, Warsaw, Indiana 46580, 574-269-3124, 574-265-7939, jim@barberfamily.org

Page 6

Produced by: James Patrick Barber, 630 Nancy Street, Warsaw, Indiana 46580, 574-269-3124, 574-265-7939, jim@barberfamily.org

Location Index

Produced by: James Patrick Barber, 630 Nancy Street, Warsaw, Indiana 46580, 574-269-3124, 574-265-7939, jim@barberfamily.org

Page 8

FAMILY GROUP WORKSHEETS

Perhaps your interest in the history of your own family has been aroused by this book – I truly hope so. Seeing your own family in the context of history can bring both the history and your ancestors to life. Genealogy can be both rewarding and frustrating. It can be a great lifelong hobby if you are so inclined. In our fast, high-tech times, it can be a way to bring your family closer together. You can dig as deep or as shallow as you want. Maybe you just want to know a little more about your grandparents, or maybe you long for more insight into the lives of other branches of your family. Whatever the case may be, it is never too late to begin.

This book and the family charts may be a good jumping off place for you. On the following pages I have included some Family Group Worksheets. You might want to use them just to add the most current information on your own family. Do it right in this book so it is contained in one central location. Or, you may want to cast your net a little further in your family search. Make copies of the worksheet, or create your own form, and jump right in.

I hope you will not wait for the "right time" to get started. It is never tool late, and it is never too soon to begin. But, if you have some older relatives who could provide some good stories on your family, don't wait. They would love to talk with you and share their own personal histories. Theirs is a history worth sharing.

Family Group Worksheet

Sheet # [ ]

1. Please enter full names, including the middle name.
2. Include wife's maiden name in this format: First Name Middle Name (Maiden Name) Last Name
3. Number each sheet completed for ease of later reference.

Parents of HUSBAND below: Father [ ]   From Sheet # [ ]
                                Mother [ ]   From Sheet # [ ]

Parents of WIFE below: Father [ ]   From Sheet # [ ]
                                Mother [ ]   From Sheet # [ ]

HUSBAND	Birth	Birth Place			Death	Death Place		
Full Name of Husband	MM/DD/YY	Town	County	ST	MM/DD/YY	Town	County	ST
	/ /				/ /			
WIFE	**Birth**	**Birth Place**			**Death**	**Death Place**		
Full Name of Wife	MM/DD/YY	Town	County	ST	MM/DD/YY	Town	County	ST
	/ /				/ /			
	Marriage	**Marriage Place**						
	MM/DD/YY	Town	County	ST				
	/ /							

OTHER SPOUSES	Birth	Birth Place			Death	Death Place		
Full Name	MM/DD/YY	Town	County	ST	MM/DD/YY	Town	County	ST
	/ /				/ /			
	/ /				/ /			

CHILDREN OF THIS MARRIAGE	Birth	Birth Place			Death	Death Place		
Name of Child	MM/DD/YY	Town	County	ST	MM/DD/YY	Town	County	ST
	/ /				/ /			
	/ /				/ /			
	/ /				/ /			
	/ /				/ /			
	/ /				/ /			
	/ /				/ /			
	/ /				/ /			
	/ /				/ /			
	/ /				/ /			
	/ /				/ /			

Compiled By: _____

Date: _____

Additional Notes or Comments:

Family Group Worksheet

Sheet # [   ]

1. Please enter full names, including the middle name.
2. Include wife's maiden name in this format: First Name Middle Name (Maiden Name) Last Name
3. Number each sheet completed for ease of later reference.

Parents of HUSBAND below: Father [   ]   From Sheet # [   ]
Mother [   ]   From Sheet # [   ]

Parents of WIFE below: Father [   ]   From Sheet # [   ]
Mother [   ]   From Sheet # [   ]

HUSBAND	Birth	Birth Place			Death	Death Place		
Full Name of Husband	MM/DD/YY	Town	County	ST	MM/DD/YY	Town	County	ST
	/ /				/ /			
WIFE	**Birth**	**Birth Place**			**Death**	**Death Place**		
Full Name of Wife	MM/DD/YY	Town	County	ST	MM/DD/YY	Town	County	ST
	/ /				/ /			

	Marriage	Marriage Place		
	MM/DD/YY	Town	County	ST
	/ /			

OTHER SPOUSES	Birth	Birth Place			Death	Death Place		
Full Name	MM/DD/YY	Town	County	ST	MM/DD/YY	Town	County	ST
	/ /				/ /			
	/ /				/ /			

CHILDREN OF THIS MARRIAGE	Birth	Birth Place			Death	Death Place		
Name of Child	MM/DD/YY	Town	County	ST	MM/DD/YY	Town	County	ST
	/ /				/ /			
	/ /				/ /			
	/ /				/ /			
	/ /				/ /			
	/ /				/ /			
	/ /				/ /			
	/ /				/ /			
	/ /				/ /			
	/ /				/ /			
	/ /				/ /			

Compiled By: _____

Date: _____

Additional Notes or Comments:

Family Group Worksheet

Sheet #

1. Please enter full names, including the middle name.
2. Include wife's maiden name in this format: First Name Middle Name (Maiden Name) Last Name
3. Number each sheet completed for ease of later reference.

Parents of HUSBAND below: Father [   ]   From Sheet # [   ]
Mother [   ]   From Sheet # [   ]

Parents of WIFE below: Father [   ]   From Sheet # [   ]
Mother [   ]   From Sheet # [   ]

HUSBAND	Birth	Birth Place			Death	Death Place		
Full Name of Husband	MM/DD/YY	Town	County	ST	MM/DD/YY	Town	County	ST
	/ /				/ /			

WIFE	Birth	Birth Place			Death	Death Place		
Full Name of Wife	MM/DD/YY	Town	County	ST	MM/DD/YY	Town	County	ST
	/ /				/ /			

	Marriage	Marriage Place		
	MM/DD/YY	Town	County	ST
	/ /			

OTHER SPOUSES	Birth	Birth Place			Death	Death Place		
Full Name	MM/DD/YY	Town	County	ST	MM/DD/YY	Town	County	ST
	/ /				/ /			
	/ /				/ /			

CHILDREN OF THIS MARRIAGE	Birth	Birth Place			Death	Death Place		
Name of Child	MM/DD/YY	Town	County	ST	MM/DD/YY	Town	County	ST
	/ /				/ /			
	/ /				/ /			
	/ /				/ /			
	/ /				/ /			
	/ /				/ /			
	/ /				/ /			
	/ /				/ /			
	/ /				/ /			
	/ /				/ /			
	/ /				/ /			

Compiled By: _____

Date: _____

Additional Notes or Comments:

Family Group Worksheet

1. Please enter full names, including the middle name.
2. Include wife's maiden name in this format: First Name Middle Name (Maiden Name) Last Name
3. Number each sheet completed for ease of later reference.

Parents of HUSBAND below: Father [ ] From Sheet # [ ]
Mother [ ] From Sheet # [ ]

Parents of WIFE below: Father [ ] From Sheet # [ ]
Mother [ ] From Sheet # [ ]

HUSBAND	Birth	Birth Place			Death	Death Place		
Full Name of Husband	MM/DD/YY	Town	County	ST	MM/DD/YY	Town	County	ST
	/ /				/ /			

WIFE	Birth	Birth Place			Death	Death Place		
Full Name of Wife	MM/DD/YY	Town	County	ST	MM/DD/YY	Town	County	ST
	/ /				/ /			

	Marriage	Marriage Place		
	MM/DD/YY	Town	County	ST
	/ /			

OTHER SPOUSES	Birth	Birth Place			Death	Death Place		
Full Name	MM/DD/YY	Town	County	ST	MM/DD/YY	Town	County	ST
	/ /				/ /			
	/ /				/ /			

CHILDREN OF THIS MARRIAGE	Birth	Birth Place			Death	Death Place		
Name of Child	MM/DD/YY	Town	County	ST	MM/DD/YY	Town	County	ST
	/ /				/ /			
	/ /				/ /			
	/ /				/ /			
	/ /				/ /			
	/ /				/ /			
	/ /				/ /			
	/ /				/ /			
	/ /				/ /			
	/ /				/ /			
	/ /				/ /			

Compiled By: _____

Date: _____

Additional Notes or Comments:

Family Group Worksheet

Sheet # [   ]

1. Please enter full names, including the middle name.
2. Include wife's maiden name in this format: First Name Middle Name (Maiden Name) Last Name
3. Number each sheet completed for ease of later reference.

Parents of HUSBAND below: Father [   ] From Sheet # [   ]
Mother [   ] From Sheet # [   ]

Parents of WIFE below: Father [   ] From Sheet # [   ]
Mother [   ] From Sheet # [   ]

HUSBAND	Birth	Birth Place			Death	Death Place		
Full Name of Husband	MM/DD/YY	Town	County	ST	MM/DD/YY	Town	County	ST
	/ /				/ /			
WIFE	**Birth**	**Birth Place**			**Death**	**Death Place**		
Full Name of Wife	MM/DD/YY	Town	County	ST	MM/DD/YY	Town	County	ST
	/ /				/ /			

	Marriage	Marriage Place		
	MM/DD/YY	Town	County	ST
	/ /			

OTHER SPOUSES	Birth	Birth Place			Death	Death Place		
Full Name	MM/DD/YY	Town	County	ST	MM/DD/YY	Town	County	ST
	/ /				/ /			
	/ /				/ /			

CHILDREN OF THIS MARRIAGE	Birth	Birth Place			Death	Death Place		
Name of Child	MM/DD/YY	Town	County	ST	MM/DD/YY	Town	County	ST
	/ /				/ /			
	/ /				/ /			
	/ /				/ /			
	/ /				/ /			
	/ /				/ /			
	/ /				/ /			
	/ /				/ /			
	/ /				/ /			
	/ /				/ /			
	/ /				/ /			

Compiled By: _____

Date: _____

Additional Notes or Comments:

www.ingramcontent.com/pod-product-compliance
Lightning Source LLC
Chambersburg PA
CBHW080046280326
41934CB00014B/3234